THE FIRST-YEAR EXPERIENCE®
& Students in Transition

NADE
National Association for
Developmental Education

Developmental Education:

Preparing
Successful
College
Students

EDITORS
Jeanne L. Higbee
Patricia L. Dwinell

National Resource Center for
The First-Year Experience & Students in Transition
University of South Carolina, 1998

Additional copies of this monograph may be ordered at $35 each from the National Resource Center for The First-Year Experience and Students in Transition, University of South Carolina, 1728 College Street, SC 29208. Telephone (803) 777-6029. Telefax (803) 777-4699.

Special gratitude is expressed to Blair Symes and Randolph F. Handel, Assistant Editors, for editing, design, and lay-out of this monograph; to Dr. Betsy Barefoot, Co-Director for Publications and Research; and to Dr. Dorothy Fidler, Senior Managing Editor.

ISBN Number: 1-889271-24-1

The Freshman Year Experience® and The First-Year Experience® are service marks of the Univeristy of South Carolina. A license may be granted upon written request to use the terms The Freshman Year Experience and The First-Year Experience. This license is not transferable without the written approval of the University of South Carolina.

378.154
D489

Table of Contents

Preface

John N. Gardner

It is a pleasure for me to introduce this, our Center's 24th monograph, in a series launched in 1987. Why is a research center housed in a flagship research university sponsoring and publishing a major monograph on developmental education? There are a number of excellent reasons. The first one—and I will make this bold assertion—is that what is good for developmental education is good for the United States. It is basic to our Center's mission to support what is the greater good, not only for the higher education community, but for the entire country. We contribute this monograph in that spirit.

Another reason we are involved in this particular project is that we have learned that often the best way for us to get our mission accomplished is by reaching out and developing partnerships with other professional associates. Since 1990, we have co-produced monographs with the Association of College and University Housing Officers-International, the National Association of Student Employment Administrators, the National Academic Advising Association, the National Orientation Directors Association, and the Association of Deans and Directors of University Colleges & Undergraduate Studies. It seems highly appropriate, therefore, that we now embrace this newest partnership with our friends and colleagues in the National Association for Developmental Education.

We have great respect for developmental education as a teaching, learning, and research culture that has been an incubator of significant experimentation and exciting assessment about student learning. This monograph will speak to that theme. We respect developmental education because of its risk taking, its fundamental value system, and its expressed commitment to an academic underclass, those students who are frequently ignored, shoved to the side, and mistreated on many campuses. We have respect for developmental educators because they also provide service as tutors, role models, peer counselors, and mentors. As the evidence continues to mount for the influence of service learning, it may be argued that the greatest beneficiaries of developmental education are the peer tutors themselves. We respect developmental education because it has enabled hundreds and thousands of students to perform far better than their initial predicted grade point averages (GPA) might suggest. Their research has shown that predicted GPAs measure neither a student's motivation nor an institution's ability to offer powerful educational interventions directed by competent personnel.

There is much about the developmental education profession that is not understood by those outside, thus leaving the profession shrouded in myth and stereotype. For example, there is the myth that developmental education occurs only in open admissions colleges. There is an additional myth that higher-achieving students do not need assistance and that learning centers serve remedial students only. I find most exciting the recent transformation in developmental education in which the client load of many learning centers now includes striking numbers of high-achieving, high-ability students who wish to develop further their potential and improve their performance. The notion that developmental educators and learning centers serve exclusively first-year students, the cohort we serve in this Center, is another myth. Increasingly, our developmental education colleagues are serving larger and larger numbers of upperclass students, for example, college seniors as they prepare to take entrance exams into graduate and professional schools.

I am particularly concerned that the mounting attacks against developmental education are based on intolerance, racism, misunderstanding, ignorance, prejudice, and selfishness. I have not devoted 30-plus years of my life to higher education to want to see the clock set back. I hope this monograph will increase the understanding, respect, and advocacy for the merits of developmental education for all types of students who need and can profit from these kinds of legitimate educational and empowering experiences. We offer this monograph for all of those reasons and in this spirit. We express our sincerest and

most profound appreciation to our colleagues of the National Association for Developmental Education for making this monograph possible. We wish you, the readers, the best as you apply on your campuses the information and inspiration contained herein.

Introduction

Jeanne L. Higbee and Patricia L. Dwinell

Developmental education has many faces. At one time perceived merely to provide remediation for academic deficiencies of college freshmen, today developmental education programs serve diverse student needs through myriad teaching and learning activities at every size and type of institution of higher education in the United States and in other countries throughout the world. The following chapters illustrate the breadth and depth of developmental education as it has evolved into an umbrella for courses and student services that promote skill development and enhance academic performance at all levels of higher education.

The first chapter, by Hunter Boylan and D. Patrick Saxon, chronicles the history of developmental education. Boylan and Saxon describe the link between achievement and noncognitive factors that inspired the use of the term "developmental" to denote a new model for facilitating academic achievement. They then provide data to support their claim that participation in developmental education courses is related to later success, "that developmental education does what it is supposed to do."

In her chapter, "Who Belongs in College: A Second Look," Carlette Hardin reprises her descriptions of different types of students served through developmental education programs. She debunks many of the myths about the needs, attitudes, and abilities of high-risk students while making a strong statement in support of educational opportunity. In her conclusion, Hardin provides brief characterizations of students who have experienced the impact of developmental education and the difference it has made in their lives.

Through her interviews with Hunter Boylan, one of the founders of the National Association for Developmental Education (NADE), and David Arendale, immediate past president of NADE, Cheryl Stratton provides a forecast for the future of developmental education in Chapter Three. She explores the political debate surrounding the existence, location, and funding of developmental programs. Stratton probes essential transitions for future programmatic success and promotes the need for ongoing research and assessment.

Chapters Four through Seven explore the role of developmental education in two very different types of postsecondary institutions: the community college and the research university. Milton (Bunk) Spann and Suella McCrimmon trace the roots of developmental education and its link to the community college. They provide information regarding several common areas of misconception, including causes of poor performance and characteristics of high-risk students, as well as logistical questions about institutional versus graduation credit and the location of programs in centralized versus decentralized units within traditional academic departments. Regarding future trends in developmental education in the community college, Spann and McCrimmon ask, "Will it succumb to the practiced values of the academy which make learning and student development a low priority, or will it take the lead in again making this the academy's first priority?"

Developmental education programs are successful in promoting the growth of college students because they encourage students to take a more active role in learning across a variety of curriculums.

Similar questions are posed by the authors of the next three chapters; they represent their programs at three research universities, where more common queries are: Should developmental education programs be relegated to the community college system? They restate the question to ask: Does developmental education serve a meaningful function in research institutions? The authors respond with data from four different types of programs. Don Garnett and M. V. Hood III evaluate a summer bridge program for provisionally admitted students at Texas Tech, while Catherine Wambach and Robert delMas describe the vast array of courses and services available to students admitted into General College at the University of Minnesota. Jeanne Higbee and Patricia Dwinell contribute data from the University of Georgia to provide

support for the value of traditional developmental freshman courses in English, mathematics, and reading; they also included information about Georgia's more recent transition to a program that serves all students.

Rita Klein, Diane Vukovich, and M. Kay Alderman shift the focus to the role of the developmental teacher in the classroom in Chapter Eight. They list characteristics of successful developmental educators—two important traits being optimism and the ability "to light the spark of hope, motivation, and achievement in each and every student." Klein, Vukovich, and Alderman discuss their own study of teacher self-efficacy and its implications for developmental educators.

In Chapter Nine, Claire Weinstein, Douglas Dierking, Jenefer Husman, Linda Roska, and Lorrie Powdrill examine the effectiveness of a strategic learning course in enhancing student retention. The course model includes four components: skill, will, self-regulation, and the academic environment. They attribute the success of their course to its foundation in learning theory and to the transferability of acquired skills to future coursework.

In her chapter on the integration of critical thinking, Linda Best also begins by providing a theoretical framework and a reminder about the necessary application of skills in other academic courses. Best is further concerned with the transferability of skills to life after college, or "the broader goal of higher education to develop skills that do not become obsolete over time." She asserts that action must be taken on both the programmatic and classroom levels to integrate critical thinking into the developmental education curriculum and makes specific suggestions for how this can be accomplished.

In her chapter on metacognition, Cynthia Craig elaborates on specific classroom practices for encouraging the development of critical thinking skills while enhancing learning. Students take a more active role in the educational process when required to use metacognitive strategies and engage in self-regulation. In addition, Craig notes that "A metacognitive perspective can also assist the teacher in diagnosis and intervention."

The next four chapters explore each of developmental education's primary teaching components—mathematics, writing, reading, and counseling—within a theoretical context. Irene Duranczyk and Joanne Caniglia distinguish between behaviorist and constructivist approaches to the teaching of mathematics. They indicate that computational skills are not enough; it is important for students to be able to interpret their results so that they become engaged "in thinking about what they are actually doing," once again emphasizing the importance of metacognition in the learning process. Duranczyk and Caniglia present results of their own research on student attitudes, which seem more compatible with behaviorist theory and a dependence on memorization. How can developmental educators prepare students to cope with philosophical differences in teaching and learning strategies?

In her chapter on teaching writing skills, Mary Deming also examines a theoretical debate. For both educational and political reasons, institutions are weighing options in their consideration of the mainstreaming of basic writers. One concern, the stigma associated with placing students in segregated basic writing classes, is balanced by another, the lack of a supportive environment for at-risk students in English composition courses in which they may be left to "sink or swim." Deming describes models that address both sides of the debate in their design and implementation.

Similarly, Martha Maxwell considers the effectiveness of separate developmental reading courses in Chapter 14. She discusses testing and placement, the stigma of participation in required reading courses, and resulting student attitudes and expectations. Like other chapter authors, Maxwell urges a focus on the skills that are needed to be successful in subsequent

coursework and offers a number of models as alternatives to the traditional "skills and drills" type reading class.

Robert Nelson's chapter promotes the concept of developmental education as "training for life." He states, "I have become increasingly aware of our students' need to witness, recognize, develop, and exercise personal management skills." Nelson outlines the behaviors of students who are successful goal setters, project planners, and time and stress managers, and he proposes seminar programs in which first-year students can learn the personal management skills necessary for success in college and in life.

The final contributor, David Arendale, expands upon the effectiveness of Supplemental Instruction (SI), a model introduced in several previous chapters. SI is popular among students, faculty, and administrators alike, targets high-risk courses rather than students, integrates skill development with course content without putting this burden on teachers who may not have appropriate training outside their disciplines, and is cost-effective. Perhaps most important, "SI encourages students to become actively involved in their own learning."

This might be considered a recurring theme of this volume, that developmental education programs are successful in promoting the growth of college students because they encourage students to take a more active role in learning across a variety of environments: the classroom, tutoring sessions, the learning center or laboratory, adjunct or paired courses or Supplemental Instruction sections, and one-to-one contact with faculty, advisors, and counselors.

We would like to express our thanks to John Gardner, Betsy Barefoot, Dorothy Fidler and the staff of the National Resource Center for The First-Year Experience and Students in Transition at the University of South Carolina and to the NADE executive board for the opportunity to compile and edit this monograph, and to our distinguished authors for their significant contributions to the field of developmental education as a whole and to this volume in particular.

The Origin, Scope, and Outcomes of Developmental Education in the 20th Century

Hunter R. Boylan and D. Patrick Saxon

Postsecondary developmental education originated in the mid-19th century in response to the presence of large numbers of unprepared students attending American colleges and universities of the 1800s. The proliferation of higher education institutions that took place following the Morrill Land Grant Act of 1862 (Brubacher & Willis, 1976) resulted in far greater numbers of students having access to college. That so many of these students were unprepared for the experience reflects the nation's failure to develop a system of public schools beyond the primary grades until the beginning of the 20th century (Maxwell, 1985).

With the exception of our most elite institutions, our colleges and universities have always needed to provide services of one kind or another to students who, for one reason or another, had difficulty doing college level academic work. These services have ranged from individual tutoring by faculty, such as that provided by Harvard as early as 1636 (Boylan & White, 1987), to contemporary comprehensive programs providing a wide range of personal and academic development activities. They have served a wide range of students, from those who are outstanding mathematicians but lack some writing skills to those who need to improve their reading rate before going on to graduate school to those who are weak in all of the basic skill areas and cannot succeed in college without a substantial amount of developmental assistance.

Throughout the history of American higher education, such students have been welcomed by admissions officers only to become the object of scorn and occasional ridicule by many faculty, administrators, and legislators. Students who need some remediation to prepare them for college are welcomed by those who recognize that postsecondary institutions need such students in order to survive financially. They are welcomed by those who believe that part of the tradition of American higher education has been helping students who are at the margins of society become part of the mainstream. They are welcomed by those who recognize that student potential for learning is not measured by standardized test scores or high school rank. They are also scorned by those who believe that our higher education system is designed for the best, the richest, or the brightest. They are scorned by those who believe that serving them takes resources that should be assigned exclusively to the best, richest, and brightest. They are scorned because much of the public believes that it is always someone else's child who is not quite "college material."

Nevertheless, a substantial number of underprepared students eventually become successful college and university graduates through a combination of their own efforts to overcome academic weaknesses and the efforts of those whose job it has been to assist them in those efforts. Today, such students are called "developmental students," and those who serve them are referred to as "developmental educators." This chapter traces the origins of modern developmental education, describes the scope of that endeavor, and provides some indication of the success of the endeavor in American higher education.

Why Are They Called "Developmental" Students?

Developmental programs and students have been described in many ways. They were known as "preparatory students" in the 1800s because underprepared students were typically assigned to a battery of courses in college preparatory departments before taking the regular college curriculum. Brier (1985) reports that the first such program was established at the University of Wisconsin in 1849 and that this innovation had spread to the majority of American colleges and universities by the 1880s.

Preparatory students were quite numerous in American higher education during the 19th century. Brubacher and Willis (1976) report, for instance, that by the 1890s more than half of the students enrolled at many colleges and universities were in preparatory departments. The fact that there were so many of them, however, did not make them welcome at our institutions of higher learning.

Henry Tappan once referred to preparatory students at the University of Michigan as "juvenile . . . raw and undisciplined youth" (Brubacher & Willis, 1976). According to Brier (1985), those who participated in preparatory programs at Vasser were considered "a vandal hoard of unconventionalities" (p. 3). Brier also suggests that most college administrators at the turn of the century regarded preparatory students as something akin to a necessary evil. They were necessary to meet admission quotas and to fill class rosters. They were evil because no one wanted to admit to that necessity.

Until the 1930s, students who lacked all the skills necessary for success in college were still generally referred to as "preparatory students." In the 1920s, however, many universities began to eliminate preparatory departments and relegate their tasks to the emerging junior colleges. Although junior colleges performed well in their capacity as preparatory institutions, they only served in this capacity for those students who did not meet university admission standards or who, for one reason or another, felt unprepared to enter the university immediately. Consequently, the presence of junior colleges did not entirely eliminate the need for providing academic help to weaker students enrolled at universities.

Many students who met the admissions requirements were still not quite ready for university-level courses. In some cases, such as that of Minnesota, state law required that all high school graduates be admitted to the university (Maxwell, 1985). As it became apparent that many of the students who met institutional admission requirements still had difficulties, universities searched for ways to assist them. The most common response was to offer remedial reading courses. In fact, by the late 1920s Ohio State University required that all students admitted on probation take "remedial" reading (Casazza & Silverman, 1996). By the 20th century, Harvard University already had remedial writing courses and, in 1938, Harvard established its first remedial reading course (Maxwell, 1985). As other institutions followed suit, remedial courses became quite common on the campuses of four-year institutions. The term "remedial students" eventually replaced "preparatory students" as the common description for those taking precollege level courses.

One of the greatest stimuli to the expansion of programs for underprepared students came as a result of the Veterans Adjustment Act of 1944, more commonly known as the "GI Bill." This act provided financial assistance enabling nearly two million former service men and women to attend colleges and universities. In responding to the needs of these adult learners, most institutions made the assumption that they simply needed review courses in basic skills and, perhaps, some training in study skills. Once returning veterans had taken a few "refresher courses" and learned study skills, it was assumed that they would be able to master college-level work. This assumption led university counseling centers to provide workshops or courses on study skills, while departments of English and mathematics provided what were known as "remedial courses." The term "remediation" was used consistently during the 1950s and 1960s to describe review courses and services designed specifically for veterans (although frequently used by nonveterans).

The term "developmental education" reflects a dramatic expansion in our knowledge of human growth and development in the 1960s and 1970s.

With the passage of the Higher Education Act of 1965, a substantial amount of financial aid was made available to "all learners who were previously underrepresented in higher education" (Cross, 1976, p. 4). This meant that many of the financial barriers to the attendance of adult learners, women, and minorities had now been removed. These students were unlike the typical college student of the times and were, consequently, often called "nontraditional students" (Cross, 1976).

These new students were also likely to have suffered from the effects of discrimination, poverty, and low family educational levels. Because of this, the term "disadvantaged" then attained popular usage as a description for students who were underprepared for college. The terms "nontraditional" and "disadvantaged" were used often and frequently interchanged to describe those

students participating in remediation in the 1960s and early 1970s.

Although many nontraditional students enrolled in remedial courses, a large number of them did not require remediation. The National Study of Developmental Education (Boylan, Bonham, Bliss, & Claxton, 1992), for instance, reported that only about 35% of those enrolled in remedial courses were from minority backgrounds.

Similarly, the term "disadvantaged" also did not apply to all those taking remedial courses. A very substantial number of those participating in remediation were White students from middle and upper class socioeconomic backgrounds. It was obvious then, that the terms "remedial" and "disadvantaged" or "nontraditional" were not synonymous.

There are those who believe that the term "developmental education" originated during the 1970s as a politically correct label coined to avoid offending minorities by referring to them as "remedial," "nontraditional," or "disadvantaged." This is a gross misconception. The term "developmental education" reflects a dramatic expansion in our knowledge of human growth and development in the 1960s and 1970s. As a result, we began to understand that poor academic performance involved far more complex factors than a student's being unable to solve for x in an algebraic equation or write a complete sentence using proper grammar. If such deficiencies were the only problems for students having difficulty in college, simple remediation would be an appropriate solution for everyone. A variety of noncognitive or "developmental" factors, however, were also discovered to be of critical importance to student success. These additional factors included such things as locus of control, attitudes toward learning, self-concept, autonomy, ability to seek help, and a host of others influences having nothing to do with students' intellect or academic skill.

By the late 1970s, educators who worked with underprepared students developed an entirely new paradigm to guide their efforts. Instead of assuming that students were simply deficient in academic skills and needed to have these deficiencies remediated, they began to assume that personal and academic growth were linked—that the improvement of academic performance was tied to improvement in students' attitudes, values, and beliefs about themselves, others, and the educational environment. This created a new model for working with those who had previously been unsuccessful in academic tasks.

The new model involved the teaching of basic skills combined with assessment, advising, counseling, tutoring, and individualized learning experiences designed not just to reteach basic content, but also to promote student development. The resulting model became known as "developmental education," and those who participated in it were described as "developmental students." Use of the term "developmental education" has continued since the 1970s and denotes an entirely different concept from "remedial education."

How Widespread Is Developmental Education?

During the 20th century, the percentage of students who need preparatory work before they can be successful in college has declined substantially. Although more than half of those entering college in 1900 took preparatory courses (Brubacher & Willis, 1976), the National Center for Education Statistics (1996) reported that only about 29% of entering freshmen took similar courses in 1995.

Interestingly enough, however, the percentage of institutions offering preparatory, remedial, or developmental courses has remained relatively constant in American higher education for most of this century. In 1915 the U. S. Commissioner of Education reported that about 80% of the nation's colleges and universities offered remedial courses (Maxwell, 1985). The National Center for Education Statistics reported in 1996 that 78% of American colleges and universities offered remedial courses (National Center for Education Statistics, 1996). Although the percentage of entering students requiring some form of developmental education has declined in this century, the percentage of institutions providing developmental education has stayed about the same.

Estimates from the National Study of Developmental Education (Boylan, Bonham, Bliss, & Claxton, 1992) indicate that about 90% of all two-year institutions and 70% of four-year institutions offer developmental courses. A breakdown of those offering developmental courses by institutional type is presented in Table 1.

In 1985 the National Center for Education Statistics reported that about 25% of students entering colleges and universities enrolled in developmental courses in reading, writing, or mathematics (Plisko & Stern, 1985). A report issued a decade later indicated that this percentage had

Table 1

Percent Offering Developmental Courses by Institutional Type

Institutional Type	Percent Offering Developmental Courses
Public 2-year	100
Private 2-year	63
Public 4-year	81
Private 4-year	63

Note. From *Remedial Education at Higher Education Institutions in the Fall 1995.* Washington, DC: National Center for Education Statistics, U. S. Department of Education.

increased slightly to 29% by 1995 (National Center for Education Statistics, 1996).

Based on this and other information, Boylan (1995) estimates that there are more than two million students participating in developmental reading, writing, and mathematics courses or services during any given academic year. This figure does not count an unknown number of students who participate in developmental courses in areas other than reading, writing, and mathematics. Also, this does not count an estimated 700,000 students participating in educational opportunity programs offering developmental courses or services (National Council of Educational Opportunity Associations, 1995). Consequently, it is reasonable to assume that about three million college students participate in some form of developmental education each year.

How Successful Are Developmental Students?

The success of developmental students is typically measured in three ways: (a) the rate at which they pass developmental courses, (b) the rate at which those who pass developmental courses later pass regular courses in the same subject, and (c) the rate at which developmental students are retained through to graduation. According to the National Center for Education Statistics (Plisko & Stern, 1985), approximately three-fourths of those enrolled in developmental courses in 1985 were able to complete them successfully. A follow-up report (National Center for Education Statistics, 1996) indicated that the same pass rate was maintained by developmental students 10 years later. Pass rates for students enrolled in developmental courses have remained consistent, therefore, at about 75% for at least a decade. A description of pass rates by institutional type and subject area is provided in Table 2.

Given that the students entering developmental courses have already been judged, according to institutional criteria, to be underprepared for academic work, these pass rates are commendable. Working with the weakest students at their institutions, developmental educators are still able to lead three out of four of their students to early academic success.

This success, however, would be pointless if it were not related to success in later courses. The efforts of developmental educators are directed, not just to help students be successful in their courses, but to help them be successful in post-secondary education. The extent to which those who complete developmental courses are successful in later courses, therefore, is a very powerful indicator of the impact of developmental education.

Using a retrospective analysis of data for students participating in developmental courses from 1986 through 1992, the National Center for Developmental Education attempted to identify how those who passed developmental courses fared in regular curriculum courses in the same or related subjects. In this analysis, all students

Table 2

Percent of Students Passing Developmental Courses by Institution and Type

Institutional Type	Reading	Writing	Mathematics
Public 2-year	72	71	66
Private 2-year	--	81	80
Public 4-year	82	81	71
Private 4-year	84	88	84

Note. From *Remedial Education at Higher Education Institutions in the Fall 1995.* Washington, DC: National Center for Education Statistics, U. S. Department of Education.

who had passed a developmental course with a grade of C or better were tracked to determine if they later took the curriculum course in that subject or a related area. Student transcripts were then used to determine how many of these students passed the curriculum course with a grade of C or better. The results are presented in Table 3 (Boylan & Bonham, 1992).

Of those students who passed the highest level developmental mathematics course with a grade of C or better, 77% eventually passed their first regular curriculum mathematics course with a grade of C or better. Of those who passed the highest level developmental writing course with a grade of C or better, 91% eventually passed their first college level English course with a

level developmental courses is related to success in the regular curriculum. Using the very powerful indicator of student success in courses taken after participation in developmental education, we know that developmental education contributes to success in college courses for a very substantial number of students. According to institutional criteria, these at-risk students were predicted to fail without the opportunity offered by developmental education courses.

Another measure used to describe the success of developmental students is their rate of retention through graduation. Although this measure is very popular among those who evaluate developmental programs, it is not a particularly powerful indicator of their impact. Developmental

Table 3
Percent of Students Passing Developmental Courses Who also Passed Their First College Level Course in the Same or Related Subject

Developmental Course Subject	Percent Passing College Level
Mathematics	77
Writing	91
Reading	83

Note. From Boylan, H. R., & Bonham, B. S. (1992). The impact of developmental education programs. *Research in Developmental Education, 9*(5), 1-3. Reprinted with permission.

grade of C or better. For reading, the first college English course was also used for the purposes of comparison. Of those who passed the highest level developmental reading course, 83% eventually passed their first college level English course.

It should be reiterated that only those who passed the highest level developmental course in a particular subject area with a C or better and then passed the regular curriculum course with a C or better were included in this study. A very substantial number of students were eliminated from the analysis because they either did not take the highest level developmental course, did not complete it with a C or better, or, having completed the developmental course, never enrolled in the related regular curriculum course. Nevertheless, it is apparent from the results of this study that success in the highest

courses are usually taken during a student's first year at an institution. Graduation typically takes place anywhere from two to eight years later. Quite a few things happen in a student's life during that period that will determine the likelihood of graduation. Students may be forced to overcome financial, personal, family, or health problems. Students may develop their noncognitive skills as a result of college attendance, or their development may be stifled as a result of their college experiences. Students may decide to postpone or quit higher education altogether for reasons having nothing to do with their academic ability. Consequently, it is probably inaccurate and definitely unfair to evaluate the worth of any single early college intervention or set of interventions on the basis of long term retention and graduation. Institutions with typically high retention and graduation rates for all students will probably have similarly high rates for developmental students. Institutions with typically low retention and graduation rates will probably have similarly low rates for developmental students. Therefore, it is best to consider retention and graduation rates for developmental students within the context of the general institutional rates of retention and graduation. This admonition should be kept in mind in reviewing the national averages for developmental students' retention and graduation rates presented in Table 4 (Boylan & Bonham, 1992).

The figures presented in Table 4 were based on the following:

♦ Retention and graduation percentages included all those who had graduated within the specified time period or who might reasonably be expected to graduate within a semester.

♦ Rates for two-year institutions were calculated at the end of three and one half years.

♦ Rates for four-year institutions were calculated at the end of five and one half years.

♦ Rates are calculated for random samples of students participating in developmental programs between 1986 and 1992 at a random sample of institutions.

Based on these data, it can be said that developmental students' retention and graduation rates tend to exceed the national average for students enrolled at two-year institutions which, according to Tinto (1986), is about 27%. This is particularly true when only those developmental students who have actually declared an intention to complete a degree are counted. When those students who do not intend to complete a two-year college degree are eliminated from the sample, the retention and graduation rates for developmental students at community colleges increase to 30% (Boylan, Bonham, Bliss, & Claxton, 1992).

The reverse of this situation appears to be true at four-year institutions. According to government figures (U. S. Office of Education, 1993), 45% of those who enter four-year colleges and universities will complete a baccalaureate degree within six years. The average retention and graduation rate for all developmental students enrolled in four-year institutions was approximately 39%. It appears that developmental students attending four-year institutions lag behind their better prepared peers in terms of graduation rates. The rates for developmental students were substantially higher at private institutions and at research universities than at public colleges and universities.

Using this indicator, several things can be said about developmental education and its contribution to the success of students. For instance, participation in developmental education appears to be positively related to retention and graduation at two-year institutions. Developmental education effectively reduces the differences in

Table 4

Percent of Retention/Graduation for Developmental Students by Institutional Type

Institutional Type	Percent of Retention/Graduation
Public Community Colleges	24
Public Technical Colleges	34
Public 4-Year	28
Private 4-Year	40
Research Universities	48

Note. From Boylan, H. R., & Bonham, B. S. (1992). The impact of developmental education programs. *Research in Developmental Education, 9*(5), 1-3. Reprinted with permission.

student graduation rates that should be expected because of measured differences in entry level skills. The relationship between participation in developmental education and graduation may be more apparent at community and technical colleges because the time required to attain the degree is shorter. Under such circumstances, whatever early impact developmental education may have is less likely to be dissipated by intervening variables.

When measured over the long term at four-year institutions, however, the initial positive results of developmental education do not appear to eliminate completely the impact of entry level differences between developmental and nondevelopmental students. Students who enter four-year institutions with strong basic skills still graduate more often than students with weaker skills even though the latter group participated in developmental education. This should not be surprising. Given the distance in time between a developmental education intervention and the outcome measure of graduation, it is unlikely that any substantial effect would be noticeable. At four-year institutions, the amount of time between developmental education and potential graduation is doubled, allowing for more mitigating variables to dilute the effects of developmental education intervention.

In spite of this latter situation, the general record of developmental students in higher education is very strong. It should be born in mind that those who participate in developmental courses and services are also those who are already having trouble in college or those who have already been identified as having weaknesses in basic academic skills. They are, consequently, the very students who are least likely to succeed in college. That three out of four of these students are able to improve their skills and complete developmental courses is noteworthy and commendable. The fact that the vast majority of those who complete developmental courses are successful in related courses in the curriculum is equally noteworthy and commendable.

When measured in terms of immediate outcomes, developmental education is obviously successful. When measured in terms of extended outcomes such as continued retention and graduation, developmental students perform slightly better than other students at two-year institutions and slightly worse at four-year institutions. Since these students were identified initially as potential failures, the outcomes certainly suggest that developmental education is positively related to favorable long term benefits for the weakest students.

Conclusion

Students entering college unprepared for college work are not a recent phenomenon. Colleges and universities have always needed to offer services to students who have difficulty performing at the college level. No doubt this will continue to be a challenge for institutions that include educational opportunity in their mission.

Although the majority of colleges have developmental programs or courses in place, these programs and the personnel within them may be handicapped by the stigmatization that they are working with the weakest students and that resources should not be used to reteach basic content. Successful developmental education, however, involves more than just the teaching of basic skills. Understanding that there is a link between personal and academic growth is the key difference between "developmental" and "remedial" education. For developmental intervention to be successful, student development must be promoted through services such as advising, counseling, and tutoring. For these treatments to be effective, developmental educators must attend to noncognitive variables.

To measure the outcomes of developmental education, we need to consider the goal of the intervention. This goal, of course, is to promote success in postsecondary education. One of the more effective ways of measuring this is to examine how developmental students perform in their first college curriculum courses. If outcomes are measured using the more popular gauge of retention through to graduation, it must be considered that over the course of a student's college career, there are many other variables that might affect one's ability to continue to graduation.

Finally, the research shows that the majority of developmental students do advance and succeed in regular college curriculum courses. Not only do the majority of the weakest students who participate in developmental courses pass, they also go on to pass their first college-level course in the same subject. Furthermore, a substantial number of these students do attain college degrees following developmental intervention.

References

Boylan, H. R. (1995). The scope of developmental education: Some basic information on the field. *Research in Developmental Education, 11*(2), 1-4.

Boylan, H. R., & Bonham, B. S. (1992). The impact of developmental education programs. *Research in Developmental Education, 9*(5), 1-3.

Boylan, H. R., Bonham, B. S., Bliss, L., & Claxton, C. S. (1992, November). *The state of the art in developmental education.* Paper presented at the First National Conference on Research in Developmental Education, Charlotte, NC.

Boylan, H. R., & White, W. (1987). Educating all the nation's people: The history of developmental education, Part I. *Review of Research in Developmental Education, 4*(4), 1-4.

Brier, E. (1985). Bridging the academic preparation gap: An historical view. *Journal of Developmental Education, 8*(1), 2-5.

Brubacher, J. S., & Willis, R. (1976) *Higher education in transition: A history of American colleges and universities 1636-1976.* New York: Harper & Row.

Casazza, M. E., & Silverman, S. L. (1996). *Learning assistance and developmental education: A guide for effective practice.* San Francisco: Jossey-Bass.

Cross, K. P. (1976). *Accent on learning.* San Francisco: Jossey-Bass.

Maxwell, M. (1985). *Improving student learning skills.* San Francisco: Jossey-Bass.

National Center for Education Statistics. (1996). *Remedial education at higher education institutions in the fall 1995.* Washington, DC: U. S. Department of Education, Office of Educational Research and Improvement.

National Council of Educational Opportunity Associations. (1995). *Introducing TRIO* [Brochure]. Washington, DC: Author.

Plisko, V. W., & Stern, J. D. (1985). *The condition of education.* Washington, DC: U. S. Department of Education, Office of Educational Research and Improvement.

Tinto, V. (1986). *Leaving college: The causes and cures of student attrition.* Chicago: University of Chicago Press.

U. S. Office of Education. (1993). *Digest of educational statistics.* Washington, DC: U. S. Government Printing Office.

Chapter 2

WHO BELONGS IN COLLEGE: A SECOND LOOK

Carlette J. Hardin

Hardin (1988) identified the characteristics of students needing academic assistance in the hope that if policy makers better understood why students take developmental courses, then those policy makers would be less critical of developmental programs. Unfortunately, in the 10 years since that article was written, the debate over the role and appropriate place for developmental education has continued. Recently, the National Association for Developmental Education (1997) recorded such debates in 31 states.

The debates encompass several themes. Some argue the philosophical issue of developmental education, suggesting that higher education should be "higher" and, therefore, limited to the financially able and academically gifted. Others argue that the American education system is based on the Jeffersonian concept that all American citizens are entitled to achieve their full academic potential. They propose that the American taxpayers paying the bill for public education have a right to the education for which they are paying. As Cross (1976) notes, educational opportunity should mean more than the right to meet minimal standards; it should mean the right to reach one's full potential. Money, it seems, is the foundation for much of the discussion concerning developmental education. Since many policy makers have the mistaken idea that most developmental students are recent high school graduates who failed to take advantage of the opportunities they were given in high school, they charge the students with "double-dipping" and question the spending of additional money for what they consider remediation.

All too often the most important element of the developmental issue, the student, is forgotten in the arguments concerning developmental education. Few policy makers have recent experience in a developmental classroom; therefore, they have the misconception that the students filling the seats are 18-year olds who slept through high school and now want a second chance to learn at taxpayers' expense. One visit to a developmental program will show the fallacy of this thinking. The students served in developmental programs come from diverse backgrounds, and the reasons they need developmental courses are as complex as the students themselves. Hardin (1988) identified the characteristics of six categories of students who participate in developmental programs. While the demographics have changed in the almost 10 years since this article was published, the categories of students identified remain valid. A seventh category, "The Extreme Case," has been added to the original list of six. The seven categories are examined below.

The Poor Chooser

The most common type of student who fills developmental classrooms is the student who made a decision or decisions that have adversely affected his or her academic future (Hardin, 1988). These "poor choosers" are misprepared rather than underprepared. Typically, poor choosers made decisions that were detrimental to their academic future for one of two reasons.

The most common type of student who fills developmental classrooms is the student who made a decision or decisions that have adversely affected his or her academic future.

Some poor choosers selected something other than a college preparatory curriculum while they were in high school and, therefore, are ill prepared for the demands made by the college environment. From 1982 to 1994, the number of students taking college preparatory courses increased from 37.9% to 43% (U. S. Department of Education, 1997b). This was due in large part to the 1983 recommendation of the National Commission on Excellence in Education, published in *A Nation at Risk*, that all students take four years of English, three years each of mathematics, science, and social studies, and a half year of computer science. For those going on to college, an additional two years of foreign language were recommended. Since then the average number of science and mathematics credits earned by high school graduates has increased substantially. The mean number of mathematics credits (Carnegie units) earned in high school

rose from 2.5 in 1982 to 3.3 in 1992, and the number of science credits rose from 2.2 to 3.3. The percentage of graduates who completed all courses recommended by the Commission on Excellence rose from 2% in 1982 to 23% in 1992 (National Center for Educational Statistics, 1997a).

While this trend would imply that students graduating from high school since 1982 are better prepared for college, this is true for only those students who selected and completed a college-preparatory curriculum. During this period, the number of students who completed a high school program classified as "general" rose from 35.2% in 1982 to 45.3% in 1992 (U. S. Department of Education, 1997b). As Hodgkinson (1993) asserts, the 45% of students tracked into the "general" curriculum in high school are prepared for neither college nor work. Hodgkinson further notes that most of these students are coming from inner cities and rural areas. Statistics from the U. S. Department of Education (1997b) confirm this analysis in that only 20.5% of those students from the lowest level of the socioeconomic scale were in a college preparatory program while 60.1% of those from the top 25% of the socioeconomic scale earned a college preparatory diploma.

The second type of poor chooser is the student who dropped out of high school. The reasons for such decisions are as numerous and varied as the students themselves. The good news is that the dropout rate among 16 to 24-year olds has fallen over the past 20 years along with the dropout rate for all races, which has dropped from 13.9% in 1975 to 10.5% in 1994 (National Center for Education Statistics, 1997a). However, in 1992 approximately 3.4 million individuals in the United States from age 16 to 24 had not completed high school and were not currently enrolled in school. This number represents approximately 11% of all individuals in this age group (*School-to-Work Opportunities Act*, 1994). Many of these students will eventually realize that their only hope for a meaningful future is to complete their education and earn a college degree. They will earn a General Educational Development (GED) diploma and enroll in college with a false sense of security about their academic ability. What they often fail to understand is a GED diploma measures their ability to complete the most basic of high school level work. It does not measure their ability to be successful in college.

Those students who earned a GED diploma are in for a rude awakening when they reach college. Since they have a high school diploma, they assume they are prepared for college. Unfortunately, that is not the case, and as Crosby (1993) notes, the gap between the knowledge required to be successful in college and what is required to graduate from high school has actually widened since the publication of *A Nation at Risk* in 1983. Since then, many colleges and universities raised their admission requirements and strengthened their core curriculum based on the assurance that students graduating from high school were entering with better skills, so students who have anything but a college-preparatory curriculum find the gap between what they know and what they need to know wider than ever before. Without developmental courses, that gap can never be closed. As Hodgkinson (1993) proposes, "having a wide range of undergraduate institutions that specialize in different kinds of students from different backgrounds is vital to success in a highly diverse nation" (p. 623).

There are five additional points that must be remembered about the students who are poor choosers:

1. Their academic decisions were made early in life. Do we want to live in a society where a poor decision made at age 14 or 15 can never be corrected? We currently have laws that seal the records of juveniles when they reach maturity so they can have a second chance in life. Should we not offer a second chance if the student's only crime was failing to learn what is needed to be successful in college?

2. Their academic inability stems from a lack of background, not competence. Twenty-five

years ago many poor choosers left high school and acquired manufacturing jobs that guaranteed them good wages, benefits, and security. They went on to be productive citizens, making a contribution to their families and the community. Between 1979 and 1985, the number of manufacturing jobs in the U. S. declined by 1.7 million (Lewis, 1988). These jobs were replaced by jobs in retail trade and service, and it takes two retail jobs to equal the wages of one manufacturing job. Displaced poor choosers learn quickly that they must acquire more education if they hope to have the standard of living that had once been available to those without a college degree. They return to school willing to work at their education with the same dedication they had devoted to their job.

3. They often had no control over the decisions that affected their lives. Decisions were made by coaches, parents, counselors, or others who thought they had the best interest of the student in mind. In some cases, decisions by policy makers of the local school system impact choice. Students from rural and inner city schools may not have the same diversity in course selection as their counterparts at comprehensive high schools in suburban areas.

4. They may be convinced by their past academic experiences that they lack academic ability; they, therefore, avoid academic challenges. Poor choosers need to see that skill comes with practice and to learn that lack of experience is not synonymous with lack of ability. Without intrusive counseling to overcome students' perceptions of themselves as academic failures, past patterns will be repeated and the students will fail.

5. They lack the skills to interact in a college classroom. Many poor choosers are first-generation college students who are not familiar with the language of higher education. Often, they fail to understand the expectations of faculty. Unless they can be provided this information in a way that is neither threatening nor embarrassing, they will leave the institution.

Poor choosers can become excellent students when provided the appropriate developmental courses. When given the proper help, these students quickly make up for the lost time caused by their poor academic decisions.

The Adult Student

The second type of student filling developmental classrooms is the adult learner who has been away from an academic setting for an extended time. The adult student population has been one of the fastest growing segments in higher education. In the late 1970s and early 1980s, older students, primarily women and part-time students, began to enroll in greater numbers (Gerald, 1997). In fact, the number of older students in college has been growing faster than the number of younger students. Between 1980 and 1990, the enrollment of students under age 25 increased by three percent. During this period, enrollment of students 25 and over rose by 34%. From 1990 to 1998, Gerald (1997) projects a 14% increase in growth in enrollments of students over 25 and an increase of 6% in the number of students under 25. The proportion of students 25 years old and over rose from 38% in 1987 to 43.8% in 1995. While the proportion of adult students is projected to drop to 40% by the year 2007 as baby boomers reach retirement, colleges can expect to continue to see large numbers of gray-haired students filling their classrooms. Many of these students feel they have wasted 20 or 30 years, and they do not want to waste another day. For many adult students, developmental education is the first step in acquiring the future they want.

The adult students who enter our colleges and universities bring unique characteristics to the campus that not only create problems for the students but also for the institution. Almost all adult students are returning to college because of some transitional state in their personal or career

Many poor choosers are first-generation college students who are not familiar with the language of higher education . . . [they] can become excellent students when provided the appropriate developmental courses.

life. Greenfeig and Goldberg (1984) found that the classification of adult students includes those who (a) are newly separated or divorced, (b) want or need a mid-life career change, (c) wish to reenter the job market, and (d) have been laid off or have chosen to leave their jobs and return to college to upgrade skills and obtain a higher level job. Therefore, while these individuals try to establish themselves as students, they are creating new identities in all areas of their lives. As these students try to deal with the emotional issues evolving from these life changes, they also must deal with the emotional challenges of being a first-time student.

Although it is common for all students to experience stress when they enter college, the amount of stress experienced by nontraditional students is tremendous. Besides being a college student, adult students can be spouses, parents, and employees. Each of these roles provides a unique set of responsibilities pulling the student away from the time needed for academic pursuits. Because of their lack of academic experience, adult students do not have the academic network that exists for their younger counterparts. Adult students often hesitate to speak up in class or seek the instructor outside class. The majority, being commuter students, leave campus when classes end and therefore never establish a network of classmates to call upon when they must miss class or fail to understand instructions. For adult students, everything from the vocabulary to the administrative structure of the academic environment is new and foreign.

Hardin (1988) found that the adult learner is often in need of developmental help. Many adult students may need such assistance because they left high school without getting the skills needed to succeed in college. Between 1980 and 1994, the National Center for Education Statistics (1997a) found that the proportion of the adult population 25 years of age and over with four years of high school or more rose from 69% to 81%. However, that means that 12% of adults in this age group are without a high school education. These students may have poor self-concepts and see themselves as less capable than their younger classmates. Other adults may have had a college-preparatory background when they were in high school, yet have not used these academic skills in many years. Cuccaro-Alamin (1997) found that many students delay their entry into postsecondary education and that delaying entry is more common among lower socioeconomic status students than those from a higher socioeconomic status. Delaying enrollment in postsecondary education by as little as one year after high school is associated with poorer persistence and attainment outcomes. The longer the delay, the more difficulties the student faces. Without the help provided by such developmental programs, adult students may become discouraged and decide they were previously wise to avoid the college environment for such a long time.

However, the picture for nontraditional students is not completely bleak. Adult students bring experiences to the classroom that add to the wealth of information available to all students. These students are often described by their instructors as more eager, motivated, and committed than their traditional age counterparts. Haponski and McCabe (1985) found that there is less absenteeism among adult students. Adult students have a greater appreciation of good teaching. Once enrolled at a college, most adult students become determined to obtain a degree.

The existence of programs to meet the needs of developmental students is often defended by pointing out that everyone deserves a second chance. For adult students on our campuses, developmental courses are their first, and possibly only, chance for an education. For many, it will also be their last.

The Student with a Disability

The third type of student in developmental programs is the student who has a physical or learning disability (Hardin, 1988). The number of students with disabilities entering postsecondary

education is increasing daily. Between 1977 and 1994 the number of learners identified with learning disabilities increased over 200% (U. S. Department of Education, 1995). Many of these students will decide to continue their educations beyond high school. The U. S. Department of Education (1997a) found that 6.3% of all undergraduates and 4% of all graduate students enrolled in postsecondary institutions in 1992-1993 had one or more of the following conditions: a specific learning disability, a visual or hearing impairment, a physical or mobility disability, a speech disability, or a health impairment. Forty-seven percent of the undergraduates with disabilities were over the age of 30 and had the added disadvantage of being nontraditional students.

Hardin (1988) found that students with physical or learning disabilities may need developmental classes because of the following three conditions:

1. The disability may have prevented the student from entering and becoming a part of the mainstream of secondary education. The educational plan developed for the student may have focused on the immediate needs of the student rather than the student's needs in the future. If the student was not enrolled in college-preparatory courses, he or she may enter college with academic deficiencies.

2. The student may have been taught in isolation, and therefore may have had little opportunity to interact with teachers or peers. Such students fail to learn to interact with their peers. They have not been exposed to a variety of teaching styles. They may have had little experience with the lecture format or the demands of the college classroom.

3. The student may have lost previously learned material if the disability is the result of an injury. Relearning becomes a frustrating experience.

Many students with disabilities find that the support provided at the elementary and secondary level is not available at the college level. Faculty members are subject-area specialists with no training in providing accommodations to students with disabilities. When faced with students who cannot learn through the common methods used each day, these teachers may feel powerless to help.

The first generation of students who entered preschool under Section 504 of the Rehabilitation Act of 1973 has now completed high school and is currently entering college. These students and their parents are knowledgeable about the law and are demanding access to a college education. It is not a question of whether students with disabilities will be admitted or not, but how colleges and universities will serve them once they are admitted. Many institutions of higher education are turning to developmental education programs to provide the required services.

The Ignored

The fourth type of developmental student, "the ignored," had academic or physical problems that were never detected while attending high school (Hardin, 1988). Many students spend their elementary and secondary years staying out of the teacher's way and, in the process, have academic and physical problems that have been ignored. These ignored students expend a great deal of energy maintaining anonymity. Of course, while being anonymous eliminates the possibility that they will be corrected or embarrassed in the classroom, it also limits what they will learn. Too often teachers view the shy or quiet student as less capable and fail to challenge or push the student. Later, when these students decide to give teachers and the educational system another try, they are behind their classmates in what they know and what they can perform.

In addition, the ignored student's passive involvement in classes often causes physical or learning disabilities to go undetected. A dramatic example was discovered when students enrolling in developmental courses at Volunteer State Community College were screened for visual and hearing

It is not a question of whether students with disabilities will be admitted or not, but how colleges and universities will serve them once they are admitted.

problems (Hiett, 1987). The screening revealed that 65% of the students enrolled in developmental courses had visual problems that had never been detected. Another 54% of the students had a hearing loss, while 41% of the students had both visual and hearing problems. Is it such a shock that these ignored students encounter academic difficulties?

Often it is a developmental educator who first suggests to adult students that they might have a learning disability or Attention Deficient Disorder (ADD). Children and Adults with Attention Deficit Disorder (1995) notes that many adults with ADD were never diagnosed as children. Thus, they are not aware of, nor do they understand, the consequences of their disability. They may have spent years being treated for depression, antisocial personality, or character disorders. Because their ADD has been undiagnosed or misdiagnosed, they may have low self-esteem and fear the academic environment. Students with physical and learning disabilities face tremendous challenges in higher education, but students who have lived with a disability that was never detected must also overcome years of self-doubt concerning their own ability and self-worth.

Most successful students remember being motivated by a teacher or a parent who saw their potential and encouraged them to go further than the student thought possible. This has never happened to the ignored student. Traditional education has failed the ignored student, and unless the student can develop new perceptions of how learning takes place, and begin his or her postsecondary education at a level where success is possible, failure will occur again.

The Student with Limited English Proficiency

The fifth type of student enrolled in developmental programs is the student who has limited English skills (Hardin, 1988). This group includes students who acquired their elementary and secondary education in a foreign country. These students usually need help in developing verbal skills and in communicating with fellow students and teachers. They may need academic assistance in the areas of reading and writing rather than mathematics.

When one thinks of students with limited English proficiency attending American universities, the foreign scholar who is an academic pursuing an advanced degree or conducting research comes to mind. However, 48% of the 453,787 international students enrolled in the United States in 1995 were undergraduates (Desruisseaux, 1996); and as Ross and Roe (1986) note, even very intelligent international students often have inadequate English communication skills.

Although statistics show international students accounted for 3.1% of the total enrollment in U. S. higher education in 1994-1995 (Desruisseaux, 1996), the number of students with limited English proficiency far exceeds this number. These figures do not account for the students who are foreign-born family members of American citizens. These family members may have very limited English skills, yet often they are not counted in the statistics of international students because they are not required to have visa privileges. The National Center for Education Statistics (1997b) found that the number of children enrolled in public schools who had difficulty speaking English increased from 1.25 million in 1970 to 2.44 million in 1995. In 1993-1994, 46% of all public schools had limited-English-proficient (LEP) students. In central cities, urban fringes, and large towns, about 60% of the schools had such students. In five states, 75% or more of the schools had LEP students. As these students graduate, they enter colleges and universities with less than sufficient English skills to be successful. Few institutions of higher education are adequately equipped to deal with these students, and administrators often turn to faculty teaching in developmental education programs to provide the assistance needed by students with limited English proficiency.

Students in the five categories listed above deserve a chance in our institutions of higher education. For the most part, their need for academic assistance is a result of a lack of preparation, not

ability. Therefore, they should not only be admitted, but also provided the necessary assistance to be successful. There are two groups, however, who take developmental courses and who may not belong in higher education. These two groups of students are classified as "users" and "extreme cases." Of all the categories of developmental students, it is the students in these categories who seem appropriate candidates to bar from the "open door" of public education.

The User

The "user" is not going to college to acquire an education but to reap the benefits of being classified as a college student. This sixth type of developmental student lacks clear-cut academic goals and intends to use the educational system for his or her own purposes (Hardin, 1988). Often these benefits are monetary, as students receive financial aid, veteran's benefits, or parental support. Sometimes these students are simply attending college as a means to avoid acquiring a job or facing their parents' wrath. Others see college as a place to hang out and play sports until spotted by a professional team, or to socialize without being required to earn the income to support their social life.

Users assess the academic climate and determine what is minimally acceptable for continued enrollment. If they must maintain a 2.0 grade point average (GPA) to stay in school, they will earn a 2.0, not a 2.1. If the syllabus says that they are allowed three absences, they perceive these as three days of escape. Once they know the ground rules, they become the most vocal in their dislike of subject matter and university requirements.

Users need much more than academic assistance. They need counseling to overcome their myopic view of life. Career counseling is also needed, as users have planned only for the immediate future and have not considered what they will do when they slip, earn a 1.9 GPA, and are suspended.

However, users can be successful, and once they become excited about the prospect of learning and decide that earning a degree is a priority in their lives, they make rapid academic progress.

The Extreme Case

Christian and Carter (1995) first identified the developmental student classified as the "extreme case." Students in this category have such extreme academic, emotional, and psychological problems that they cannot be successful in higher education. These students not only create problems for themselves, but they prevent faculty members from teaching and fellow students from learning.

Usually, these students meet the admission requirements, and the depth of their problems is not discovered until they create a disturbance in the classroom. An example of such an extreme case was 40-year-old Roy. Roy was struggling in the most basic developmental math class and was constantly interrupting the instructor because he failed to understand the information presented. Roy demanded an inordinate amount of time from the instructor as he camped out in her office whenever she was not in class. A review of Roy's admission records not only showed that Roy had earned a regular high school diploma in the early 1970s, but that he had a respectable GPA. Bewildered, the instructor questioned Roy about his math background and was told that when Roy was in school, he was enrolled in all "special" classes and that he had not had "hard math," such as simple multiplication.

There is no legal or ethical way to prevent most students who can be classified as extreme cases from attending an institution. When a student who is in a fragile emotional state applies to the institution, there is no way to know if the pressure to perform will be what pushes the student over the edge. When a student with severe psychological problems applies, there is no admission standard that detects if the student will eventually become a danger to him or herself, to faculty, or to fellow students. As George W. Young (1992) of Broward Community College notes,

We're talking about those who should be institutionalized, who are out of control and desperate to get their hands on $4,000 to $5,000. Problems arise when people who are not functioning emotionally or intellectually show up in class or financial aid offices and become disruptive. (p. A21)

To establish an admission screening process restrictive enough to identify and restrict the extreme cases would be detrimental to students who can successfully attend college. There are students who have severe intellectual, emotional, and psychological disabilities who function very well in an educational setting. Somehow, we have to balance access to those who want and need to go to college with the denial of those students who are only there because they were told to be in school by their probation officer or social worker. Therefore, our goal should not be to close the door to opportunity for the extreme cases, but to train faculty to identify such students so they can be counseled early in their academic careers. This prevents the heartache often felt by these students when they cannot succeed.

In the past, many labels have been used to describe developmental students . . . Most of these labels focus on weaknesses rather than strengths.

Perhaps higher education has been "higher" because colleges and universities were able to stay above the problems of society; however, this is no longer possible. The problems of poverty, violence, drugs, mental illness, and homelessness are being brought to institutions of higher education by these extreme cases. While the number of students in this category has been small, it is growing daily. Because developmental programs are the entry points for so many of the students who fit the extreme case classification, developmental faculty face these students every day. Most students in developmental courses are underprepared, and this does not equate to being incapable or ineducable (Hardin, 1988). Most live productive lives outside the institution. They can raise families, hold down jobs, or join the military. However, this is not true for the extreme case. The extreme case often decides to go to college because he or she is not functioning outside the institution. These students are in grave need of intervention, but the college environment is not the place where it should be provided.

In the past, many labels have been used to describe developmental students, such as disruptive, probationary, remedial, alternative, high-risk, at-risk, and nontraditional. Most of these labels focus on weaknesses rather than strengths. The purpose of this article is not to add new labels by listing the categories of students in developmental programs. However, by focusing on the characteristics of these categories, one can see that the backgrounds and needs that put developmental students at a disadvantage can be overcome.

Those who support access to higher education must remind policy makers that the issue of access is a bigger issue than an individual student. If we deny admission to students who are underprepared, we have narrowed our vision of the society we want to foster. When policy makers see our students as developmental students rather than students who need a developmental course or courses, it is because of their limited experience with these students. They have not met the music student who earned her music degree and traveled the world with the university choir after taking one developmental math course. They have not met the professional basketball player who read his first novel in a developmental reading course and earned his degree while playing collegiate ball. They never met the 30-year-old father of three who accepted his company's offer to pay for an engineering degree, and after taking developmental mathematics, not only earned a bachelor's degree in engineering, but a master's as well. They have had no interaction with the director of a crisis line who took developmental writing before going on to complete her degree in social work and change the lives of countless individuals. When they meet these students, they will come to understand the impact developmental education has in the lives of students each and every day.

References

Children and Adults with Attention Deficit Disorder. (1995). *Adults with attention deficit disorder*. [On-line]. Available: http://www.chadd.org/factsy.html

Christian, A., & Carter, S. (1995). *Extreme students who will never succeed academically*. Unpublished manuscript, Austin Peay State University, Clarksville, TN.

Crosby, E. (1993). The at-risk decade. *Phi Delta Kappan, 74,* 598-604.

Cross, K. P. (1976). *Accent on learning.* San Francisco: Jossey-Bass.

Cuccaro-Alamin, S. (1997). *Postsecondary persistence and attainment*. [On-line]. Available: http://nces01.ed.gov/NCES/pubs/cc/c97007.html

Desruisseaux, P. (1996, December 6). A record number of foreign students enrolled at U. S. colleges last year. *The Chronicle of Higher Education,* A64-A68.

Gerald, D. E. (1997). Chapter 2: Higher education enrollment. *Projections of education statistics to 2007.* [On-line]. Available: http://nces01.ed.gov/NCES/pubs/pj/p97c02.html

Greenfeig, B. R., & Goldberg, B. J. (1984). Orienting returning adult students. In M. L. Upcraft (Ed.), *Orienting students to college.* San Francisco: Jossey-Bass.

Haponski, W. C., & McCabe, C. E. (1985). *The education and career planning guide for adults.* Princeton, NJ: Peterson's Guides.

Hardin, C. J. (1988). Access to higher education: Who belongs? *Journal of Developmental Education, 12,* 2-6.

Hiett, J. (1987). *Results of vision and hearing screening.* Unpublished research, Volunteer State Community College, Gallatin, TN.

Hodgkinson, H. (1993). American education: The good, the bad, and the task. *Phi Delta Kappan, 74,* 619-623.

Lewis, A. (1988). Barriers in the path of the non-college-bound. *Phi Delta Kappan, 69,* 396-397.

National Association for Developmental Education. (1997). *1997 leadership manual.* Chicago: Author.

National Center for Education Statistics. (1997a). *Educational outcomes.* [On-line]. Available: http://nces01.ed.gov./NCES/pubs/minidig95/outcome.html#17

National Center for Education Statistics. (1997b). *Public schools with bilingual or ESL programs*. [On-line]. Available: http://nces01.ed.gov./NCES/pubs/ce/c9745a01.html

National Commission on Excellence in Education. (1983). *A nation at risk*. Washington, DC: Author.

Ross, E. B., & Roe, B. D. (1986). *The case for basic skills programs in higher education*. Bloomington, IN: Phi Delta Kappa.

School-to-Work Opportunities Act of 1994. (1994). Public Law 103-239, 108 Stat 568, May 4, 1994.

U. S. Department of Education. (1995). *Seventeenth annual report to Congress on the implementation of the Individuals with Disabilities Education Act*. Washington, DC: Author.

U. S. Department of Education. (1997a). *The digest of education statistics 1996/Table 206*. [On-line]. Available: http://nces01.ed.gov./NCES/pubs/D96/d96t206.html

U. S. Department of Education. (1997b). *Youth indicators 1996/Indicator 26*. [On-line]. Available: http://nces01.ed.gov./NCES/pubs/yi/9626a.html

Young, G. W. (1992, September 30). Ways and means. *The Chronicle of Higher Education*, p. A21.

Chapter 3

Transitions in Developmental Education:
Interviews with Hunter Boylan
and David Arendale

Cheryl B. Stratton

Developmental educators are constantly reinventing themselves. In a time when student populations and missions are changing, and administrative and legislative support is questionable, many traditional programs are searching for identity. In the National Association for Developmental Education's first monograph, Higbee (1996) asks, "How do we want to define ourselves? Is our mission to promote the growth of students to their highest potential or to correct a previous wrong?" (p. 63). This question implies that developmental educators have control of their destiny. To a great extent they do. The repurposing of their current efforts is leading to expanded missions to serve broader populations.

The Strategic Plan of the National Association for Developmental Education (*NADE's Strategic Plan*, 1997) suggests that "by 2003, NADE will be a nationally recognized association of professionals with expertise to help students succeed academically throughout their entire educational experience from high school through college and graduate/professional schools" (p. 1). The role of developmental education is changing to include more comprehensive designs and services that can affect the growth of all postsecondary students. These new self-directed definitions of the breadth and scope of our mission can provide models for the 21st century.

This chapter asks two leaders in developmental education to do some future forecasting. Commenting about the role of developmental education in the future, Hunter Boylan and David Arendale discuss influences on the profession, requirements for success, and a view of expanded missions to promote the cognitive and affective growth of all students.

Hunter Boylan, one of the founders of the National Association for Developmental Education, served as President of NADE from 1981 to 1983. He is currently the director of the National Center of Developmental Education at Appalachian State University and editor of *Research in Developmental Education*. He has also served as the director of the doctoral program in developmental education at Grambling State University and director of the Kellogg Institute at Appalachian State University. Since 1990 Boylan has been the principal investigator for a study funded by a grant from the Exxon Education Foundation to determine the efficacy of developmental education programs in the United States; his findings have been reported in numerous publications (Boylan, Bliss, & Bonham, 1997; Boylan & Bonham, 1992; Boylan, Bonham, & Bliss, 1994).

David Arendale is the immediate past president of NADE and has served as the associate director of the Center for Academic Development at the University of Missouri-Kansas City (UMKC) since 1991. As National Project Director for Supplemental Instruction, he also has published extensively (Arendale, 1997a, 1997b, 1997c; Martin & Arendale, 1993; Martin & Arendale, 1994) and is a major contributor to the NADE web page (http://www.umkc.edu/centers/cad/nade.htm). The following statements are Arendale's and Boylan's responses to interview questions posed during conversations with them in the summer of 1997.

Cheryl Stratton: Dozens of U. S. Department of Education programs that have historically funded academic support programs have been eliminated over the past years. Some political officials argue that developmental education should be shifted from four-year to two-year institutions. Others wishing to reduce or eliminate affirmative action policies believe that affirmative action mandates developmental education. Politicians are discussing eliminating student financial aid for developmental education (Arendale, 1997d). Even so, many learning support programs are actually expanding. What are your general feelings about the future of developmental education?

David Arendale: I am cautiously optimistic for the future of the profession. I think that developmental education is at a crossroads. The choices that developmental educators make in the next few years will decide whether the professionals are change agents for the next phase of service or whether they are assigned tasks by

others. It is exciting to see what some institutions are already doing to transform their departments and centers to meet new needs more effectively.

Hunter Boylan: At this moment, developmental education is more in the forefront of the public debate on higher education than at any other time in the history of American higher education. This is basically good news in spite of the fact that the debate sometimes includes negative comments about developmental education. The fact that it is being debated means that attention is being focused on it. The number of times remedial or developmental education has been mentioned in the news media during the last two years is greater than the number of times it was mentioned in the media during the entire past decade. That attention will help legislators, higher education executives, and the public understand our field better.

In states where developmental education is part of the higher education debate, it is incumbent upon professionals in our field to contribute to that debate, to explain why we need remediation, to provide data demonstrating the efficacy of what we do, to demonstrate how developmental education contributes to an educated citizenry, and to show how developmental education contributes to opportunity for people of all colors and socioeconomic backgrounds.

I regard the fact that the debate over the role and scope of developmental education is taking place as good for the field politically. It will only be bad for the field if we allow those who don't understand what we do, don't want us to do it, or don't value the outcomes of what we do to be the only voices heard in that debate. We have a very good case. We just have to make it.

Stratton: What changes in the political environment will have an effect on the profession?

Boylan: The major change in the political environment is that legislators are becoming more aware of developmental education. As a result of that awareness, some are supporting it and some are opposing it. Some are advocating legislation that will strengthen developmental education, and some are advocating legislation that will weaken it. Some are advocating legislation that won't have any effect on it. But because developmental education is becoming more of a legislative issue, we will probably have more legislative allies as well as legislative opposition.

Arendale: There are numerous trends at the state and national level that are having an important, and generally negative, impact upon our profession. Understanding the trends will enable us to anticipate some of the changes ahead and provide time for us to adapt our programs to meet these changes. It is dangerous to be in a reactive mode regarding policy makers. Change takes much time and energy.

Following are some of the trends that will have an impact upon our service to students. There will be fewer grants from the federal government for academic support programs at individual campuses. Due to the federal budget crunch, dozens of U. S. Department of Education programs have been eliminated. There are strong discussions whether the Title III Strengthening Institutions Program should be phased out. Title III, along with other programs, has been critical for beginning academic assistance programs at hundreds of colleges across America. Along with less money, there will be less influence by the federal government and more directives by the states. This will result in uneven regulations regarding developmental education across the United States. There will be pockets of great support for developmental education in sections of the country.

There is a trend to curtail or eliminate developmental education at public four-year institutions and direct students needing help to local two-year colleges. Reports indicate that Colorado already has instituted such a policy. The latest example of this trend is South Carolina, which plans to phase out developmental courses at the public four-year institutions in the next few years. While traditional forms of academic service may be curtailed, other opportunities will

While traditional forms of academic service may be curtailed, other opportunities will be available. The need for academic assistance will still exist, if not increase.

be available. The need for academic assistance will still exist, if not increase.

In *NADE's Strategic Plan* (1997), there is a section devoted to identifying internal and external forces that will impact upon the developmental education profession over the next decade. The trend areas considered are student-related, political, institutional, economic, and instructional. The document is available for review at the NADE homepage (*NADE's Strategic Plan*, 1997).

Stratton: Arendale discussed the trend of some states moving developmental education to two-year colleges. I find it surprising that four-year colleges and universities would want to release control of their developmental education programs. Do you think that moving developmental education to two-year colleges is a viable idea?

Boylan: I do not support the notion of relegating developmental education to the community colleges. Although this issue will be brought up in many state legislatures during the coming years, it is not an educationally sound idea. It is difficult for a community college to teach basic English and mathematics at a level that would prepare students for a university without a great deal of collaboration between the community college and the university. Although I have seen several state legislatures attempt to mandate that developmental courses be taught exclusively at community colleges, I have yet to see any of these legislatures attempt to mandate the collaboration required to make this work.

Furthermore, community colleges have a very difficult task in facilitating college transfer for weaker students. Successful developmental education for the weakest students requires that these students invest a great deal of time in academic support activities, frequently outside of class. Developmental education is best carried out in environments where students are also immersed in the culture of academe.

Unfortunately, about a third of the underprepared students at community colleges are enrolled only part-time, and the vast majority of all underprepared students at community colleges are commuters (Boylan, Bonham, & Bliss, 1994). Consequently, it is difficult for them to put the time into developmental education or to be immersed in the academic culture.

At this point, the majority of those who start out at a two-year institution never receive a baccalaureate degree. Unless the resources and support are provided for community colleges to enhance their college transfer programs, forcing underprepared students to take remediation at two-year schools will probably reduce the number of university graduates in this country. It will particularly reduce the number of low income and minority students who receive university degrees.

Relegating remedial education to two-year schools has the potential of turning these institutions into remedial colleges. This, in turn, degrades the very important comprehensive and transfer missions of the two-year schools. Those who want to initiate a future trend of relegating developmental education exclusively to community colleges should be forewarned that this is a dangerous trend.

Stratton: At Georgia State University (a large, urban, mainly commuter campus) we are seeing a changing student population. The average age of undergraduates is 27. The average age of students enrolled in developmental courses is 23. This means the majority of first-year students have been out of high school for five years. How does this increase in population of nontraditional students and of those high school students who did not take college preparatory courses affect developmental education?

Boylan: Eventually even state legislators will figure out that only 43% of high school graduates take a full battery of college preparatory courses, yet 62% of graduates go on to college within a year after completing high school. In addition to that 62%, the numbers go up substantially when you take into account those who work for a while, join the military, or drop out of education until later in life. The notion that

"We've already paid for this once" is what my father used to refer to as "horse feathers." We paid to have college preparatory courses delivered to fewer than half of our high school students. Now we're paying to have much of the other half do preparatory work in college.

Let's see, 43% of our young people take college preparatory courses in high school while 62% go to college. That's a difference of 19%. Another 10% or so of entering students are those who are going to college later in life. That's about 30% differential between those who take college preparatory courses and those who actually go on to college. The National Center for Education Statistics reports that about 30% of entering college students need one or more remedial courses. So why is anyone surprised at the need for remediation?

Arendale: There is a false belief that by raising graduation requirements for high school students there will be no need for developmental education at the postsecondary level. This fails to account for the many students who enroll in college who have been out of high school for years.

It also makes an assumption that higher exit requirements from high school will automatically enable these students to achieve high academic achievement at the college level. While the general public's expectation level for high school graduates has risen, professionals in postsecondary education continue to raise their expectation levels for college students. Recently, when entrance standards were raised at one of the campuses of California State University, the mathematics department raised their required pass rate for the department screening test even higher. More students were placed into the college developmental courses after the increased college entrance standards than before! I think that there will be a greater need for developmental education in the future, not less. But the form of assistance must be acceptable to the policy makers who will regulate us.

As in far too many areas of American life, there are many who prefer to blame others rather than seeking creative solutions to problems. Rather than agreeing that more resources need to be provided to college students to help [them] reach higher levels of academic achievement, some would prefer to blame others for providing "damaged goods." Seeking someone to blame, some policy makers want to levy a monetary fine on high schools that produce students who need academic assistance or developmental courses at the college level. Such plans are being considered in Florida, Montana, New Jersey, Washington, and West Virginia. Other policy makers want to force students who enroll in developmental courses to pay higher tuition, thereby paying the "true" cost of their education. In Florida, students who retake a developmental education course for the third time pay a higher tuition fee. In Oklahoma, developmental education courses at most two- and four-year institutions carry a surcharge of between $10 and $20 per credit hour. In Wisconsin, students must pay the "full cost" of the developmental courses.

Stratton: Dr. Boylan, in your article, "Who are the Developmental Students?" (Boylan, Bonham, & Bliss, 1994), you state:

> By all accounts, one thing that has increasingly come to characterize American higher education in the past 25 years has been the diversity of its students. Developmental education programs not only reflect but also contribute to this diversity . . . Just as its students are diverse in their characteristics, developmental programs ought also to be diverse in their characteristics. (p. 3)

What are your thoughts about the multicultural nature of our students?

Boylan: A great many developmental programs, particularly those in urban areas or on campuses on the east or west coasts, are experiencing an influx of students even more diverse and less traditional than those we've served in the past. After years of effort, we've finally *almost* learned how to work with a diverse student population including African Americans or Mexican Americans. We haven't mastered that yet, but we're getting better. We are still learning to work with those groups, while simultaneously being inundated with Asians,

Russians, Cubans, Haitians, and a host of South American refugees.

The need for ESL [English as a Second Language] courses and programs as part of developmental education is increasing. The need for us to understand multiculturalism in its truest and most international sense is increasing. The need for us to look beyond our own culture for solutions is increasing. Unfortunately, there are very few opportunities for us to learn how to do these things. There are very few people out there who know how to do these things. Even more unfortunately, we're still trying to learn how to do developmental education right, at the same time we need to learn the lessons necessary to serve newly diverse populations.

Stratton: I agree, Dr. Boylan, however one of the findings from your national study is that it is important to help others understand the nature of developmental students. You quoted Abraham (1991), saying, "Many people probably believe that remedial/developmental work began as a response to the Civil Rights movement or the equal opportunity legislation of the 1960s and 1970s" (p. 1). Some believe that students participating in these programs are from minority backgrounds. However, your study shows that the majority (62.5%) of developmental students are White (Boylan, Bonham, & Bliss, 1994).

Boylan: That is true. The preponderance of developmental students has always been from majority backgrounds (i.e., White students). However, the 37.5% of minority students in our programs is becoming increasingly diverse, no longer representing simply African Americans and Hispanics but a host of other groups. These students of color who populate our programs are still very deserving of our best efforts.

Stratton: What components do you see as necessary to make developmental education programs successful into the 21st century? What transitions do you see as essential?

Arendale: It is essential that our profession continue to grow to meet new needs and to learn from research that is being conducted concerning effective practices. Rather than reacting to the mandates of policy makers, it is critical that we help shape the agenda.

The following three areas are ones that I hope developmental educators will consider: reinventing their departments into comprehensive teaching and learning centers, becoming an integral part of campus enrollment management programs, and developing programs that embed study strategy development into college-level content courses.

Stratton: Please discuss further your idea of comprehensive teaching and learning centers.

Arendale: We need to reinvent ourselves as resources for the entire campus, students and faculty alike, in renewing the learning environment. Our institutions need our centers and departments to expand our services to include academic enrichment for all students. In the past, some institutions focused their attention by serving only students at the far extremes, developmental students and honors students. We can become comprehensive teaching and learning centers. Whatever name we have, we need to become more comprehensive in service. I believe that is the bright future for our profession.

We [learning center programs] need to reinvent ourselves as resources for the entire campus, students and faculty alike, in renewing the learning environment.

Faculty development activities are a natural fit for many of us in the profession. Many professors are searching for effective ways to change the classroom focus from how faculty lecture to how students learn. Faculty have the content knowledge. We, as learning assistance professionals, possess knowledge and skills that would be helpful to faculty members as they improve the learning environment within their classrooms. Many developmental educators possess knowledge and skills in one or more of the following areas: peer collaborative learning, informal classroom assessment techniques, new paradigms of student learning pedagogy, instructional technology, affective needs of students, curriculum development, peer review of

teaching activities, professional developmental activities, adapting instruction for diverse learning styles, and many others.

At my own campus we often consult with faculty members regarding instructional delivery, computer-based instruction, and integration of technology with distance education. We conduct new faculty member orientation and host faculty development workshops. This has allowed us to become more deeply integrated into the academic fabric of the institution. We are partners in the learning process.

Stratton: Arendale suggests comprehensive teaching and learning centers for the whole campus. Your research (Boylan, Bliss, & Bonham, 1997) confirms that centralized developmental programs are more effective than decentralized programs. What other components do you see as necessary for these centers?

Boylan: Insofar as program components are concerned, I believe that in the future learning assistance centers will become an increasingly important part of developing those skills, particularly at universities. Computer-based assessment and diagnosis will become a critical component of successful programs at all levels. Ongoing, intensive, and systematic faculty and staff development will also be important factors for successful developmental programs everywhere. Our students, our research and theory base, and our technology will all change, and we must learn to change with them. Evaluation of our outcomes—not only to demonstrate accountability, but also to strengthen our programs—will also become more important in the future.

Stratton: Could you elaborate on your statement about developmental educators being partners with enrollment management programs?

Arendale: Developmental educators possess many of the skills and the knowledge needed for successful enrollment management programs.

When reviewing concurrent session topics at the recent Noel-Levitz National Conference on Student Retention, I was struck that developmental educators already possess many of the skills showcased at the conference. Some of these skills included establishing computer-based instruction, small peer-led study groups, academic alert programs, academic intervention strategies, intrusive academic advising, academic assessment, and new student orientation. Developmental educators must be players in this important activity. It is critical that we do research concerning our programs and their impact on higher levels of reenrollment and graduation of our students when compared with others. Administrators expect quantitative studies to document our claims. This will provide the needed credibility in their eyes. We need to volunteer to serve on enrollment management task forces and be willing to take on additional responsibilities. A quality learning assistance program can serve as the centerpiece for an effective enrollment management program.

Stratton: Georgia State University is trying several new methods to reach students who need academic assistance, including offering Supplemental Instruction and learning support co-courses for such high-risk courses as American History, English Composition, and College Algebra (Commander, Stratton, Callahan, & Smith, 1996; Stratton, 1996). Would you elaborate on some of the successful programs that you have seen?

Arendale: I think that concurrent development of learning strategies is essential for a variety of reasons. Students need to apply immediately learning strategies with college-level content material to make a difference for higher academic achievement and student persistence rates. The professional literature suggests that students need to make direct applications of these skills (Kerr, 1993; Martin, Blanc, & DeBuhr 1983; Rafoth & DeFabo, 1990; Stahl, Simpson, & Hayes, 1992) or they will be unable to transfer them for use in other classes. Offering traditional study skill classes that are isolated from course content is not in step with the research. Of all the developmental courses that are offered, they are the most vulnerable for elimination by institutions.

Two ways to embed study strategies into the curriculum are paired classes and Supplemental Instruction. Paired classes are those that enroll students in two courses. One course is the regular college-level content course (e.g., history, chemistry). The other is an adjunct course that uses the content course as the base to teach study strategies. A recent article by Commander and Smith (1995) describes this method. At Georgia State University, an adjunct course (Learning Strategies for History) was paired with American History. Most of those enrolled in the adjunct course were developmental students. Though these students were less academically prepared, they achieved nearly the same final course grade in history as the other students. This is an excellent example of concurrent development of learning strategies while [students are also] enrolled in college-level course work.

The second way to embed study strategies into the curriculum is through Supplemental Instruction (SI) for historically difficult courses. The SI program was developed at University of Missouri-Kansas City in 1973 by Deanna C. Martin. Rather than targeting at-risk students, the SI program provides services to courses that have a high rate of final course grades of D or F and course withdrawals (e.g., Anatomy, General Chemistry, College Algebra). A student who has already been successful in the targeted course is hired by the department. After extensive training in collaborative learning and modeling of study strategies, the student (called the SI leader) attends the class again. Three to five times a week the SI leader facilitates study review sessions where course content is reviewed along with modeling of appropriate study strategies by the SI leader and others in the group. SI sessions are focused on what to learn along with how to learn it. Research from UMKC and other institutions suggests that SI participation is correlated with higher final course grades, higher reenrollment rates, and higher graduation rates. Since its development in 1973 at UMKC, faculty and staff from more than 800 colleges in the U. S. and 12 other countries have received training to implement their own SI programs. In addition to the benefit to SI participants, other colleges have reported using SI to create an environment for

SI leaders and faculty members to develop professionally.

Another variation of the paired class model is the Video Supplemental Instruction (VSI) program that is being used at the University of Missouri-Kansas City and several other sites in the United States. With VSI, students enroll in two courses, a core course and a paired critical thinking course. At the present time, students can enroll in either Western Civilization I, General Chemistry, or Introduction to Physics. The students also enroll in a critical thinking course that is paired with one of these three courses. Rather than attending two separate class lectures for the two classes, the classes have been integrated together. All class lectures of the content course (e.g., Western Civilization I) have been placed on videotape by the regular course instructor. They are identical in content to the ones delivered live in the large class. The VSI students attend class eight hours each week (two hours a day, four days a week). A paid facilitator that has been trained in the VSI methodology serves as facilitator for the VSI class sessions. The facilitator helps to regulate the flow of information to the learner. The lectures are stopped and started as needed (e.g., every 10 to 15 minutes), allowing the facilitator to verify that students have comprehended one idea before moving on to the next. During the times that the videotape is stopped, the facilitator uses a variety of activities to develop learning strategies and writing skills of the students.

VSI students take the same examinations as students in the live section. Even though students enrolled in the live sections have statistically significantly higher college entrance test scores and high school percentile rank (as well as lower rates of students on academic probation), the developmental education students who are enrolled in the VSI courses receive higher final course grades than students enrolled in the large live sections of the same class. More information about the VSI program is available on the homepage for Supplemental Instruction: http://www.umkc.edu/cad/si.htm.

At University of Missouri-Kansas City, the VSI model is another way of doing developmental education that will be politically acceptable to policy makers. It allows for students to be enrolled in college-level coursework while they develop the study strategies and academic power needed to graduate with academic achievement. It more closely places academic assistance into the heart of the academic program of the campus.

It is exciting for me to review the professional literature and hear conference presentations that illustrate other ways to embed study strategies within course content. The previously mentioned three methods are just part of some of these strategies.

Stratton: How can departments that offer developmental education and other types of learning support best evaluate their programs?

Boylan: We are, primarily, in the business of teaching and learning. In evaluating our programs, we need to prove that we have taught and that students have learned. We have to do that first. Whatever evaluation we do should be built upon a foundation of teaching and learning.

I do not believe that developmental programs should be held any more accountable for retention than other components of the institution. The admissions office, the registrar's office, the English department, the counseling center, and the financial aid office, for instance, all can contribute to or detract from student retention. For reasons that escape my comprehension, however, no one ever goes to the chairperson of the English department and says, "Well, how much have your courses contributed to the retention of our students lately?"

I believe that developmental programs can reasonably be held accountable for the following: (a) providing remedial or developmental services to all those who need them in order to be successful, (b) encouraging students to participate fully in developmental courses and services, (c) helping students complete developmental courses and services, (d) insuring that the exit standards of developmental courses are consistent with the entry standards for the regular curriculum, and (e) insuring that students completing the program have met these standards.

If developmental programs do these things, they will at best contribute to retention by reducing the number of students who drop out because they are academically underprepared for college level work. Developmental programs will not reduce the attrition of those who leave because of insufficient financial aid, personal and family problems, or illness. Unfortunately, these latter causes of attrition tend to be the most common. Consequently, I would not encourage developmental educators to sell their programs exclusively on the basis of retention. They should document that they make a contribution to it, but that should not be their primary reason for being.

Stratton: Does reporting on research in this field have any impact on the success of programs?

Arendale: It is important that research studies [on developmental education] be ongoing. These research studies must be conducted in a rigorous fashion. Studies need to account for a variety of issues (e.g., student motivation, previous levels of academic achievement, research design).

Most policy makers want to see a blend of quantitative and qualitative research studies [on which] to base their decisions. Too often our profession has relied on student testimonials, Likert scale survey forms, and the like to document the impact of our profession. Policy makers are required, due to a tight financial environment, to make difficult choices about which programs to fund and which to curtail or eliminate. We, as educators, have assumed that everyone would agree that developmental education is essential. No longer. Policy makers want to see research showing that our programs are contributing to behavioral changes in our students. Some examples of these behavior alterations might include: (a) students in developmental education programs who had lower academic predictors (e.g., entrance test scores) later earning comparable grade point averages with other students who had higher initial

For reasons that escape my comprehension, however, no one ever goes to the chairperson of the English Department and says, "Well, how much have your courses contributed to the retention of our students lately?"

predictors; (b) students who participate in the programs earning higher grades and reenrolling at higher rates than students who do not take advantage of the services; and (c) the reduction in the number of failing course grades and student withdrawals in specific courses for which academic support services are provided.

Boylan: An essential component of a successful program in the future will be research and development. The most successful programs are theory based. They don't just provide random intervention; they intervene according to the tenets of various theories of adult intellectual and personal development.

These theories will undergo further research and refinement as time passes, and we will, as a consequence, understand much more about human learning and development. If we wish to serve students with the best of our knowledge, developmental programs will need to have a component charged with studying our knowledge base. That component will also be charged with incorporating it into the training of faculty and staff so that it can be applied to practice.

Stratton: What do you believe is the best measure of success for developmental programs?

Boylan: Developmental programs exist because we have large numbers of students who are underprepared for success in college courses. The most direct measure of our impact, therefore, is the extent to which those who complete our programs are able to pass regular college classes. If those who complete English 090 can pass English 101, then we have succeeded. If those who complete our courses and participate in our services are able to remain in good standing or maintain a 2.0 GPA or better, then we have succeeded. If we do this and students still leave because they found a higher paying job or they had to return home to care for ailing parents, then we have not failed.

Stratton: What specific ideas can you give us to "spread the word"?

Boylan: If we are to make our case to institutional decision makers through evaluation, we must involve those decision makers in the evaluation process. We must ask them what they desire as outcomes of developmental education. We must discuss with them whether or not these desires are reasonable. We must ask them to review our evaluation plans and make suggestions. We must share the results of our implementation of these plans and ask for comments.

We must also share what we do with the rest of our colleagues in academe. Every developmental program should have a newsletter or similar type of communication that goes out to all faculty and administrators on campus. Every developmental program should have at least one person, usually the director, who is responsible for communicating and maintaining a liaison with other programs and departments on campus as well as community agencies. Every developmental program should have a public relations plan designed to explain what the program does, to articulate its needs, and to describe its successes to the campus community. This plan should also include communication with local legislators and other political decision makers.

Arendale: For us at the University of Missouri-Kansas City, we do rigorous studies every academic term that we offer Supplemental Instruction or Video Supplemental Instruction (VIS) to our students. Those studies are distributed to all faculty members that had SI or VSI associated with their course. These reports are also provided to their department chairs, deans, and vice chancellors. We publish a 100-page annual report containing research studies every year and distribute it to all the upper level policy makers at our campus. We also have established a departmental web page, with an address of http://www.umkc.edu/cad/ nade.htm to provide this information to anyone from on or off the campus. While time consuming, this level of reporting has been critical for maintaining our credibility with the policy makers and providing needed feedback to us to

guide revisions and improvements of the program.

Boylan: State professional associations in developmental education must also take a leadership role in communicating the aims, role, scope, and successes of developmental education to legislators. Every state chapter should appoint a political liaison officer to communicate with legislators.

Almost every state legislative body has an education subcommittee. The political liaison officer should insure that the chair and the members of this committee regularly receive material describing developmental education efforts and their outcomes in state colleges and universities. There is generally a legislative staff member assigned to this subcommittee. The political liaison officer should meet with that staff member to discuss developmental education at least twice a year.

Evaluation and public relations activities ought to be delivered at two levels: the cognitive and the affective levels (i.e., "the head and the heart"). Administrators, legislators, and other decision makers are influenced by facts, figures, and data. They have an intellectual need to justify their support for or opposition to developmental education on the basis of rational, objective, scientific evidence. We must provide this evidence. In the past, we have failed to do [so].

Nevertheless, decision makers are also human beings who relate to human interest stories as much as anyone else. Last year I read a dozen or so stories about developmental education that appeared in major national newspapers such as *The New York Times*, *The Boston Globe*, or *The Los Angeles Times*. More than half of these pieces featured the story of some[one] . . . who had participated in developmental education and later graduated from college and established a successful career. The obvious point to these stories was that developmental education contributes to opportunities for the poor and the powerless. Most people cannot help but be moved by these stories.

Stratton: In closing, what thoughts would you like to leave with the readers?

Arendale: We are in the midst of a major transition for developmental education. While the need for learning assistance will increase, the form of service must change; for example, some institutions have already changed to other forms of service, such as SI. However, major upheaval and conflicting events often accompany transition phases before most stakeholders embrace the new paradigm.

Recently, secondary education has realigned its curriculum to achieve new state and national educational standards. Some standards emphasize integrating career information within content subjects to support the school-to-work transition. Other standards support an inclusive classroom for all students, despite disability. A central theme to these changes is providing an effective learning environment for all students without need for separate tracks that often led to stigmatization, segregation, uneven results, and lack of support by policy makers and the public.

I think that we are seeing the "mainstreaming" of developmental education within postsecondary education.
Best parts of our practice are being embedded into college-level courses at more institutions through linked courses, adjunct courses, Supplemental Instruction, and other similar programs. Integration of learning strategies into core-curriculum, college-level courses is the most effective way to meet the needs of students and satisfy the expectations of policy makers. The past developmental education paradigm often included a separate track of developmental courses, and this often placed developmental education at the outside edge of the academic community. Now we have the opportunity to become central players for an enriched learning environment for all college students.

Through my work with NADE, I met with many educators across the United States. It was encouraging to see that many of them are already finding ways to mainstream their developmental education programs.

The obvious point to these stories was that developmental education contributes to oppportunities for the poor and the powerless.

Boylan: I say all this to suggest that developmental education makes a positive difference, not just because of what goes on in a given class period, but also because of what goes on before and after that class period. I refer here to personal support from developmental instructors, monitoring and advising from developmental educators, learning assistance services provided by centers and laboratories, as well as both the formal and informal tutoring that accompanies developmental education.

The fact that all this support is provided is commendable. Unfortunately, it's usually provided on a more or less random basis. Some students get the support, and some don't. Some students get the support they need, and some students get support they don't need. Some students are directed by faculty or advisers to participate in tutoring, some wander into the tutoring program on their own, and some never get within 50 yards of a tutor. Most programs just take whatever they have "on the shelf" and give it to students without determining how much of what's on the shelf is needed, if they need what's on the shelf at all, or if they need something from some other shelf.

If developmental education is to achieve its potential for helping students be successful in college, it will have to be delivered more systematically. Treatment must be grounded in theory and based on assessment of both the cognitive and affective components of learning. That also means that courses and support services, remedial classes and learning centers, assessment, placement, and advising will all have to be integrated with each other and into the total institutional endeavor.

We can do a better job of remediation and development by targeting our services more specifically, by doing a better job of assessment, by measuring both cognitive and noncognitive factors of student learning, by giving more remediation to those with the greatest need and less remediation to those with the least need, by integrating theory and research to build sound practice, and by advocating the position that personal and academic development is everyone's business in academe. We need our institutions to understand that developmental educators are leading the way and taking the risks for all of academe.

References

Abraham, A. A. (1991). *They came to college? A remedial/developmental profile of first-time freshmen in SREB states.* Atlanta, GA: Southern Regional Education Board. (ERIC Document Reproduction Service No. ED 280 369)

Arendale, D. (1997a). Leading the paradigm shift from teaching to learning. *National Association for Developmental Education Newsletter,* 20(2), 1.

Arendale, D. (1997b). Learning centers for the 21st century. *Journal of Developmental Education,* 20(3), 16.

Arendale, D. (1997c). Preface. In P. L. Dwinell & J. L. Higbee (Eds.), *Developmental education: Enhancing student retention* (pp. v-vi). Carol Stream, IL: National Association for Developmental Education.

Arendale, D. (1997d). *Survey of education policies concerning developmental education at the state and federal level in the U. S.* [On line]. Available: www.umkc.edu/centers/cad/nade/nadedocs/devstate.edu

Boylan, H. R., Bliss, L. B., & Bonham, B. S. (1997). Program components and their relationship to student performance. *Journal of Developmental Education,* 20(3), 2-8.

Boylan, H. R., & Bonham, B. S. (1992). The impact of developmental education programs. *Research in Developmental Education,* 9(5), 1-3.

Boylan, H. R., Bonham, B. S., & Bliss, L. B. (1994). Who are the developmental students? *Research in Developmental Education,* 11(2), 1-4.

Commander, N. E., & Smith, B. D. (1995). Developing adjunct reading and learning courses that work. *Journal of Reading, 38*(5), 352-360.

Commander, N. E., Stratton, C. B., Callahan, C. A., & Smith, B. D. (1996). A learning assistance model for expanding academic support. *Journal of Developmental Education, 20*(2), 8-16.

Higbee, J. L. (1996). Defining developmental education: A commentary. In J. L. Higbee & P. L. Dwinell (Eds.), *Defining developmental education: Theory, research, & pedagogy,* (pp. 63-66). Carol Stream, IL: National Association for Developmental Education.

Kerr, L. (1993). Content specific study strategies: A repertoire of approaches. *Journal of College Reading and Learning,* 26(1), 36-43.

Martin, D. C., Blanc, R. A., & DeBuhr, L. (1983). Breaking the attrition cycle: The effects of Supplemental Instruction on undergraduate performance and attrition. *Journal of Higher Education, 54*(1), 80-89.

Martin, D. C., & Arendale, D. (Eds.). (1993). *Supplemental Instruction: Improving first-year student success in high risk courses* (Monograph No. 7). Columbia, SC: National Resource Center for The Freshman Year Experience.

Martin, D. C., & Arendale, D. (Eds.). (1994). Supplemental Instruction: Increasing student achievement and retention. *New Directions in Teaching and Learning, No. 60.* San Francisco: Jossey-Bass.

NADE's Strategic Plan. (1997). National Association for Developmental Education. [Online]. Available: www.umkc.edu/centers/cad/nade/nadedocs/straplan.htm

Rafoth, M. A., & DeFabo, L. (1990). *What research says to the teacher: Study skills.* Washington, DC: National Education Association.

Stahl, N. A., Simpson, M. L., & Hayes, C. G. (1992). Ten recommendations from research for teaching high-risk college students. *Journal of Developmental Education, 16*(1), 2-4, 6, 8, 10.

Stratton, C. B. (1996). Effects of learning support on college algebra. In J. L. Higbee & P. L. Dwinell (Eds.), *Defining developmental education: Theory, research, & pedagogy,* (pp. 29-37). Carol Stream, IL: National Association for Developmental Education.

Chapter 4

REMEDIAL/DEVELOPMENTAL EDUCATION: PAST, PRESENT, AND FUTURE[*]

Milton G. Spann, Jr. and Suella McCrimmon

Remedial/Developmental Education in the Community College

Traditionally, the community college has performed a number of curricular functions: college transfer preparation, vocational technical education, continuing education, community service, and remedial/developmental education (Cohen & Brawer, 1982). With the breakdown of basic academic education at the secondary level, remedial/developmental education emerged in the late 1960s and the early 1970s as a major function of community colleges and it remains so today. As long as the majority of students entering open-door community colleges continue to come from the lower half of the educational and socioeconomic spectrum, they will probably need heavy doses of effective remedial/developmental education.

Historically, remedial/developmental education has concerned itself primarily with the remediation of academic skill deficiencies. However, since the 1970s, the field has expanded to include all forms of learning assistance and personal development suitable to the needs of at-risk college students. Borrowing from a variety of theories and concepts of learning and human development, the field advocates placing the low-achieving learner at the center for the teaching/learning process, believing that, despite the extent of technology available, personal involvement with the learner and conscious attention to the student's developmental needs are essential if meaningful learning is to occur.

As an evolving field in the postsecondary sector, remedial/developmental education is still in a state of transition and is likely to be so well into the 21st century. While its philosophical roots are humanistic, its practices are quite diverse and often centered in the experience of its practitioners who come from a wide variety of backgrounds and do not have a set of clearly articulated assumptions about education.

The extensive curriculum of remedial/developmental education is perhaps the largest "hidden curriculum" in American postsecondary education. That is, remedial/developmental courses and services are frequently scattered throughout the institution with various administrative units responsible for a portion of them.

Whether these courses, services, and activities are brought together under one administrative umbrella or simply viewed collectively, they often affect, particularly in community and technical colleges, a significant portion (from 30-90%) of the student body (Richardson & Bender, 1987). Educational assessment and demographic projections support the view that high percentages (from 25-30%) of students will enter America's postsecondary institutions with some academic, psychological, or physical challenge significant enough to impair their success if not compensated for or corrected (Hodgkinson, 1985).

While the remedial/developmental function has become more acceptable to community college educators, it has drawn its share of critics. McGrath and Spear (1987) have discussed the politics of remedial/developmental education and have suggested that its presence in the community college has contributed to the perpetuation of a dual-class structure in American postsecondary education which has resulted in the tracking of the lower socioeconomic classes away from the professions and toward serving the lower-level technical and semiprofessional needs of society. Remedial/developmental education is identified as a contributing factor in the channeling of lower-class students toward the same relative position in the social structure their parents occupy and thus leaving the essential shape of the social structure unchanged. It appears that community colleges in general and remedial/developmental programs in particular may serve to lower the aspirations of individuals who have made the mistake of aspiring too high. Clark (1960) first de-

scribed this process of lowering aspirations as the "cooling" function and believed it to be one of democracy's major problems—the inconsistency between encouragement to achieve and the realities of limited social mobility. Echoing Clark's observations, Zwerling described the community college counselor as playing the key role in redirecting low-achieving students away from aspirations to higher education and professions and toward the semiprofessional vocations more in keeping with their actual abilities. Test scores are frequently used to show the student that remediation is essential and "cast doubt on the students' feelings that they can do bona fide college work" (Zwerling, 1976, p. 18). Zwerling also suggested that although remedial/developmental education may serve to remediate isolated low-level academic skill deficiencies, it usually fails to initiate the student into the intellectual community which has become necessary for access to the professions.

Clark (1960) first described this process of lowering aspirations as the "cooling" function and believed it to be one of democracy's major problems—the inconsistency between encouragement to achieve and the realities of limited social mobility.

If community colleges are to remedy the cooling-out function, they must not only know how students learn and develop, they must also believe that these students can learn the higher-order thinking skills necessary for upward mobility in a modern society. Others would argue that teaching low-achieving students to think critically and reason carefully is beyond the scope of remedial/developmental education. Visionaries such as Curtis Miles at the Center for Reasoning Studies, Piedmont Technical College, and John Chaffee (1992), director of Creative and Critical Thinking Studies at LaGuardia Community College, argue that higher-order cognitive skills are the very essence of a successful basic skills program and within the reach of most low-achieving students. Remedial/developmental programs of the future must move beyond rote learning, isolated skills training, and the memorization of isolated facts to a focus on learning how-to-learn skills and processes.

Regardless of what the critics say, there is little evidence that remedial/developmental education is declining in importance among community colleges or that it will do so in the future. In fact, the remedial/developmental function has become so pervasive that Richardson and Bender (1987) claim that the college transfer curriculum has now been displaced by this function. Accompanying the displacement of the transfer function has been the challenge of teaching the academically and psychologically underprepared college student, a challenge that Cohen and Brawer (1982) described as "the thorniest single problem for community colleges" (p. 231).

History and Background

Helping underprepared students prepare themselves for college has been a feature of American higher education since Harvard opened its doors in 1636. The place of remedial/developmental education in the educational community proved increasingly tenuous, however, as higher education abandoned its roots in the more holistic English residential model of education for the research-oriented German model which prevailed following the Civil War. As faculty interest shifted from student "whole-person" development to intellectual development, from religious to secular concerns, and from small intimate learning communities to larger, more complex institutions (Brubacher & Rudy, 1976; Delworth & Hanson, 1989), higher education struggled with the appropriateness of admitting students not adequately prepared for the college experience. The issue was often controversial and found expression through major reports and prominent speeches by educational leaders.

As far back as 1828, the Yale Report called for an end to the admission of students with "defective preparation" (Brier, 1984). The sentiment was echoed in 1852 by the president of the University of Michigan, Henry P. Tappan (Maxwell, 1979). Charles Elliot (1869), on the other hand, stated in his inaugural address as president of Harvard that "the American college is obliged to supplement the American school. Whatever elementary instruction the schools fail to give, the college must supply." Harvard, along with oth-

ers, instituted programs to remediate deficiencies, and by 1870 only 23 colleges reported no college preparatory program (Losak & Miles, 1991).

After 1920, higher educational institutions left most of the preparation and remediation to the two-year college, but, prior to the 1960s, the success of remedial education programs must be questioned. Roueche (1968) found that as many as 90% of all remedial students in California community colleges failed or withdrew from remedial courses. A more recent study conducted by the National Center for Developmental Education showed examples of success in preparing low-ability students for successful entry into the college-level curriculum of choice (Spann & Thompson, 1986). A few of the most successful programs have been able to prepare and then see graduate previously low-achieving students at rates equal to students not in need of remediation. Several community colleges in Ohio reported that the percentage of students using developmental services was greater among graduates than among the general student body, implying that students utilizing these services (i.e., preparatory courses, tutoring, and specialized counseling) were more likely to remain in college and earn a degree (Braswell, 1978).

Causes of Poor Performance

Various reasons have been offered to explain the cause of poor academic achievement. Cross (1976) outlined several explanations for poor academic performance in the period between 1930 and 1980.

From 1894, when the first remedial course was offered at Wellesley College, until the 1930s the perceived cause for poor performance was thought to be poor study habits. The typical response to this problem was to offer voluntary, noncredit courses or workshops. In the late 1930s and early 1940s, remedial reading courses, clinics, and workshops were added to the existing how-to-study courses. Students were placed in those courses based largely on a single test score. After 1945, millions of veterans swelled the ranks of colleges and universities, and their need for remedial/developmental education was extensive, particularly the need for counseling.

Limited higher-education resources, along with an abundance of students seeking entry to college, produced increased political pressure to determine who was best suited for the college experience. Test results were used to separate "underachievers" from "low-ability" students with colleges admitting the more promising underachievers and rejecting most of the low-ability students as unsuitable for higher learning (Maxwell, 1979). Many of these low-ability students enrolled in community colleges and technical institutes. With the passage of Higher Education Act of 1965, the U. S. Congress provided greater access to more minority and, later, to handicapped students. Government-supported programs, particularly Upward Bound and Special Services, proved unusually effective in bringing the children of noncollege graduates to the campus. During this period (1940-1975), socioeconomic factors were regarded as the principle cause of poor academic performance, and compensatory academic and cultural enrichment programs were designed to bring deprived students into the mainstream of American society.

Today, we perceive the cause of poor academic performance as multifaceted and multidimensional, a combination of socioeconomic, cultural, and individual differences. Cognitive and affective dimensions of learning are increasingly diagnosed and treated. Particularly in large urban centers, student socioeconomic and sociocultural background is viewed as an important factor is planning and individualizing the program of study. Personality types, learning style, and other noncognitive factors may also be diagnosed and the results utilized in the development of a personalized learning plan for students.

The Professionalization of Remedial/Developmental Education

In the 1970s the numbers of students needing remediation sharply increased, and postsecondary institutions began to recognize and accept remedial/developmental education as a legitimate, even permanent, part of their mission. Programs were staffed by persons who accepted the challenge as a career opportunity rather than as a stepping stone to teaching regularly admitted students. Today more than 50% of those working in remedial/developmental education think of it as their career of choice. Referred to as developmental educators or learning skills specialists, they attend professional meetings and workshops on ways to teach, motivate, and assess at-risk students.

Beginning in the early 1970s, several professional organizations for remedial/developmental education practitioners emerged. At the national level, there are two major organizations: the National Association of Developmental Education and the College Reading and Learning Association. Each organization hosts a number of state or regional chapters. Specialized practitioner and research-oriented publications, such as the *Journal of Developmental Education* and the *Review of Research in Developmental Education*, are published by the National Center for Developmental Education at Appalachian State University. Such other key publications as *Research and Teaching in Developmental Education* (New York Learning Skills Association) and *Journal of College Reading and Learning* (College Reading and Learning Association) have been published since the mid-1970s. There are graduate-level programs specifically designed to prepare college-level remedial/developmental education professionals at Appalachian State University and Grambling State University.

Student Characteristics

The academically underprepared college student may be defined as one who fails to meet the established entrance criteria for a beginning college-level course or entry-level program of choice. Maxwell characterized underprepared students as those "whose skills, knowledge, and academic ability are significantly below those of the 'typical' student in the college or curriculum in which they are enrolled" (1979, p. 2). Low-achieving students tend to avoid what they perceive to be painful or threatening. For example, underprepared students who come to college with a weakness in reading, writing, or mathematics, when given a choice, will often put off taking the needed basic skills courses or try to bypass them. They may attempt to enroll in the regular beginning level course and thus try to avoid the pain of embarrassment and feelings of inadequacy they believe will come should they actually enroll in one of these courses (Maxwell, 1979). Given the self-esteem issues associated with enrollment in basic skills programs, institutions should be more sensitive to the psychological dimensions of student behavior as they consider such things as the titles of basic skills programs, the numbering of basic skills courses, and the attitudes of basic skills faculty and staff.

Earlier, Pritchard and Bloushild (1970) researched the characteristics of low-achieving students and found the following: lack of academic potential, inadequate understanding of the work required for college success, failure to make studying the first priority, interference from psychological problems, failure to assume responsibility for learning and success, poor communication skills, and failure to select a college where they can be successful. Those descriptors are as valid today as they were in 1970.

Academically underprepared students are not the only at-risk students served by the modern developmental education or learning assistance program. Other at-risk populations include the learning disabled, the visually and hearing impaired, the mobility handicapped, the English as a second language student, the student-athlete, the returning adult student, and the first-generation college student. These and other at-risk populations may receive a variety of educational services, for example, counseling or instruction, designed to reduce the risk and maximize the potential for the successful completion of anything from a single course to a complete program of study leading to a certificate or a degree.

Evolution of Terms

Historically, three terms—remedial, compensatory, and developmental—have dominated the literature and vocabulary of those concerned with the education of the academically underprepared college student. The term "remedial education" is based on the idea of a deficit in students' academic backgrounds. To remediate is to remedy the problem, to build the skills necessary for success in a college entry level course or program of study.

The term "compensatory education" is of more recent origin. According to Clowes (1982), this term emerged in precollegiate settings after World War II. In both England and America, compensatory education was associated with the lessening or removal of "environmentally induced" achievement deficits and later with the push to break the cycle of disadvantagement associated with President Lyndon Johnson's war on poverty. Compensatory education was essentially a middle-class response to a perceived cultural deficit in the educational and social background of lower-class persons. Compensatory education was designed to bring them into the culture of the middle class by providing a variety of educational, cultural, and personal growth experiences not available in their home environment.

In the 1970s "developmental education" became the preferred term among postsecondary faculty associated with courses and programs for academically at-risk college students. This term was first popularized by faculty at open-access colleges, particularly community colleges, and evolved from dissatisfaction with the negative connotations and limited meaning of the term remedial. The term developmental, at least in the context of the postsecondary developmental education movement, focused on the student's potential rather than the student's deficit. Since the goal of developmental education is a fully developed and fully functioning person, focusing on academic skills alone is insufficient if students are to make the transition to all-around effective students and involved citizens.

More recently, Losak and Miles (1991) defined developmental education as "those services and policies needed to help students develop the baseline academic intellectual and affective capabilities which are prerequisites to achieving

Academically underprepared students are not the only at-risk students served by the modern developmental education or learning assistance program.

their postsecondary educational goals" (p. 22). This definition suggests a largely preparatory function and thus adheres strongly to the historical emphasis within the field. In the 1990 document *A Learning Assistance Glossary: Report of the CLRA Task Force of Professional Language for College Reading and Learning,* developmental education is given a threefold definition: "(1) a sub-discipline of the field of education concerned with improving the performance of students; (2) a field of research, teaching, and practice designed to improve academic performance; (3) a process utilizing principles of developmental theory to facilitate learning" (College Reading and Learning Association, 1990, p. 3). The CLRA definition appears to turn away from the historical function and focuses instead on students as developing persons and on the principles of teaching and learning. It speaks to the learning and human development needs of all students at all levels rather than to the particular needs of the at-risk students.

An example of a definition with a distinguishing focus is the one offered in a recent study by the Southern Regional Education Board (SREB) of college-level remedial and developmental programs: "Remedial or developmental education refers to programs, courses, and activities designed specifically for first-time entering students who lack minimum reading, writing, or oral communications, mathematical, or study skills, and/or basic skills necessary to do freshman-level college work as defined by the institutions" (Abraham, 1986, p. 19).

Status of Developmental Education Activity in the United States

A recent nationwide study of 546 randomly selected institutions conducted by the National Center for Education Statistics (NCES) (1991) described the current status of remedial/developmental education in community colleges. Results revealed that 90% of community colleges offered this type of education in 1989, compared with 88% in 1983. The data also indicated that 36% of all entering community college freshmen enrolled in a remedial reading, writing, or math course. Of those freshmen taking these courses, 73% passed reading, 70%

passed writing, and 65% successfully completed mathematics. On the average, two-year colleges offer 2.8 courses in each of these areas, with most colleges offering at least two levels of remedial/developmental work.

When asked how many faculty were involved in the teaching of remedial/developmental education courses, respondents failed to distinguish community college faculty alone. However, for all types of postsecondary institutions, nearly 31,000 taught one or more basic skills courses. These numbers were up considerably over the 26,000 faculty identified by the College Marketing Group of Winchester, Massachusetts, in 1985. However, the data did reveal the average number of persons in community colleges teaching basic skills courses. In the 139 two-year colleges surveyed, an average of 20 faculty members taught one or more remedial/developmental courses. Of those 20, an average of 11.5 were employed specifically to teach remedial/developmental courses, however, only 4.6 of them had degrees or credentials specific to remedial or developmental education.

Credit for Remedial/Developmental Courses

When asked what kind of credit institutions offered remedial/developmental students, respondents to the NCES (1991) survey reported the following: Among community colleges, 76% offered institutional or transcript credit in reading, 78% offered institutional or transcript credit in writing, and 79% offered institutional credit in mathematics. Among those community colleges offering degree credit for remedial/developmental courses, the data revealed that 14% offered degree credit in reading, 11% in writing, and 13% in mathematics. It is clear that institutional credit for remedial/developmental courses is offered more frequently than degree credit.

A comparison of data gathered in 1989 by NCES with data gathered by Cross (1976) in early 1970s revealed a dramatic decline in the percent of institutions currently offering degree credit for remedial/developmental courses and a significant increase in those offering institutional or transcript credit.

Location of Remedial/Developmental Programs

In community colleges nationwide, NCES (1991) data revealed that 28% of remedial/developmental reading programs, 23% of writing programs, and 25% of mathematics programs were associated with a separate basic skills or developmental studies unit; while 55%, 63%, and 64%, respectively, were housed in traditional academic departments. Learning centers were the only other administrative unit to house these functions to any significant extent with 16% responsible for reading, 14% for writing, and 10% for mathematics. The trend since the 1970s has been to restore remedial/developmental course responsibility to the traditional academic departments.

Extent of Evaluation Studies

With increased demands for accountability from the public at large and by public agencies at the state and federal levels and with the growing need to determine the outcome or results of educational inputs, the evaluation of remedial/developmental programs is increasingly being emphasized. When Spann and Thompson (1986) reviewed documents from over 500 colleges and universities, they found evidence of ongoing written evaluation reports in less than one-third of all instructions submitting documentation. This study revealed a generally low level of sophistication in carrying out evaluation procedures and raised questions about the extent to which institutions were taking seriously the obligations they have to assess adequately their remedial/developmental courses and programs.

NCES (1991) data revealed that a variety of evaluation measures were used by community colleges including student opinion surveys, teacher effectiveness, student completion rates, and follow-up studies involving student grades, among others. It is evident that a significant majority were carrying on evaluation efforts, but it remains to be seen how sophisticated these studies are. At least one study of 29 institutions in Michigan reinforces the perception that evaluation studies of remedial/developmental services in community colleges

need improvement. This study, conducted by the Michigan State Board of Education (1990), produced several recommendations regarding the adequacy of current evaluation practices. The study recommended that community colleges improve records and data-keeping procedures to determine the impact of remedial/developmental services on various student populations and that they utilize stronger evaluation methods to determine the effectiveness of developmental efforts and incorporate the results into their decision-making process. Historically, evaluations of remedial/developmental programs have consisted of little more than solicited opinions and frequency counts. Comparative studies and investigations of student success in subsequent courses, while seldom available, are on the increase. We believe that more sophisticated studies will be required in the future.

Recommendations for Reducing the Demand for Remedial/Developmental Activities

Two recommendations appear in the NCES (1991) study regarding ways to reduce the escalating demands for remedial/developmental education within the community college. One of the recommendations is to improve communications with high school students and their parents describing in various ways and through various means the knowledge, skills, and attitudes necessary for success in college. In 1989, 71% of all public colleges, including community colleges, reported that they were communicating with high schools about this subject. The second recommendation is that college and university personnel would benefit from attending organized workshops with high school faculty to discuss what a student must do to be ready for college. The NCES study found that only 24% of public college personnel have actually attended workshops of this type. In all cases, large institutions (5,000+) led the way in communicating and working with colleagues in the public schools.

In addition to NCES information regarding current practices designed to reduce the need for remediation, the SREB has offered 11 recommendations to help ensure quality undergraduate education and to reduce the number of inadequately prepared college students:

1. Require that higher-education institutions identify and implement statewide minimum standards and assessments for college courses that earn credit toward baccalaureate or associate degrees. These should represent a consensus by higher education on the basic academic skills students need to begin to study at the college level, especially in reading, writing, and mathematics.

2. Require secondary and postsecondary educators to work collaboratively to identify basic academic skills needed for college-level study.

3. Require students who do not meet minimum standards to take nondegree credit courses/programs that provide further preparation.

4. Require that minimum standards and procedures for placement and assessment be consistent statewide for all public institutions of higher education.

5. Recognize remedial/developmental education as an essential element of the mission of all public institutions of higher education that admit students who are not ready to begin college-level work.

6. Ensure that students not qualified to begin degree-credit study are within commuting distance of programs that will prepare them to qualify.

7. Initiate and maintain effective remedial/developmental programs that uphold institutional integrity and standards for quality undergraduate education.

8. Provide adequate funding for remedial/developmental programs, recognizing that it can require comparatively greater efforts and cost to develop instruction and programs for teaching students who are academically deficient.

9. Clearly state and make known to schools, high school students, and their parents the skills needed to pursue college-level course work.

10. Require that faculty and staff who teach remedial/developmental courses be fully trained and qualified.

11. Provide annual review and evaluations of remedial/developmental programs to ensure academic integrity and to ensure that students who complete those courses have competencies that are equivalent to entrance requirements for "regular" college-level students. (Abraham, 1988)

If the developmental education movement is to be a part of the reform so necessary in higher education, it must be willing to risk itself for the well-being of students.

Challenges to Developmental Education

The field of developmental education currently faces an identity crisis. For the most part, it has little knowledge of its roots or a widely understood and articulated philosophy, a body of common knowledge, or a commonly accepted set of theoretical assumptions congruent with that philosophy. Like the academy, its guiding principles are largely based on folklore about "good education" and "good teaching" rather than on empirical evidence and a clear understanding of human needs. If the developmental education movement is to be a part of the reform so necessary in higher education, it must be willing to risk itself for the well-being of students and identify itself even more closely with an expanding list of basic skills and attitudes necessary for personal, academic, and vocational success in the 21st century. It is a field struggling with its identity with one foot in the traditionalist camp and one in the reformer camp. Its greatest challenge is to resist the call of acceptance and respectability and step forward as an articulate and enthusiastic representative for the long-term educational goals of the next century. Along the way it may raise the level of the dialogue regarding the art and the science of teaching, learning, and human development.

Summary

This chapter attempts to lay the foundation for an understanding of the evolution of remedial/developmental education in the community colleges. A review of the historical context of remedial/developmental education in American higher education is used to set the stage for the dominant role played by the two-year college beginning in the 1920s.

The evolution of remedial/developmental education was influenced by increasingly complex reasons regarding the need for such services. These reasons parallel an increasingly sophisticated understanding on the part of social scientists about how persons learn, grow, and develop.

The field of developmental education was founded on the democratic ideals of justice, freedom, and opportunity for all citizens. The practice of remedial/developmental education has not only been influenced by these ideals but also by metaphors like oneness, wholeness, and community. These powerful ideas make the field of developmental education a natural ally with those proponents of an egalitarian educational system. It is, therefore, understandable why the developmental educator has often been a protector and defender of the open-access college and why these educators may be among those persons best equipped philosophically and theoretically to deal with the coming demographic changes likely to bring large numbers of at-risk students into every level of education.

In spite of its belief in providing postsecondary education for all who can benefit, the adolescent field of developmental education faces an identity crisis. Will it succumb to the practiced values of the academy which make learning and student development a low priority, or will it take the lead in again making this the academy's first priority? Should the field choose the latter course, it may well become a major force in restoring the integrity of American higher education and thereby make the effective teaching of students the high priority it must become if the United States is to prepare its citizens for leadership and competition in the global society that is now upon us.

Bibliography

Abraham, A. (1986). *A report on college level remedial/developmental programs in SREB states.* Atlanta, GA: Southern Regional Education Board.

Abraham, A. (1988). *Remedial education in college: How widespread is it?* Atlanta, GA: Southern Regional Education Board.

Astin, A. W. (1984). Student involvement: A developmental theory for higher education. *Journal of College Student Personnel, 24,* 297-308.

Bliss, R. W. (1986). *Intellectual development and freshman English.* Paper presented at Project MATCH conference, Davidson College, Davidson, North Carolina.

Braswell, W. (1978). *Report on admissions and developmental education.* Columbus, OH: Ohio Board of Regents.

Brier, E. (1984). Bridging the academic preparation gap. *Journal of Developmental Education, 8*(1), 2-5.

Brubaker, J. S., & Rudy, W. (1976). *Higher education in transition.* New York: Harper & Row.

Buerk, D. (1985). *From magic to meaning: Changing the learning of mathematics.* Paper presented at ISEM Workshop on Teaching and Learning Mathematics, Saint Paul, Minnesota.

Burnham, C. (1984). *The Perry scheme and the teacher of literature.* Paper presented at Conference on College Composition and Communication, Las Cruces, New Mexico.

Chaffee, J. (1992). Critical thinking skills: The cornerstone of developmental education. *Journal of Developmental Education, 15*(3), 2.

Chickering, A. W. (1969). *Education and identity.* San Francisco: Jossey-Bass.

Clark, B. (1960). The cooling-out function in higher education. *American Journal of Sociology, 65,* 569-76.

Clark, B., & Trow, M. (1966). The organizational context. In T. M. Newcomb & E. K. Wilson (Eds.), *In college peer groups: Problems and prospects for research.* Chicago: Aldine.

Claxton, C. S., & Murrell, P. H. (1987).

Learning styles: Implications for improving education practices. ASHE-ERIC Higher Education Report No. 4. Washington, D.C.: Association for the Study of Higher Education.

Clowes, D. A. (1982). More than a definitional problem: Remedial, compensatory, and developmental education. *Journal of Developmental and Remedial Education, 4*(2), 8-10.

Cohen, A. M., & Brawer, F. B. (1982). *The American community college.* San Francisco: Jossey-Bass.

College Reading and Learning Association. (1990). *A learning assistance glossary: Report of the CLRA task force of professional language for college reading and learning.* Minneapolis, MN: Author.

Copes, L. (1982). The Perry developmental scheme: A metaphor for learning and teaching mathematics. *For the Learning of Mathematics, 3,* 38-44.

Cross, K. P. (1971). *Beyond the open door: New students to higher education.* San Francisco: Jossey-Bass.

Cross, K. P. (1976). *Accent on learning: Improving instruction and reshaping the curriculum.* San Francisco: Jossey-Bass.

Delworth, U., & Hanson, G. R. (1989). *Student services: A handbook for the profession.* San Francisco: Jossey-Bass.

Drucker, P. F. (1989). How schools must change. *Psychology Today, 23, 5.*

Elliot, C. W. (1869). *A turning point in higher education: The inaugural address of Charles William Elliot as president of Harvard college.* Cambridge, MA: Harvard University Press.

Erikson, E. H. (1950). *Childhood and society.* New York: Norton.

Erikson, E. H. (1968). *Identity: Youth and crisis.* New York: Norton.

Fetters, W. B. (1977). *Withdrawal from institutions of higher education.* National Center for Educational Statistics. Washington, DC: U. S. Government Printing Office. (ERIC Document Reproduction Service No. ED 150 913)

Glasby, M. K. (1985). *An analysis of cognitive development and student profiles on three levels of mathematics courses at a selected community college (Perry scale).* Unpublished doctoral dissertation, University of Maryland, College Park.

Glasser, W. (1984). *Take effective control of your life.* New York: Harper & Row.

Haisty, D. B. (1983). *The developmental theories of Jean Piaget and William Perry: An application to the teaching of writing.* Unpublished doctoral dissertation, Texas Christian University, Fort Worth.

Havingshurst, R. J. (1953). *Human development and education.* New York: Longmans, Green.

Heard, F. B. (1988). *An assessment of the Tennessee statewide school-college collaborative for educational excellence: The middle college high school.* Fort Lauderdale, FL: Nova University. (ERIC Reproduction Service No. ED 294 637)

Heath, R. (1964). *The reasonable adventurer.* Pittsburgh: University of Pittsburgh Press.

Hodgkinson, H. L. (1985). *All one system: Demographics of education, kindergarten through graduate school.* Washington, DC: Institute for Educational Leadership.

Hunt, D. E. (1970). A conceptual level matching model for coordinating learner characteristics with educational approach. *Interchange, 1,* 68-72.

Katz, J., & Sanford, N. (1962). *The American college.* New York: Wiley.

Keniston, K. (1971). *Youth and dissent.* New York: Harcourt Brace Jovanovich.

Kiersey, D., & Bates, M. (1978). *Please understand me: Character and temperament types* (3rd ed.). Del Mar, CA: Prometheus Nemesis Books.

King, P. M. (1982). *Perry's scheme and the reflective judgment model: First cousins once removed.* Paper presented at annual conference of Association for Moral Education, Minneapolis, Minnesota.

Kitchhener, K. S., & King, P. M. (1981). Reflective judgement: Concepts of justification and their relationship to age and education. *Journal of Applied Educational Psychology, 2,* 89-116.

Kirchhener, K. S., & King, P. M. (1985). *The reflective judgment model: Ten years of research.* Paper presented at Beyond Formal Operations Systems.

Kneflkamp, L., Widick, C., & Parker, C. (Eds.). (1978). Applying new developmental findings. *New Directions for Student Services, No. 4.* San Francisco: Jossey-Bass.

Kohlberg, L. (1969). Stage and sequence: The cognitive developmental approach to socialization. In D. Godlin (Ed.), *Handbook of socialization theory and research.* Chicago: Rand McNally.

Kohlberg, L. (1972). A cognitive developmental approach to moral education. *Humanist, 6,* 13-16.

Kohlberg, L. (1975). The cognitive developmental approach to moral education. *Phi Delta Kappan, 10,* 670-77.

Kolb, D. A. (1976). *Learning styles inventory technical manual.* Boston: McBer.

Lawrence, G. D. (1982). *People types and tiger stripes* (2nd ed.). Gainesville, FL: Center for Applications of Psychological Type.

Lawrence, G. D. (1984). A synthesis of learning style research involving the MBTI. *Journal of Psychological Type, 8,* 2-15.

Levinson, D. J. (1978). *The seasons of a man's life.* New York: Knopf.

Loevinger, J. (1976). *Ego development: Conceptions and theories.* San Francisco: Jossey-Bass.

Losak, J., & Miles, C. (1991). *Foundations and context of developmental education in higher education.* Boone, NC: National Center for Developmental Education.

Marcia, J. (1966). Developmental and validation of ego-identity status. *Journal of Personality and Social Psychology, 35,* 551-58.

Maxwell, M. (1979). *Improving student learning skills.* San Francisco: Jossey-Bass.

McGrath, D., & Spear, M. B. (1987). The politics of remediation. In K. M.Ahrendt (Ed.), *Teaching the developmental education student.* San Francisco: Jossey-Bass.

McGrath, D., & Spear, M. B. (1991). *The academic crisis of the community college.* Albany, NY: State University of New York Press.

Michigan State Board of Education. (1990). *Survey of student assessment in Michigan's public community colleges.* Lansing, MI: Michigan State Board of Education. (ERIC Document Reproduction Service No. ED 320 624)

Myers, L. B. (1980). *Gifts differing.* Palo Alto, CA: Consulting Psychologists Press.

National Center for Educational Statistics. (1991). *College level remedial education in the fall of 1989.* Washington, DC: U. S. Department of Education.

Neugarten, B. L. (1976). Adaption and the life-cycle. *Counseling Psychologist, 6,* 16-20.

Newcomb, T. M., Koenig, K. E., Flacks, R., & Warwick, D. P. (1967). *Persistence and change.* New York: Wiley.

Perry, W. G. (1970). *Forms of intellectual and ethical development in the college years.* New York: Holt, Rinehart and Winston.

Piaget, J. (1964). Cognitive development in children. In R. Ripple & V. Rockcastle (Eds.), *Piaget rediscovered: A report on cognitive studies in curriculum development.* Ithaca, NY: Cornell University School of Education.

Pritchard, R. W., & Bloushild, B. (1970). *Why college students fail.* New York: Funk and Wagnalls.

Project synergy: Software report for underprepared students. (1991). Miami: Miami-Dade Community College.

Reid, G. B. (1986). *The use of Perry scheme in the teaching of freshman English.* Unpublished doctoral dissertation, Memphis State University.

Richardson, R. C., & Bender, L. (1987). *Fostering minority access and achievement in higher education.* San Francisco: Jossey-Bass.

Roberts, G. H. (1986). *Developmental education: An historical study.* (ERIC Document Reproduction Service No. ED 276 395)

Roueche, J. E. (1968). *Salvage, redirection, or custody? Remedial education in the community/ junior college.* Washington, DC: American Association of Junior Colleges.

Sanford, N. (1966). *The American college.* New York: Wiley.

Sanford, N. (1967). *Where colleges fail: A study of the student as a person.* San Francisco: Jossey-Bass.

Spann, M. G., & Thompson, C. G. (1986). *The national directory of exemplary programs in developmental education.* Boone, NC: The National Center for Developmental Education.

Van Hecke, M. (1985). The work of William Perry, Part II: Teaching psychology to dualistic level students. *Illinois Psychologist, 24,* 15-20.

Wright, D. A., & Cahalan, M. W. (1985). *Remedial/developmental studies in institutions of higher education: Policies and practices.* Paper presented at the annual conference of the American Educational Research Association, Chicago, Illinois. April 1.

Zwerling, L. S. (1976). *Second best: The crisis of the community college.* Boston: McGraw Hill.

*Reprinted by permission: Greenwood Press. Originally published in *A Handbook on the Community College in America.* (1994).

Chapter 5

Provisionally Admitted College Students: Do They Belong in a Research University?

Don T. Garnett and M. V. Hood III

Beginning in the mid-1960s in the United States with the enactment of civil rights legislation and subsequent explosion in college enrollments through open door policies, millions of new underprepared students were identified at secondary and post-secondary levels. Maxwell (1994) refers to TRIO programs as compensatory education that attempts to do in college what low-income parents who never attended college failed to do at home: provide the encouragement and support children need to reach their potential. TRIO programs such as Talent Search, Upward Bound, Student Support Services, and McNair Scholars are examples of federally supported compensatory efforts to assist relatively small numbers of high school and college students.

TRIO programs have been successful, but they have reached only a fraction of the students who need the kind of support provided. Some states and individual institutions have attempted to meet the needs of underprepared students through a variety of initiatives including state-mandated assessments. At the same time, the dissolution of families, rise in teenage pregnancy, and increases in crime have further reduced the number of adequately prepared, college-bound students. As state expenditures for developmental programs consumed more of the budgets of colleges and universities, legislators and administrators began to ask if the states can afford open door policies. Legislators are asking the same question that Hardin reported 10 years ago: "Can we justify allowing students needing remedial or developmental courses to enter institutions of higher learning?" (Hardin, 1988, p. 2). Arendale (1996) found a general mood at the federal and state levels to reduce the cost of remediation, cut developmental programs and faculty, and remove developmental courses from four-year campuses. Since 1985, Florida public universities have not been allowed to teach remedial courses.

University administrators and legislators are concerned about the length of time students require to graduate. Astin (Henry, 1996) reported that slightly less than 40% of college students in the United States complete a bachelor's degree within four years after entering college, down nearly 7% from 20 years ago. After six years the number rises by five points to 44.9%. Allowing up to nine years brings the number up less than one point more to 45%.

In an attempt to increase graduation rates, the Texas Legislature in 1997 passed the "slacker" bill that limits undergraduate students to a maximum of 170 hours of credit attempted that can be paid for by the state before graduation. Developmental courses are counted in this limit. After the limit is reached, students begin to pay out-of-state tuition rates. Another bill proposed to award students a $1,000 rebate if the degree is completed without taking more than one course outside those required. Other states are considering measures such as basing funding on the number of students who graduate rather than the number enrolled.

When public university administrators hear about Ivy League colleges that graduate 95% of their students in four years, they are tempted to respond by raising admission standards in an attempt to raise graduation rates. Focusing only on admission standards misses the fact that many selective admissions colleges also traditionally have used a strategy of "front-loading" services, which is the allocation of faculty and other institutional resources to better serve entering students (Noel, 1987). If students arrive on highly selective campuses lacking certain basic skills or competencies, the institution pro-

vides whatever is needed to help those students succeed. The most selective, often private, colleges know that it is less expensive to help students already enrolled than to recruit replacements for students who leave college. There is an expectation that students who are admitted will graduate.

Problem

The question raised by this research is whether or not provisionally admitted students belong in a four-year university. Provisional admission may have a variety of definitions at institutions across the country, but at Texas Tech University the term implies students who do not meet "assured admission" criteria and are allowed to enroll during the summer immediately following high school graduation to attempt to prove that they can handle rigorous college courses. At Texas Tech, assured admission is based on a combination of class standing and standardized test scores, as indicated in Table 1.

Students who do not meet the criteria may apply for the provisional program. Provisionally admitted students must pass six semester hours of college work with a grade point average of 2.0 or higher prior to their initial fall enrollment. One three-hour course must be taken in either mathematics, English, or a laboratory science. One other course must meet general education requirements, such as history, political science, foreign language, psychology, or sociology. Remedial or developmental courses may be used to satisfy the six-hour requirement.

Nationwide, provisionally admitted students range widely from "at-risk" individuals whose

Table 1

Class Standing and Standardized Test Scores Used for Assured Admission

| High School Class Rank | Minimum Test Scores for Assured Admission | |
	ACT	SAT
Top 10%	22	1010
First Quarter	25	1140
Second Quarter	28	1230
Lower Half	29	1270

standardized test scores throughout their academic careers, high school transcripts, college admission test scores, and graduation class standing provide a consistent profile of under-achievement, to the well-prepared students who may have good high school grades but graduated sixth in a class of 10. Provisional admits might include students who have difficulty with standardized tests as well as some with undiagnosed learning disabilities.

Regardless of how provisionally admitted students are defined and identified, many public research universities have an alternate enrollment for students who want to enter during the summer to attempt to qualify for fall. Support for these provisionally admitted students can range from none, in a "sink or swim" or "right to fail" environment, to extensive support systems in which the university invests heavily in provisionally admitted students who have been identified as having the potential to graduate.

Methodology

Beginning in the summer of 1996, provisionally admitted students who elected to enroll at Texas Tech were required to enter as arts and sciences undeclared students to be advised by the University Transition Advisement Center (UTAC). Prior to 1996, provisionally admitted students were allowed to choose majors from any of the seven undergraduate colleges at Texas Tech. In 1996, 244 students entered Texas Tech labelled provisionally admitted. These students are being tracked in a longitudinal study that will follow them for a 10-year period or until graduation.

Provisionally admitted students at Texas Tech are identified through the Office of Under-graduate Admissions. Once students are classified as provisional, they receive a letter from the Director of Undergraduate Admissions informing them of their status and identifying the University Transition Advisement Center (UTAC) as their point of contact on campus. In January, UTAC begins to send personalized letters to provisionally admitted students who have indicated their intention to enroll at Texas Tech during the summer. On or about May 1,

students planning to enroll for the first summer term receive a packet of materials that includes a survey of the student's perceived strengths and weaknesses and an opportunity to request any special services (such as learning and testing accommodations) for the summer classes in which they plan to enroll. Provisional students may elect to live in campus housing or off campus. Students are required to arrive on campus the day before registration in order to participate in an orientation conference that includes mathematics assessment and personal assistance with course selection based on a review of high school transcript and standardized test scores.

In the fall of 1996, a total of 271 students were identified through the Texas Tech student record system as having attended one or both summer terms at Texas Tech, or as having transferred credit from another institution in order to be eligible for fall enrollment. Of those, 104 (38.4%) attended the first summer session only; 120 (44.3%) attended the second summer session only; 19 (7.0%) attended both sessions at Texas Tech; 27 (10.0%) transferred six or more hours from other institutions; and 1 (0.4%) completed one course at Texas Tech and one course at another college or university.

To create a comparison cohort for the provisional admittants, a random sample of 280 students with assured admission was drawn from a population of approximately 6,000 entering freshmen. Comparisons of the two populations included data on the following items: demographic profile, GPA breakdowns for the fall and spring semesters, the mean number of hours attempted, cumulative grade point distributions following the spring semester, and scholastic probation and suspension rates at the end of the spring semester (see Table 2).

Consistent with findings of other studies (Lewis, Farris, & Greene, 1996), significantly higher percentages of minority students were among provisional admittants: 25.9% Black and Hispanic compared to 12.5% of the comparison group. More males were provisional admittants than assured admission: 57.6% compared to 43.6%.

Table 2

Demographic Data for Provisionally Admitted (n = 243) and Regularly Admitted (n = 280) Students

	Provisional	Regular Admittants
Race:		
White	71.6% (n = 174)	83.6% (n = 234)
Hispanic	22.2% (n = 54)	10.0% (n = 28)
Black	5.3% (n = 13)	2.5% (n = 7)
Other	0.8% (n = 2)	3.9% (n = 11)
Sex:		
Male	58.0% (n = 141)	43.6% (n = 122)
Female	42.0% (n = 102)	56.4% (n = 158)
Mean SAT Composite Score	827.5	1125*
Mean Hours Attempted—Fall 1996	12.7	14.4
Mean Hours Attempted—Spring 1997	12.3	14.4
Mean GPA Fall 1996	1.73	3.0
Mean Cumulative GPA Fall 1997	2.11	---
Mean GPA Spring 1997	1.79	2.98
Mean Cumulative GPA Spring 1997	1.98	3.04

*Figure is average SAT score for all students admitted to Texas Tech in Fall 1997.

To fulfill the math, English, or science requirement, provisional admittants chose English more often than the other two courses: math, 18%; English, 71%; science, 5.8%. Nearly 5% of the students enrolled for math and English; none registered for math and science or science and English. The mean high school class rank was 42.38 and the mean SAT Composite score was 827.46. These students would be classified as "at risk" by the two primary criteria for admission to Texas Tech: high school class rank and SAT score.

Results

Provisionally admitted students attempted fewer hours than the comparison group: in the fall of 1996, 12.69 compared to 14.37; and in the spring of 1997, 12.27 compared to 14.39. Cumulative GPAs compared as follows: the Fall 1996 mean was 1.73 compared to 3.00; and the Spring 1997 mean was 1.98 compared to 2.98. The gap suggests that the provisionally admitted students were identified correctly as "at risk" and that they will need strong support systems if they are to make progress toward a degree.

At the end of the fall semester, 38.7% of the provisional admittants were placed on probation because their cumulative grade point averages dropped below 2.00. Under Texas Tech University requirements, students whose cumulative GPA is below 2.0 must earn at least 2.0 for each semester thereafter or be placed on suspension. First-time suspension students must stay out of the university two summer terms or one regular semester. At the end of the spring semester of 1997, 31.8% of the remaining provisional admittants were suspended. Ten percent who were eligible to return in the spring semester elected not to enroll at Texas Tech and may have enrolled at some other institution. Table 2 compares demographic data between provisionally admitted students (*n* = 244) and regularly admitted students. Among the control group, 8.6% were placed on probation after the fall semester and 7.5% of those students were suspended at the end of the spring semester. Retention rates for provisional students are provided in Table 3.

Discussion

This is the first attempt to track provisional admittants to Texas Tech over the course of an entire year. As the results of this analysis indicate,

calculation of a summary statistic for the number of students who meet the requirements for provisional credit can be highly misleading. For example, calculations indicate that during the first and second summer terms at Texas Tech, 75.3% of the provisional admittants completed at least six required hours while maintaining a 2.0 GPA or better. Yet, because they enrolled for the second summer term and did not achieve a 2.0 in one or more classes, 23.5% were placed on academic probation at the beginning of the fall semester of 1996. This pattern continued throughout the fall and spring semesters, with 38.7% and 46.4% of the Texas Tech provisional population being placed on probation. Scholastic suspension rates also took a high toll, claiming 1.5% following the fall semester and 28.8% after the spring of 1997. By contrast, only 8.6% of the assured admission cohort were placed on probation following the fall semester. At the end of the spring semester, only 7.5% of this group were on probation, and only 3.6% had been suspended for academic deficiencies.

Unfortunately, this research does not reveal a very optimistic picture of success for the majority of provisional admittants who entered Texas Tech in the summer of 1996. By the end of a single academic year more than half of these students left Texas Tech, either voluntarily or involuntarily. Of those who enrolled in courses in the spring of 1997, none had a cumulative GPA

Table 3
Retention Rates for Provisionally Admitted Students

	Start	Provisional Requirements	Scholastic Suspensions	Other	Finish
Summer 1996	244	60 (24.6%)	---	10 (4.1%)	174 (71.3%)
Fall 1996	174	---	3 (1.7%)	17 (9.8%)	154 (88.5%)
Spring 1997	154	---	49 (31.8%)	NA	105* (66.2%)
Total	244	60 (24.5%)	52 (21.3%)	27 (11.1%)	105 (43.0%)

*At this date we do not know how many provisionally admitted students will register for the Fall 1997 term. Therefore, end numbers for Spring 1997 are calculated by subtracting known suspensions from beginning totals.

of 3.5 or better; only 6.5% had earned a GPA between 3.0 and 3.49 (corresponding figures for the comparison cohort are 31.6% with GPAs of 3.5 or better and 29.2% with GPAs between 3.0 and 3.49).

The 1996 provisional admission cohort will continue to be tracked through 10 years or until graduation. Efforts will be made to identify students who have transferred from Texas Tech to another institution to determine success rates of this population more accurately, but the results of this study speak for themselves. It should be obvious that provisional students at Texas Tech should be classified as being at risk of scholastic failure and that steps should be taken to assist these students to a greater degree than regular admittants. Summer, fall, and spring advising should be intrusive in nature, with much more frequent contact between students and advisors. All provisionally admitted students should be required to enter Texas Tech in the summer as arts and sciences undeclared majors and remain with UTAC for at least the first year. In addition to the two courses required for qualification, we recommend that each provisionally admitted student should be required to complete a course entitled XL 0201: Strategies for Academic Success. At the end of the spring semester of the first year, students with 2.5 or higher GPAs who have not failed any classes would be allowed to declare a major.

References

Arendale, D. (1996). *Unpublished survey of education policies concerning developmental education at the local, state and federal level in the U. S.* [On-line]. Available: http://www.umkc.edu/nade.htm

Hardin, C. J. (1988). Access to higher education: Who belongs? *Journal of Developmental Education, 12*(1), 2-6, 19.

Henry, T. (1996, October 14). More in college: Fewer graduate. *USA TODAY*, 1-2.

Lewis, L., Farris, E., & Greene, B. (1996). *Remedial education at higher education institutions in fall 1995.* Washington, DC: U. S. Department of Education.

Maxwell. M. (Ed.) (1994). *From access to success.* Clearwater, FL: H & H.

Noel, L. (1987). Increasing student retention: New challenges and potential. In L. Noel, R. Levitz, R. Saluri, & Associates, *Increasing student retention* (pp. 1-25). San Francisco: Jossey-Bass.

Senate Bill 148 (1997). Texas Legislature, 75th Session.

Chapter 6

Transitions in Developmental Education at the University of Georgia

Jeanne L. Higbee and Patricia L. Dwinell

As might be expected, trends in developmental education reflect changes in higher education as a whole. Numerous factors have influenced the direction of programs and services in recent years, including legislative demands for accountability, a new focus on workplace literacy, an influx of students with disabilities due to the mandate of the Americans with Disabilities Act (1990), and the increased availability and affordability of new technologies. Levine and Cureton (1998) point to the changing undergraduate demographics in American institutes of higher education, stating that less than one sixth of these students are the stereotypical "18 to 21 years of age, attending full-time, and living on campus" (p. 5).

Levine and Cureton (1998) report that close to one third of all undergraduate students today respond that they have taken at least one developmental course in reading, writing, or math. Furthermore, increasing levels of underpreparedness are not limited to two-year institutions. Levine and Cureton state, "Nearly three fourths (73%) of deans report an increase within the last decade in the proportion of students requiring remedial or developmental education at two-year (81%) and four-year (64%) colleges" (1998, p. 8).

Thus, developmental education programs may be even more important to the success of students at research universities than in the past. However, legislators balk at being required to "pay twice" to prepare students for higher education. In several states including Georgia, it has been proposed that developmental education be offered only at two-year institutions; yet large numbers of students who meet and exceed admissions requirements at four-year colleges and research universities are unable to pass placement tests for entry-level writing and mathematics courses. This chapter describes how the Division of Developmental Studies at the University of Georgia has metamorphosed to respond to internal and external demands. Now called the Division of Academic Assistance, the program has transformed and grown from a successful series of classes for provisionally admitted students to a broad range of courses and services for all students at the university.

Division of Developmental Studies: 1976-1993

From 1976 to 1993, the Division of Developmental Studies provided an opportunity to attend the University of Georgia to students who otherwise would not have been admitted. The academic environment in the Division of Developmental Studies was planned and implemented to maximize learning and to help students develop effective study strategies necessary for academic success. Class sizes were small (i.e., fewer than 20 students) to promote interaction between faculty members and students and to encourage student involvement in the classroom. Students were also able to seek individual academic assistance outside the classroom during the daily office hours maintained by their own teachers and in the Developmental Studies (DS) learning laboratory. Adjacent to the DS learning lab was the University's tutorial center, where students could continue to receive academic assistance after they exited the Developmental Studies program.

Four Teaching Components

The Division of Developmental Studies consisted of four components. The curricula in English, mathematics, and reading were designed to enhance students' academic competencies and to enable them to compete successfully in the University's rigorous academic program. The counseling curriculum focused on reducing or eliminating affective barriers to achievement.

English. The objective of the English Program was to teach students to write fluently, correctly, and effectively. English course activities included peer review, word processing instruction and practice, and both classroom and writing center instruction in all aspects of the composing process. The English courses were designed to teach students to use details, to show rather than tell the action, to develop organized structure, to achieve purpose, and to incorporate logical thinking and support. The English Program's purpose was to teach writing and

critical thinking competence that would empower students in their personal, academic, professional, and public lives.

Mathematics. Three objectives of the Mathematics Program were:

♦ to develop and strengthen the mathematics skills of students so that they could be successful in their entry-level mathematics courses and other courses requiring elementary mathematics reasoning;

♦ to develop and strengthen the thinking, reasoning, and problem-solving skills of students and thus promote the ability to make analytical transferences; and

♦ to develop and strengthen the mathematical work and study habits of students.

Reading. The overall objectives of the Reading Program were to increase the reading proficiency of students and to teach them reading and study strategies needed for success in university courses. Instruction and practice were given in text comprehension, reading speed and flexibility, strategies for textbook reading and studying, concentration techniques, note-taking and test-taking strategies, vocabulary, and techniques for mastering specialized discipline-area terms and concepts. Because instruction was linked to University reading demands, courses incorporated applications of reading techniques to university-level texts, novels, and supplementary content and news materials.

Counseling. The objective of the Counseling Program was to promote development of those psychological, social, and vocational life skills that facilitate success and achievement in a college setting. In addition to group and individual counseling, the component offered a course titled "Strategies for Academic Success," which included instruction in self-awareness, goal setting, determining priorities, anxiety management, academic planning, utilization of campus resources, and effective time management. DS counselors also served as their students' academic advisors as long as the students were enrolled in the Division.

Placement and Exit. Student placement in the appropriate course in each component was determined by Scholastic Aptitude Test (SAT) scores, high school grade point average (HSGPA), Collegiate Placement Exam (CPE) scores, and other placement measures such as a writing sample. Students exited the Division of Developmental Studies when they achieved within four attempts the exiting criteria for each of the program areas in which they were placed. Students who did not exit a program area in four attempts were dismissed from the university. Counselors assisted dismissed students in developing alternative educational or occupational plans.

Development of the Program

In the early 1970s, the Board of Regents of the State of Georgia determined that any student who graduates from a Georgia high school should have the opportunity to pursue a program of study in a postsecondary educational setting. Recognizing that many students may be unprepared in the fundamental core curriculum necessary for successful entry into higher education, the Board of Regents mandated all institutions within the system to establish a program of Special Studies (changed to Developmental Studies in the fall of 1981), which would be an integral component of the institution's academic program. These programs would provide systematic academic services to entering students with deficient academic skills to enhance their ability to succeed in regular college work. The program at the University of Georgia began in 1976 with a staff of five graduate assistants and a student population of 50. By the fall of 1990, the program had an enrollment of 454 students served by a staff of 17 full-time faculty members (15 of whom had earned doctoral degrees), 29 part-time faculty, and a support staff of five.

Goals and Objectives

The goal of the Division of Developmental Studies was to enable students who did not meet regular admissions requirements for the University of Georgia to develop the skills necessary to matriculate and ultimately to graduate. Complementary goals were to enhance cultural diversity at the institution and to provide a wider choice of educational opportunities to Georgia's youth.

Students selected to participate in the Division of Developmental Studies had narrowly missed regular admission to the institution. A predicted freshman grade point average based on SAT scores and HSGPA was used to rank applicants to the University. After the cutoff for regular admission was determined, the group of students just below the cutoff was admitted to the Division of Developmental Studies. Affirmative action guidelines were applied to the admission of qualified Black candidates. The DS Minority Enrollment Committee, a group of DS faculty members, telephoned prospective Black DS students to respond to questions and encourage Black students to enroll.

> *The program has transformed and grown from a successful series of classes for provisionally admitted students to a broad range of courses and services for all students at the university.*

Results and Outcomes for Students and the Institution

Students enrolled in the Division of Developmental Studies had a lower mean high school grade point average, and a mean SAT composite score typically 200 points lower than students admitted as freshmen. The mean SAT composite score for students admitted to the Division of Developmental Studies in the Fall Quarter of 1990 was 831; for regular freshmen, the mean score was 1045. The mean HSGPA was 2.41 for developmental students compared to 3.2 for regularly admitted freshmen.

Between 85% and 90% of the students who matriculated in the Division of Developmental Studies fulfilled the requirements to enroll in regular coursework. The remainder of the students (fewer than 1%) either withdrew from the University or were dismissed because of failure to complete requirements within the allotted four quarters of DS coursework.

Retention rates compiled by the University's Office of Retention and Advising indicate that DS students persisted at rates comparable to those of other entering freshmen. For the period of 1985 to 1990, one-year retention rates (fall to fall) ranged from 78.6% to 84.6% for DS students; rates for regularly admitted freshmen ranged from 81.4% to 84.5%.

Because the mission of the Division of Developmental Studies was to prepare students with the skills to succeed in college-level work, one of the best measures of the program's success was the performance of students once they entered the regular curriculum. Each quarter the performance of developmental students was compared with the performance of regular enrolled students in selected core courses. Although SAT scores and HSGPA were lower for developmental students, there were usually no significant differences in the performance of the two groups of students in introductory English, mathematics, and social science courses as indicated in Table 1.

Graduation rates also indicate that developmental students were successful in the college curriculum. The Office of Institutional Research and Planning compiled data during the Fall Quarter of 1990 on developmental students who were enrolled during the period ranging from the summer of 1976 to the spring of 1985. These matriculants would have been enrolled long enough to have completed the requirements for graduation. Of the 1,954 Developmental Studies students who completed the program, 901 (46.1%) graduated from the University of Georgia. The graduation rate for all freshman matriculants during the same period was 59.9%. However, for a comparable size group of the lowest ranking freshmen, the graduation rate was 41.6%. The lowest ranking freshmen were predicted to succeed; the Developmental Studies freshmen had predicted grade point averages below the 2.0 required to graduate.

Many institutions provide programs to ameliorate academic deficiencies and facilitate skill development, but few can boast the University of Georgia's success rate. Several factors may be particularly significant in contributing to program effectiveness. Perhaps the most important

of these was the developmental nature of the Division's course offerings, characterized by the focus on process in addition to content mastery. This developmental focus on process skills (i.e., learning strategies) plus content mastery is beyond mere remediation. Another critical aspect of the program was its duration. Students could exempt (i.e., place out of) one subject and exit another in one quarter, yet require four quarters for completion of another DS component. Students could begin taking regular university courses in each area after DS prerequisites had been met, and meanwhile continue to receive support services throughout the period they were enrolled in one or more DS courses.

The full-time faculty had both expertise and interest in enhancing the academic potential of high-risk students. The counseling component, made up of doctoral-level faculty members employed specifically to teach, counsel, and advise the target population, was a unique feature of this program. Counseling faculty members were knowledgeable about the specific needs of high-risk students; they engaged in intrusive advising practices and communicated student progress through an early warning system devised by the Assistant to the Director for Research and Evaluation to utilize student performance data provided each week by the members of the English, mathematics, and reading faculties.

Developmental theory and recent research support the value of the following: (a) a developmental focus, (b) opportunities for assistance over an extended period of time, (c) intrusive advising with an emphasis on affective barriers to achievement, and (d) an early warning system. These variables, combined with low student/teacher ratios, extensive opportunities for individual assistance both with the faculty member and in the lab, a committed faculty, and an expectation of excellence, contributed to the Division's success.

Division of Academic Assistance: 1993-Present

In 1993, in response to a change in priorities perceived by the state legislature and the University System of Georgia Board of Regents, the Division of Developmental Studies at the University of

Table 1

A Comparison of the Performance of Developmental Studies Students and Regularly Enrolled Students in Selected Core Curriculum Courses: Summer 1989 - Winter 1990

Selected Core Curriculum Courses	Total Enrollment[a]		Grade of D or Better[b]		Grade of C or Better	
	Regularly Enrolled Students	Developmental Studies Students	Regularly Enrolled Students	Developmental Studies Students	Regularly Enrolled Students	Developmental Studies Students
ENG 101	2562	256	97.9	96.9	94.0	92.2
ENG 102	1970	120	99.0	98.3	96.3	90.8
MAT 102	1988	249	81.1	80.3	65.3	61.0
SOC 105	1790	120	98.0	93.3	90.3	81.7
PSY 101	1847	168	96.6	92.3	82.9	68.5
POL 101	2107	109	98.0	91.7	91.4	77.1
HIS 251	1770	141	95.9	90.0	82.4	70.2
HIS 252	1624	105	96.6	94.3	88.5	74.3
SPC 108	430	27	98.8	100	95.3	92.6

Note. The data for Developmental Studies include students currently enrolled in the program as well as former Developmental Studies students.

[a] W, I, AV, NR, and K are not included in calculations. Data provided by Institutional Research and Planning.

[b] The University considers a C or better in ENG 101 as passing.

Georgia began its transformation to the Division of Academic Assistance. Significant changes in the structure of the program have included the elimination of a separate admissions procedure, the expansion of course offerings, and relocation to a centralized facility that houses the Division's administrative and faculty offices, the new Academic Center, Tutorial Services, TRIO programs, one multimedia classroom, a multipurpose room with media capabilities, and numerous small group rooms. The Division is now perceived as a developmental program that serves all students at the University of Georgia, regardless of class level, rank, or academic standing.

Placement in Academic Assistance Courses

Upon admission to the University of Georgia, students may be placed in one or more Academic Assistance (ACA) courses in English, mathematics, or reading depending upon high school grade point average (GPA), standardized admissions test scores, and scores on a variety of placement tests in English, mathematics, and reading. Any student who is placed in two or more Academic Assistance courses is also required to enroll in the ACA counseling course. These courses are comparable to the former DS courses, though geared to a higher level of student abilities. Based on standardized test scores and scores on the Collegiate Placement Exam (CPE), a series of tests in English, mathematics, and reading developed for the University System of Georgia by Educational Testing Service (ETS), a very small number of especially high-risk students (approximately 10 to 20 per year) are designated as DS students, and are also advised and monitored by an ACA counselor. The State Board of Regents has mandated that by the fall of 2001 there will no longer be DS students enrolled in research institutions in the state of Georgia. Originally considered the death knell of developmental education at research universities in the state, this mandate has instead inspired developmental education program administrators and faculty members at the state's research institutions, including Georgia State

University (Commander, Stratton, Callahan, & Smith, 1996; Stratton, Commander, Callahan, & Smith, 1996) and the University of Georgia (UGA), to think creatively with a focus on program development. At UGA approximately 15% of the freshmen tested during summer orientation sessions are required to enroll in one or more academic assistance courses. During the past four academic years, the number of students enrolled in ACA courses ranged from 717 to 1,246, with the greatest enrollment in the area of mathematics.

University (UNV) Courses

At UGA two new courses were piloted in the summer of 1991, and have proven very popular and successful ever since. University (UNV) 102: Learning to Learn, taught by ACA reading faculty, addresses reading and study strategies. UNV 103: Strategies for Academic Success, taught by ACA counseling faculty, is a self-awareness course that enables students to explore the relationship between attitudes (and other noncognitive factors) and academic performance. Special sections of these courses have been made available to students participating in an early enrollment summer program at UGA. In 1997 a special section was also provided for students with disabilities, at the request of UGA's Office of Disability Services. Participants evaluated this special section very favorably, reporting that they felt more comfortable discussing their specific academic needs in a class in which every student had a disability of some kind.

In recent years numerous other courses have been piloted under the UNV course prefix, including "Problem Solving," "Grammar Review," "Preparation for Statistics," "Writing the Research Paper," and "Enhancing Thinking Skills." Students receive institutional rather than degree credit, but their grades are calculated into their cumulative GPAs. In Georgia, where many college students are attending on HOPE scholarships and must maintain a 3.0 average, UNV courses are perceived as having the dual benefits of enhancing skill development and bolstering students' GPAs. The courses are highly structured, with a strong emphasis on attendance and participation, so that students who meet course expectations can anticipate earning high grades. During the 1996-97 academic year, 1,145 students enrolled in at least one

UNV course. At present enrollment is limited by resources of the Division; however, it is anticipated that more sections of the UNV courses will be offered in the future.

Academic Center and Tutorial Services

The former DS learning laboratories for students enrolled in DS English, mathematics, reading, and counseling have been converted into a centralized Academic Center that serves all students at the institution. Relocation to the new building prompted the receipt of a technology grant to create a computer network with all new equipment. Students utilize the Academic Center for assistance in writing papers, computer-assisted career exploration, self-assessment in such areas as learning styles and academic strategies, and computer-assisted preparation for graduate and professional school admissions tests, as well as for instructional support for ACA courses. Students may also use Academic Center computers to access the Internet for email and course registration. Many students visit the Academic Center frequently during a term either because of courses in which they are enrolled or because the Center is generally conducive to studying and learning. It is estimated that 1,200 students used the resources during the 1996-97 academic year.

Students visit the Academic Center for skill development; for assistance in specific non-ACA courses, they can seek free peer tutoring two times per week per course at University Tutorial Services, where there are private rooms for one-on-one and small group sessions. Tutoring is available for most core curriculum requirements and other high-risk courses. Although it may change from quarter to quarter depending on the availability of tutors, tutoring is available for approximately 90 courses in 22 subject areas. Sixteen tutors served over 900 students for a total of 3,100 peer tutoring contacts during 1996-1997.

Other Services

The Division of Academic Assistance sponsors numerous other services including community outreach programs, adjunct courses pairing study strategies with high-risk core courses, in-class workshops on such topics as reducing test anxiety or algebra review for astronomy students, and individual counseling. Perhaps one of the most popular programs is the Academic Success Series. ACA faculty present several late after-noon workshops per week on a variety of topics of interest to students, such as time management, taking lecture notes, learning styles, and critical thinking. Sessions for relaxation training held during the weeks before midterm and final exams have attracted as many as 50 students per workshop.

The expansion of developmental education services at the University of Georgia is consistent with the National Association for Developmental Education's (1995) revised definition statement that encompasses academic support for all students, regardless of their year in school or level of preparedness. Although it is more difficult to monitor and measure the impact of these programs, their popularity with students is well documented by participant evaluations. A survey of UGA faculty (Higbee, Thomas, Glauser, Hayes, & Hynd, 1996) indicated that academic departments appreciate the centralized provision of support services. The demand for courses and programs continues to grow.

References

Americans with Disabilities Act. (1990). Public Law 101-336, 42 U. S. C. Sec. 12101.

Commander, N. E., Stratton, C. B., Callahan, C. A., & Smith, B. C. (1996). A learning assistance model for expanding academic support. *Journal of Developmental Education, 20*(2), 8, 10, 12, 14, 16.

Higbee, J. L., Thomas, P. V., Glauser, A. S., Hayes, C. G., & Hynd, C. R. (1996). *Final report of the Division of Academic Assistance Semester Conversion Grant Committee*. Athens, GA: The University of Georgia.

Levine, A., & Cureton, J. S. (1998). What we know about today's college students. *About Campus, 3*(1), 4-9.

National Association for Developmental Education (1995). *Definition and goals statement*. Carol Stream, IL: Author.

Stratton, C. B., Commander, N. E., Callahan, C. A., & Smith, B. D. (1996). From DS to LS: The expansion of an academic preparation program from developmental studies to learning support. *Selected Conference Papers, 2*, 42-44.

Chapter 7

Developmental Education at a Public Research University

Catherine Wambach and Robert delMas

Although developmental education is generally associated with open-access postsecondary institutions, it is also present in most four-year colleges and research universities. A National Center for Educational Statistics survey of postsecondary institutions (Lewis, Farris, & Greene, 1996) found that about three quarters (78%) of higher education institutions that enrolled freshmen offered at least one developmental reading, writing, or mathematics course in the fall of 1995. Among public four-year institutions, 81% provided at least one developmental reading, writing, or mathematics course. In a recent investigation of developmental education in Big Ten research universities, Wambach (1997) found that all but one had developmental courses and support services for a segment of their freshmen identified as underprepared. The most comprehensive and ambitious of these programs is located at the University of Minnesota's General College. This chapter will describe the University of Minnesota's approach to serving underprepared students and present what is known about the program's outcomes.

The University of Minnesota's approach to developmental education is unique in several respects. First, students are admitted to a college designed to meet their needs in a comprehensive way. The curriculum and student services are coordinated to a greater extent than is possible in most developmental programs. Second, developmental education is delivered by regular faculty in the context of college-level, credit-bearing courses. Skills are not taught in stand-alone courses, but instead are integrated into the regular curriculum. Third, preparation for transfer is the primary function of General College. The salience of transfer has created a focus on student academic planning and monitoring of student progress. Fourth, and perhaps most important, the location of General College in a major research university has created a context and climate where research on developmental education can and does occur.

General College and Its Students

At the University of Minnesota, freshmen can be admitted into any of seven colleges. Most students enter either the College of Liberal Arts or the Institute of Technology. A handful of new students are admitted very selectively each year to the Carlson School of Management, the College of Biological Science, the College of Human Ecology, and the College of Agriculture, Forestry and Environmental Sciences. These colleges grant degrees and admit only highly qualified freshmen. Students who fall below these colleges' selective admissions criteria are admitted to the University's General College.

The mission of General College is to prepare underprepared students for transfer to the degree granting colleges of the University of Minnesota. The college recruits students from the Twin Cities metropolitan area, with a special emphasis on recruiting students of color. However, the student population represents a broad cross section of students from Minnesota and neighboring Wisconsin. General College receives about 3,000 applications each fall and enrolls about 850 freshmen. The actual number varies somewhat from year to year depending on the admissions office's ability to accurately forecast enrollment. Of the enrolled freshmen, about 30% to 35% are students of color, as indicated in Figure 1.

Although General College admits underprepared students and serves a key role in University of Minnesota access strategies, it is not an open admissions college. The University uses a formula for determining eligibility for admission called the Academic Aptitude Ratio (AAR). The AAR is the high school rank plus twice the ACT composite score. For example, a student who graduated at the 45th percentile of her high school class with an ACT composite score of 19 would have an AAR score of 45 + (2x19), or 83. Most students admitted to General College have AAR scores between 70 and 110. Such students represent the middle third of their high school graduating classes. In addition, about 140 students per year are admitted with scores below 70. A variety of strategies have been used to select these students. Research on these methods shows that none of these strategies improve our ability to select students who are more likely to succeed (delMas & Kroll, 1996). The average high school ranks and ACT test scores for General College students are presented in Table 1.

High school rank, high school grade point average (GPA), and admissions test scores have not been found to be powerful predictors of success for General College students. Table 2 presents results from a study recently conducted in the College. Although all of the correlations are statistically significant (primarily due to the large sample sizes, all between 2,500 and 5,500), the correlations are all quite weak. None of the

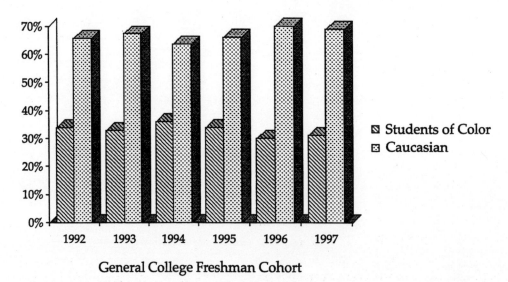

Figure 1. Percent students of color within General College entering freshman cohorts.

Table 1

Average High School GPA, High School Percentile Rank, and ACT Composite Score of General College Entering Freshmen

Precollege Measure	Freshman Cohort					
	1991	1992	1993	1994	1995	1996
High School GPA	2.21	2.26	2.23	2.44	2.48	2.57
High School Percentile Rank	42.4	41.2	39.0	44.5	43.8	46.3
ACT Compostie Score	19.0	19.1	18.7	19.5	19.5	20.1

precollege predictors, either individually or in combination, accounted for more than 10% of the variance in any of the outcome measures. The findings are consistent with the conclusion that the General College developmental program has a similar effect on all students regardless of their prior academic performance.

Research on developmental education suggests that General College students are not as well qualified as developmental students in other research universities. In a national study of education (Boylan, Bonham, & Bliss, 1994), the mean high school GPA for students enrolled in developmental courses at research universities was 2.83 and the mean for students in two-year colleges was 2.44. The mean high school GPA for General College students was 2.21 in 1991, rising to 2.57 in 1996 (see Table 1). One of the reasons

for the difference between the GPAs of General College freshmen and developmental students at other research universities is structural. Because admission to General College is considered a *de facto* placement in developmental education, all General College students are identified as developmental students, even if they take only college-level courses. In addition, students from other University of Minnesota colleges who take General College precollege-level courses, primarily in mathematics, are not described as developmental students, though they would be at other institutions. If the non-General College students enrolled in developmental courses were counted, the number of developmental students described as such at the University of Minnesota would be considerably higher, as would the average high school GPA.

Table 2

Bivariate and Multiple Correlation Coefficients Between Precollege Predictors and Academic Outcomes

College Outcomes	Predictor Variables				
	HS GPA[a]	HS PR[b]	ACT	ACT & HS GPA	ACT & HS PR
Retention	.146	.141	.031	NA[c]	.133
Transfer	.280	.237	.125	.318	.275
Good Standing	.202	.212	.078	NA[c]	.216
Cumulative GPA	.279	.255	.108	.325	.284

[a]HS GPA = high school grade point average
[b]HS PR = high school percentile rank
[c]NA = only high school grade point average accounted for a significant amount of variance in the outcome measure

Curriculum

The mission of the college is to prepare students for transfer into University of Minnesota degree programs, and so the curriculum is designed to prepare students for work in traditional majors. The college offers freshman courses in mathematics, basic writing, social sciences, sciences, and humanities. The courses are taught by 32 tenured and tenure-track faculty along with numerous appointed faculty and graduate students representing a variety of disciplines. The typical teaching load for faculty is two courses per quarter (six per year), while full-time teaching specialists teach three (nine per year).

The General College faculty is committed to offering freshmen a set of courses described as the "Base Curriculum" that integrates the goals of liberal and developmental education. Base Curriculum courses are introductory courses in the humanities, sciences, social sciences, mathematics, and composition that incorporate instruction in the skills necessary for success in these disciplines. Base Curriculum courses are intended to improve students' reading, writing, and study skills through direct instruction, the design of appropriate assignments, use of active learning strategies, and frequent feedback. Because the faculty represent a wide variety of disciplines, the instructional strategies used reflect disciplinary differences. These differences have been described in the higher education literature and observed in surveys of University of Minnesota faculty (Wambach, Woods, & delMas, 1996). Examination of General College courses suggests the following:

1. Writing is an important component of most General College courses. The base curriculum commits the faculty to the development of literacy skills through content instruction.

2. Multicultural education approaches are incorporated into many General College courses. The General College student body is diverse, and many General College courses acknowledge this in the selection of course content and pedagogy.

3. Many faculty use technology to support instruction. Computer-assisted instruction is used in highly innovative ways in the instruction of writing, psychology, biology, art, and statistics.

4. Technology is also used to enhance the delivery of lectures in a variety of subjects. Most General College classes enroll fewer than 40 students. Class size reflects the practice of assigning large amounts of written homework to students, which must be graded and returned in a timely fashion. Since frequent, meaningful assessment and feedback are important elements of the college's curriculum, class size reflects the faculty's capacity to process and return assignments with limited help from teaching assistants.

5. The informal lecture combined with class discussion is the most frequent format for class meetings (Wambach, 1992). Most General College faculty use active learning strategies of some kind to involve students in the class. These strategies include Socratic questioning, small group work, in-class writing, and simulations.

Mathematics

General College offers precollege-level courses in mathematics for all students at the University. The course offerings begin with arithmetic and extend through high school upper algebra. The college also offers one course in college level statistics. General College precollege-level mathematics courses do not count for credit toward graduation.

Students who enter the University without having completed two years of high school algebra must do so to graduate. General College mathematics courses also enroll students who have completed algebra, but have not mastered the content sufficiently to continue mathematics study. General College students must take a mathematics placement test before their initial registration. Scores on this test, combined with the student's high school record, are used to make recommendations about initial registration in mathematics. Students and their advisors ultimately decide when—and at what level—the student should begin mathematics instruction.

Cut scores for placement in General College mathematics courses are determined by the General College mathematics faculty. The validity of the placement process has been continuously tested through research. The most recent validity study (delMas, 1995) suggests that the placement test is making accurate predictions for placement into intermediate algebra and is less valid for beginning algebra.

Mathematics is considered to be one of the more challenging subject areas for General College students. General College students are more likely to be underprepared in mathematics and science than they are in other areas of the curriculum. Many General College students have successfully avoided mathematics instruction and have negative attitudes towards the subject matter. Mathematics courses have the lowest completion rate among General College courses—73% compared to an average of 83% for all General College courses (Wambach & delMas, 1995). This has been a cause of concern for the mathematics faculty and advisors. Completion rates for General College mathematics courses are, however, slightly higher than the national average of 65% for developmental mathematics courses (Boylan, Bonham, & Bliss, 1992). Efforts to increase completion, such as hiring instructors with more mathematics education training and reducing class size, have had modest, positive effects.

Writing

In the mid-1980s, the General College basic writing faculty made a radical decision. Rather than continue a curriculum that relied on paper and pencil tests to place students into a variety of precollege- and college-level reading and writing courses, the faculty decided to place all students in college-level writing and eliminate the reading curriculum. They based this decision on evidence that the tests General College used to place students in reading and writing courses were not valid and that students who took these courses did not appear to benefit from them. The faculty argued that small classes, with enrollments less than 20, supported by computer technology, were more likely to facilitate the development of student writing than were a proliferation of literacy skills courses. The writing

courses were revised to reflect theory and research on basic writing.

The results of eliminating precollege reading and writing courses for all students (besides those in English as a Second Language) have been very positive. About 87% of the students who register for the first quarter of freshman composition, General College 1421, pass the course. One study conducted by the College found evidence that students performed better in the General College freshman composition course than students with similar precollege scores who were placed into a non-General College composition course at the University of Minnesota (delMas, 1994). Student surveys suggest that students find the course extremely challenging, but view it positively (Wambach, Thatcher, & Woods, 1996).

One of the major issues surrounding writing instruction is its cost relative to the rest of the curriculum. The writing courses are small and are offered in computer classrooms. The small class size means that tuition covers only the basic instructional cost. Computer classrooms require continual upgrades of hardware and software and technical support. The problem of technical support has been softened by the imposition of a technology fee; however, equipment replacement is an ongoing issue.

English as a Second Language

General College offers a special program for English as a Second Language students called "Commanding English." The program serves students with Michigan English Language Assessment Battery (MELAB) scores from 65 to 77, just below the threshold for admission to the University. The goal of the program is to strengthen students' academic English to enable them to succeed in college. Most of the 45 to 60 students admitted each year are recently arrived refugees who are permanent residents. They take a prescribed curriculum consisting of courses in speech communication, reading, writing, literature, general arts, anatomy and physiology, and sociology. The humanities, social science, and science courses are paired with reading courses.

Student Support Services

General College offers students a variety of academic support services, including advising, career services, walk-in tutoring in mathematics and writing, Supplemental Instruction, and support for student parents. The advising model used by the college has been described as "intrusive advising." Advisors are expected to monitor student progress and intervene proactively when evidence suggests that students need assistance. Evidence comes from a system of academic alerts, such as midquarter reports and communiques from instructors to advisors indicating that a student is having problems. Midquarter reports are used to design interventions to improve student success and plan for the next quarter's registration.

Career services are also important contributors to the college's mission. A transfer and career center is located in a prominent part of the college's home building. Students must visit the center at important points in their academic career to file plans for transfer to one of the degree-granting colleges of the university. Filing transfer plans provides a context for informing students about the transfer process and requirements of the myriad majors and programs available.

Tutoring and academic support are available through the Academic Assistance Center, which provides walk-in tutoring in writing and mathematics and access to computers. Additional instruction in selected courses is available to TRIO eligible students through the Student Support Services office. The TRIO program identifies and serves GC freshmen who are TRIO eligible (first-generation college students, low income students, and students with disabilities). General College is home to one of the oldest TRIO programs in the country. The program has been identified by U. S. Department of Education researchers as one of the most successful in the nation in promoting the achievement of highly at-risk students.

General College is also the home for the Student Parent HELP Program. This program helps students who are also parents pay for child care expenses; the program also provides academic advising and counseling related to the challenges of raising children while attending college. Many of the participants in the program are single parent clients of Aid for Families with Dependent Children and related welfare programs.

Outcomes

Research on the outcomes of developmental education suggests that it contributes to student retention, at least for the short term, and increases student performance (Kulik, Kulik, & Schwalb, 1983). However, developmental students tend to have lower GPAs and graduation rates than do their better prepared peers. For example, Boylan, Bonham, and Bliss (1994) reported that the average cumulative college GPA for developmental students at four-year public institutions was 2.03, and at research universities it was 2.10. At four-year public institutions, 28.4% of the developmental students had graduated or were still in school at the end of five and one-half years. At research universities the persistence and graduation rate for developmental students was 48%.

General College students tend to persist in higher education, though not necessarily at the University of Minnesota. Typically 65% to 75% of General College freshmen reenroll at the University of Minnesota during their second year of college, while 70% or better continue enrollment beyond the first year (see Figure 2).

Wambach and delMas (1996) found that 62% of the 1988 cohort of General College freshmen had earned a degree or were still enrolled in postsecondary education somewhere in Minnesota five years after entering. However, only 9% earned bachelor's degrees from the University of Minnesota in that time, compared to 36% of the students who entered the selective College of Liberal Arts.

Because the mission of General College is to prepare students for transfer, successful transfer is an important outcome. In order to transfer to a degree-granting college, students must earn a GPA of 2.5 on 36 quarter credits. The same standard is used to evaluate transfer students from outside the University of Minnesota, regardless

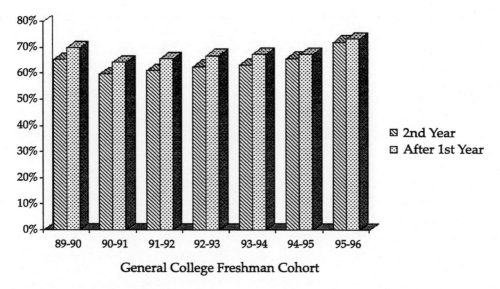

Figure 2. Retention of General College freshmen.

of transferring institution. Intra-University transfer rates for General College students are presented in Figure 3. Since 1991, General College students have transferred sooner and in larger numbers than previous cohorts; this coincides with structural changes in the University of Minnesota which codified the General College mission as a developmental studies program. After transfer, former General College students (90% or better; see Figure 4) tend to maintain satisfactory academic standing and graduate at the same rate as other transfer students, as depicted in Figure 5. Although only 13% of students who transfer to the College of Liberal Arts come from General College, they account for nearly one third of the students of color who transfer (see Figure 6). This suggests that General College makes an important contribution to the diversity of the University of Minnesota student body.

One possible explanation for the increase in the transfer rate and decrease in time to transfer is that the college is admitting a slightly more qualified student body. However, recent research (Wambach & delMas, 1996) found that transfer rate and time to transfer were not highly related to precollege entrance

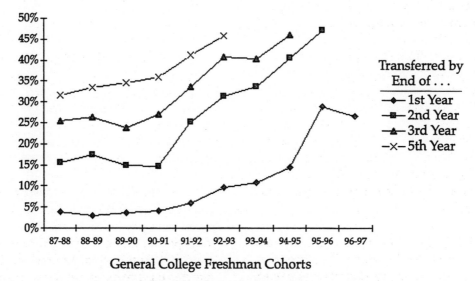

Figure 3. Intra-university transfer rates of General College freshman cohorts.

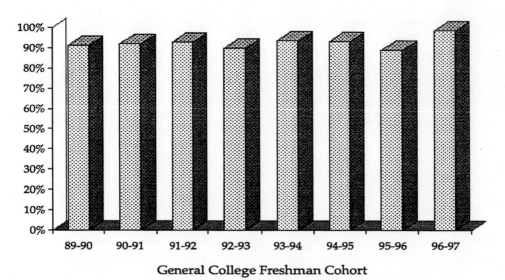

Figure 4. Percent of General College intra-university transfers in good academic standing as of the last term of registration.

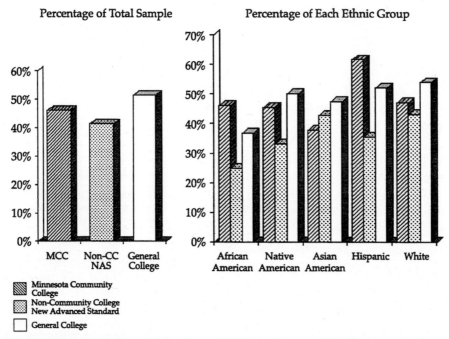

Figure 5. Percent of New Advanced Standing (NAS) and General College transfers to the College of Liberal Arts who graduated within five years of transfer.

characteristics (see Table 2), again suggesting that the college programs, not the student characteristics, were responsible for the improvements.

Conclusions

Although many lawmakers decry the use of public funds to support underqualified stu-dents' pursuit of postsecondary education, many of these students can succeed in the most competitive postsecondary environments, given the opportunity and appropriate instruction and support. However, since national rankings and other prestige factors are based on the qualifications of the freshman class, research universities have little incentive, and powerful disincentives, to admit less qualified students.

70

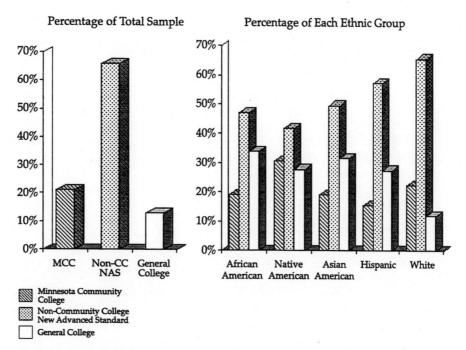

Percentage of Total Sample   Percentage of Each Ethnic Group

Minnesota Community
College

Non-Community College
New Advanced Standard

General College

Figure 6. Distribution of ethnic backgrounds among New Advanced Standing (NAS) and General College students who transferred to the College of Liberal Arts.

Given a political climate that is hostile to the principles of affirmative action, it is likely that prestigious universities will be given permission, and in some cases will face mandates, to reduce their commitments to more diversity and to less well-qualified students. Increasingly, two-year open admissions colleges are expected to bear the entire burden of developing underprepared students. Because the social and demographic correlates of underpreparation are well known, we as a society have to ask ourselves if stratifying our postsecondary education system along lines of race and class is a tolerable outcome, or if all postsecondary institutions will be called upon to make some effort to accommodate students who, for a variety of circumstances, are not adequately prepared to achieve their goals.

References

Boylan, H. R., Bonham, B. S., & Bliss, L. B. (1992, October). *National study of developmental education: Students, programs and institutions of higher education.* Paper presented at the First National Conference of Research in Developmental Education, Charlotte, NC.

Boylan, H. R., Bonham, B. S., & Bliss, L. B. (1994). Who are the developmental students? *Research in Developmental Education, 11,* 2.

delMas, R. C. (1994). *The relationship between GC 1422 and other composition courses offered at the University of Minnesota.* Unpublished research report. Minneapolis, MN: General College, University of Minnesota.

delMas, R. C. (1995). *Preliminary report on the validity of the General College mathematics course placement system.* Unpublished research report. Minneapolis, MN: General College, University of Minnesota.

delMas, R. C. (1997). *When no relationship is a good relationship.* Unpublished research report. Minneaolis, MN: General College, University of Minnesota.

delMas, R. C., & Kroll, P. (1996, October). *The use of non-cognitive variables in admission decisions for high at-risk college applicants.* Paper presented at the 1996 annual meeting of the Minnesota Association for Developmental Education, Rochester, MN.

Kulik, J., Kulik, C. L., & Schwalb, B. (1983). College programs for high risk and disadvantaged students: A meta-analysis of findings. *Review of Educational Research, 53,* 397-414.

Lewis, L., Farris, E., & Greene, B. (1996). *Remedial education at higher education institutions in fall 1995* (National Center for Educational Statistics No. 7-584). Washington, DC: U. S. Government Printing Office.

Wambach, C. (1992). *Observing the base curriculum.* Unpublished report to the General College Curriculum Committee. Minneapolis, MN: General College, University of Minnesota.

Wambach, C. (1997). *Programs and services for underprepared students in the Big Ten.* Unpublished research report. Minneapolis, MN: General College, University of Minnesota.

Wambach, C., & delMas, R. C. (April 1995). *Preliminary report on completion rates for General College courses.* Unpublished research report. Minneapolis, MN: General College, University of Minnesota.

Wambach, C., & delMas, R. C. (1996). *Should developmental education survive at the University of Minnesota?* Paper presented at the national Annual Forum of the Association for Institutional Research (AIR), Albuquerque, NM.

Wambach, C., Thatcher, K., & Woods, M. (1996). *Transition to college courses: General College students' perceptions of the relationships between high school and college courses.* Unpublished research report. Minneapolis, MN: General College, University of Minnesota.

Wambach, C., Woods, M., & delMas, R. C. (1996). *Characteristics of selected lower division courses at the University of Minnesota.* Unpublished research report. Minneapolis, MN: General College, University of Minnesota.

Chapter 8

A Charge to Developmental Educators:

Ignite the Spark

Rita Klein, Diane Vukovich, and M. Kay Alderman

> I've come to the frightening conclusion that I am the decisive element in the classroom. It's my personal approach that creates the climate. It's my daily mood that makes the weather. As a teacher, I possess a tremendous power to make a . . . [student's] life miserable or joyous. I can be a tool of torture or an instrument of inspiration. I can humiliate or humor, hurt or heal. In all situations, it is my response that decides whether a crisis will be escalated or de-escalated and a . . . [student] humanized or dehumanized. (Ginot, 1972, pp. 15-16)

How important are the teachers in our developmental classrooms? What role do they play in the success or failure of their students? What characteristics define successful developmental educators? What guidelines can administrators use to select developmental educators from pools of applicants? In the growing body of literature on developmental education, very few studies shed light on these questions.

The National Association for Developmental Education's (1996) goals outline a challenging role for developmental educators. The goals charge us to (a) preserve and make possible educational opportunity for each postsecondary learner, (b) develop in each learner the skills and attitudes necessary for success in the classroom as well as career, (c) assess each learner's preparedness for college work, (d) maintain academic standards, (e) enhance retention, and (f) develop and apply cognitive and affective learning theory. This is a tall order to be sure, but it is one that we as developmental educators are asked to embrace.

Couple these lofty demands with the diversity and complexity of the developmental student population, and our task becomes more challenging still. Developmental students have been described as students with skills much lower than those of the "typical" college student (Maxwell, 1988). More recent studies have indicated that developmental students do not display a common profile (Boylan, Bonham, & Bliss, 1994). How can we characterize developmental students? They may be traditional students who have had a past history of low achievement or poor grades before entering college. They may be students who consistently experience difficulty in college courses involving heavy reading requirements. They may be repeating a class due to a withdrawal or a failure the previous term. Some have poor attendance or habitually arrive late. Others may put in good effort and study time but with poor results. Some have come from low socioeconomic backgrounds. A growing population among developmental students is the older, returning adult who, while sharing many of the same academic problems as the traditional-age college student, is also burdened with work and family responsibilities. In addition, the self-doubt, anxiety, and fear of the college environment, which are common among freshmen, often escalate and overwhelm the returning adult student.

Developmental educators must always be ready to light the spark of hope, motivation, and achievement in each and every student.

Looking at both the goals of developmental education and the description of our students, the magnitude of the task facing developmental educators becomes crystal clear. What kind of person can shoulder this task? Developmental educators must be personally committed to the educational opportunity of each and every student who walks into their classrooms. They must believe that it is possible for all learners to develop the skills they will need to be successful in school as well as in a career. In order to begin the process toward college-level work, they must be willing to start with each student at that individual's level, regardless of his or her level of preparedness. They need to demand that all students keep working until they measure up to the competencies needed for college. Developmental educators must keep all their students in school so that the above issues will have time to take root and grow; learning is something that takes time, and time requirements are not uniform among students. Finally, in order to do all these things, developmental educators must be

professionals who are interested in the use and refinement of modern learning theory.

Are we asking for the impossible from mere human beings? Are we looking for a superhuman who is immune to adversity, setbacks, and failure? We are looking for someone willing to try again when others before them have not been successful. The source of this lack of success is not the true issue. What really matters is that developmental students need the partnership of instructors willing to set the past aside and begin working with them toward a future. Developmental educators must be professionals with an optimistic sense of efficacy about themselves and their students. They must believe there is the potential for success in each student they see; they must believe they have the capabilities to help students discover that potential. Developmental educators must always be ready to light the spark of hope, motivation, and achievement in each and every student. Some will ignite and burn brightly, some will flicker on and off, and still others may not be ready to catch fire yet; but the developmental educator persists.

In pursuits strewn with obstacles, realists forsake the venture, abort their efforts prematurely when difficulties arise, or become cynical about the prospects of effecting significant changes. An optimistic belief in one's efficacy is thus a necessity, not a character flaw. (Bandura, 1997, p. 72)

A Teacher's Self-Efficacy

Teacher efficacy, a construct widely researched in elementary classrooms, may be the spark in the soul of developmental educators. Teacher efficacy refers to a teacher's belief that he or she has the capacity to make a difference in students' lives and the belief that all teachers in general can do so. The research on teacher efficacy received national attention when the Rand Corporation sponsored two evaluative studies (Armor, Conry-Osequera, Cox, Kin, McDonnel,

Pascal, Pauly, & Zellman, 1976; Berman, McLaughlin, Bass, Pauly, & Zellman, 1977) in which teacher efficacy was identified as the best predictor of student achievement in the classrooms studied. Research continued resulting in the discovery of interesting relationships and sometimes interesting contradictions from study to study.

Teacher efficacy seemed to influence teacher behaviors (Denham & Michael, 1981), but it was not a stable trait because it appeared to be affected by other factors (Ashton, Webb, & Doda, 1983). This instability made sense within the framework of social cognitive theory. In social cognitive theory (Bandura, 1978; 1986), behavior is seen as an interdependent part of a triadic process involving personal factors (such as self-efficacy) and the external environment. The three factors—(a) observable behaviors, (b) personal beliefs and attitudes, and (c) the environment or context—affect each other bidirectionally in continuous interaction. Bandura (1978) refers to them as "interlocking factors," signifying their interdependence and mutual influence (p. 346).

The research on teachers' sense of efficacy has produced evidence validating this interdependence of efficacy, teaching behaviors, and the teaching environment. High-efficacy teachers referred fewer students for special education services, believed they could make a difference with all students, expressed a strong sense of responsibility for student achievement, and persisted when faced with difficult students (Miller, 1991). Another study found that high-efficacy teachers maintained an accepting, open, and warm climate in their classrooms, used fewer harsh control tactics, maintained high academic standards, monitored more closely their students' on-task behavior, and worked at building friendly, nonthreatening relationships with their low achievers. Low-efficacy teachers used more ability grouping in their classroom and tended to give their high-ability students preferential treatment through feedback, instruction, and interaction (Ashton, 1984; Ashton, Webb, & Doda, 1983).

High-efficacy teachers have been characterized in the literature as: (a) maintaining an academic emphasis (Hoy & Woolfolk, 1993); (b) holding an internal locus of control and exhibiting less stress (Greenwood, Olejnik, & Parkay, 1990); (c) having a more humanistic orientation toward pupil control and a preference for "activity based" instruction (Enochs, Scharmann, & Riggs, 1995); (d) using a greater variety of teaching strategies in their classroom and reporting more time spent in instructional planning (Miller, 1991); and (e) being more trusting of students (Midgley, Feldlaufer, & Eccles, 1988). Those teachers rated highest by their superintendent expressed high efficacy and appeared most satisfied with their career choice (Trentham, Silvern, & Brogdon, 1985). The behaviors described in all these studies are particularly significant for developmental education and are closely aligned with the national goals.

Teachers with high efficacy have also been shown to be more responsive to teaching innovations (Guskey, 1988). If teachers believed they were instrumental in the learning of their students, they were most likely to undertake attempts to improve their teaching behaviors through new practice (Fritz, Miller-Heyl, Kreutzer, & MacPhee, 1995; Smylie, 1988). High-efficacy teachers believed that staff development was an important factor in student achievement (Wax & Dutton, 1991).

> We have found that teachers' sense of efficacy is of significant value in understanding teachers' definitions of their role, their attitudes toward their work, and their interactions with students. As a consequence, we believe that teachers' sense of efficacy shows promise as a useful indicator for guiding and evaluating school wide innovations and classroom improvements; and most important, we believe that developing teachers' sense of efficacy is critical for attaining the goal of equal educational opportunity. (Ashton & Webb, 1986, p. ix)

Theories of Intelligence

Teacher-held beliefs about intelligence continually surface in the research as a critical, underlying issue in teacher efficacy (Bandura, 1993;

Fletcher, 1990; Miller, 1991). Two theories of intelligence have been identified in the literature: the entity theory of intelligence (refers to the belief that intelligence is a stable, unchangeable trait) and the incremental theory (takes the position that intelligence is a developed capacity) (Dweck, 1986; Dweck & Leggett, 1988).

The development of cognitive science during the last decade has revealed the critical role that accumulated knowledge plays in human intelligence. This key element has led to the understanding that intelligence may be a developed competency rather than a static, innate trait (Lohman, 1989).

Slate, Jones, and Charlesworth (1990) found that preservice teachers holding an incremental view of intelligence were most likely to employ teaching behaviors characteristic of effective teaching, such as using a variety of teaching strategies, rewarding effort, and encouraging cooperation. Preservice teachers with incremental beliefs had better study skills. Therefore, the authors concluded that teachers holding the opposite view (i.e., the entity perspective) might be less likely to keep up with change in their profession and content area.

> To provide intellectual support for a strong sense of efficacy, a teacher education program would need to introduce and foster commitment to conceptions of ability that recognize the human potential for learning and development. Teachers' belief in intelligence as a stable trait is one of the most serious obstacles to increasing their sense of efficacy. (Ashton, 1984, p. 29)

Effects of Underachievers on Teacher Efficacy

Student ability has been cited as one of the more significant environmental characteristics affecting teacher efficacy (Ashton, 1985) and could pose a serious problem for those of us in developmental education. Teachers who taught basic skills classes reported lower personal efficacy than teachers who taught heterogeneous classes (Ashton et al., 1983). Cultural stereotypes may affect teachers' sense of efficacy (Midgley, Feldlaufer, & Eccles, 1988; Pang & Sablan, 1995)

as well as the practice of tracking students: "Our data imply that the assignment to low track classes presents challenges to teachers that make it difficult for them to maintain elevated perceptions of self-efficacy. This tendency appears most pronounced for teachers of mathematics and science" (Raudenbush, Rowan, & Cheong, 1992, p. 166).

Bandura (1993) discussed the effects of perceived self-efficacy in terms of faculty beliefs in their collective school-wide efficacy. He proposed that student body characteristics may alter teachers' beliefs of collective efficacy. However, Bandura believed these beliefs can be changed.

> Indeed, with staffs who firmly believe that, by their determined efforts, students are motivatable and teachable whatever their background, schools heavily populated with minority students of low socioeconomic status achieve at the highest percentile ranks based on national norms of language and mathematical competencies. (Bandura, 1993, p. 143)

Teacher Efficacy and Developmental Educators

In a preliminary and ongoing study of developmental mathematics instructors at a large metropolitan state university in northeastern Ohio (Klein, 1996), a survey was administered that contained teacher efficacy measures (Armor et al., 1976; Berman et al., 1977; Gibson & Dembo, 1984; Woolfolk & Hoy, 1990), theory of intelligence statements (Dweck & Henderson, 1989), and other questions concerning personal, behavioral, and environmental factors.

As one would expect from the type of person willing to take on the role of a developmental educator, the results of this study indicated that the majority of the instructors held efficacy beliefs at the high end of the scale. As indicated in Figure 1, the high-efficacy developmental instructor at this institution could be described as a person holding a graduate degree who participates in several professional conferences each year. This person has high interest in learning

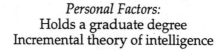

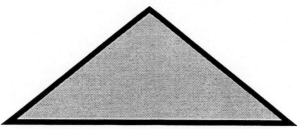

Personal Factors:
Holds a graduate degree
Incremental theory of intelligence

Teaching Behaviors:
Involves students in application.
Holds high expectations.
Focuses on all students, even the unmotivated.
Considers self a hard grader.
Participates regularly in professional

Teaching Environment:
Believes students at concrete level.
Feels work environment is cooperative.

Figure 1. Profile of the high-efficacy instructor arranged in Bandura's "interlocking factors" format.

more about teaching the at-risk student. Believing that their students were at the concrete level in cognition, they were more likely to hold an incremental theory of intelligence, believing that ability is something that can be improved with hard work. They tended to involve their students in the application of concepts rather than listening to lecture. They held high expectations for their students in spite of the label "developmental." The high-efficacy developmental instructors did not focus their attention only on those students who appeared motivated or interested. In other words, they reached out to all their students, isolating or ignoring no one. They tended to focus and interact with all students, even if the students appeared disinterested or unmotivated. They considered themselves hard graders, and they believed their work environment and interaction with colleagues was cooperative rather than competitive. The use of activity based instruction was favored by the high-efficacy instructors, suggesting that they were making efforts to move away from the traditional lecture in the college classroom.

It was also interesting to note that the high-efficacy instructors saw the University's mission statement as relevant in the work of the department. Boyer (1987) noted, "An effective college has a clear and vital mission. Administrators, faculty, and students share a vision of what the institution is seeking to accomplish" (p. 58). As might be expected from the results of previous research (Higbee & Dwinell, 1994), the nearly exclusive use of part-time faculty at the institution studied did not deteriorate the sense of culture and mission so important in institutions of higher education. Therefore, encouraging a high sense of efficacy among instructors may be a viable means for administrators to create and support the institution's mission, even with a part-time faculty.

Low-efficacy developmental instructors at this institution were more likely to hold a bachelor's degree rather than a master's degree. They participated in few, if any, professional conferences and were less interested in professional development concerning the at-risk student. They were more likely to see their students as capable of some abstract thought and held an entity or stable view of ability or intelligence (Figure 2). They typically lectured and admitted to lowering their expectations for their students. They reported that they, in fact, did ignore those students who appeared uninterested or unmotivated and rated themselves more toward the easy side of the

Personal Factors:
Holds a bachelor's degree, maybe master's
Entity theory of intelligence

Teaching Behaviors:
Uses large group instruction.
Lectures.
Holds lower expectations.
Tends to ignore the unmotivated students.
Is an easy grader.
Participates in few, if any, professional

Teaching Environment:
Believes students at abstract level.
Feels work environment is somewhat
  cooperative.
Sees mission statement as less relevant.

Figure 2. Profile of the low-efficacy instructor arranged in Bandura's "interlocking factors" format.

grading scale. They believed their work environment and interaction with colleagues were only somewhat cooperative.

Interestingly, this study did not replicate the positive relationship between teaching efficacy and student achievement that is so prevalent in the literature. Rather, student achievement, as measured by a departmental final examination minus a departmental pretest, was higher in the low efficacy teachers' classrooms. Research is ongoing to explain these unexpected results. The time factor may be one issue important to teacher efficacy yet difficult to deal with within the higher education structure. The time frame involved in this study was 15 weeks with the final exam being administered on the first day of the 16th week. The lack of significant achievement results for high-efficacy teachers may be due to the shortness of interaction time between the instructors and the students.

Teacher efficacy does not have an immediate impact on students as might be the case with more easily observed teacher beliefs and behaviors such as trust, friendliness, fairness, or ability grouping practices. Students moving to a new classroom may be immediately aware

that they have been assigned to a low-ability or high-ability math class or may be quickly affected by the warmth or fairness of their teachers. However, teacher sense of efficacy is evidently a somewhat subtle belief that is manifested in ways that are not immediately apparent to students. This finding points to the importance of taking time of year into consideration in studies of the effects of teacher efficacy. If only one measurement point during the year is planned, the study would point to waiting until the second semester. (Midgley, Feldlaufer, & Eccles, 1989, p. 255)

However, preliminary results seem to indicate that the low-efficacy teachers had more low entry skill students drop out before the end of the term. More students with low pretest scores persisted through the semester and took the final exam in high-efficacy classrooms.

A closer look at the group of students who officially withdrew (rather than just dropping out) revealed that in Basic Mathematics I, those who withdrew had a pretest mean similar to students who persisted and earned As in the class. High-efficacy teachers lost a total of two such students, while low-efficacy behavior teachers lost six.

In Basic Mathematics II, three students officially withdrew from high-efficacy classrooms, but the mean of their pretests was lower than the mean of students earning Ds and Fs as a final grade. In low-efficacy classrooms, 10 students withdrew with a mean pretest score falling between the C and D range for those students who persisted. Thus the low-efficacy teachers had three times as many students withdraw from their classes, and some of the students they lost may have had the computational skills to finish the course.

Teacher Efficacy and the Retention Issue

Low-efficacy teachers in previous research and in the study of developmental educators behaved in ways that ignored the at-risk students and focused their attention only on those students appearing motivated and interested; this finding suggests that teacher efficacy may be a key variable in retention. When addressing the topic of college teaching in general, Astin (1985) suggested that high priority be given to efforts at the college level to identify and train faculty who can work effectively with the new population of underprepared students. This task must be the highest priority for developmental administrators and instructors. Improving teachers' sense of efficacy must become an integral part of successful interventions with those who teach at-risk students (Miller, 1991).

Enhancing Teacher Efficacy

Teacher efficacy is consistently associated with teacher-held theories of intelligence, cooperative work environments, and teacher willingness to use new teaching strategies and to hold high expectations of all their students. Therefore, teacher efficacy should be a focal point for faculty development within departments of developmental education.

By analyzing their own teaching, by encouraging collegial interaction, and by sharing, teachers may be able to solve problems and in turn increase their own personal teaching efficacy

(McDaniel & DiBella-McCarthy, 1989; Volkman, Scheffler, & Dana, 1992). Reflective activities, such as keeping a journal, can be an effective means for addressing teacher beliefs and feelings of efficacy.

Theory of intelligence has been repeatedly related to the teacher efficacy factor. Therefore, this should also be an area receiving specific attention through faculty development efforts. Ashton (1984) indicated that a belief in stable intelligence could be one of the "most serious obstacles" in increasing teachers' sense of efficacy. Teachers in the study of developmental instructors (Klein, 1996) holding an entity (stable) theory of intelligence were more likely to lecture rather than provide opportunities for their students to apply the concepts. They lowered their expectations for their students as well. Such attitudes run contrary to program goals established by the National Association for Developmental Education (1996). Increasing teachers' understanding of student ability and how it interacts with other "competencies needed for success" (NADE, 1996) is an important concern for administrators in developmental education.

One way to approach theories of intelligence is through attributions. Instructors must be encouraged to become sensitive to the types of attributions they make for student performance. Attributions to stable ability must be consciously replaced with attributions to effort (Tollefson, Melvin, & Thippavajjala, 1990). The continuous association of changes in effort with changes in achievement should form a natural bridge to an incremental theory of intelligence.

The contribution metacognitive knowledge makes toward student achievement (Alderman, 1990; Fulk & Mastropieri, 1990; Swanson, 1990; Weinstein & Underwood, 1985) must be made clear and strategies toward that end made feasible for developmental instructors. Helping instructors identify students' "Zone of Proximal Development" (Vygotsky, 1978) and providing a forum for the exchange of viable teaching and metacognitive strategies will assist instructors in their endeavor to take students from where they are to where they need to be in order to be successful. As instructors witness the success of such strategies and the gradual improvement in their students, teacher efficacy and a belief in incremental intelligence will be strengthened.

Staff development projects focusing on teachers and their environment have been considered since the early years of research as a viable method to increase teacher efficacy (Berman et al., 1977). Participative decision making, support from peers, as well as support and recognition from administrators, have been suggested as impacting teacher efficacy (Ashton, 1985; Ashton et al., 1983; Denham & Michael, 1981; Hoy & Woolfolk, 1993; Miller, 1991; Raudenbush et al., 1992) along with availability of resources (Fuller, Wood, Rapoport, & Dornbusch, 1982). Providing opportunities for collaboration and problem solving among peers will increase teachers' sense of support and comfort at work. An open, fair, and supportive administrator is necessary to keep the environment on an even keel with everyone working in unison.

Care must be taken, however, not to underestimate the complexity of teacher efficacy (Ross, 1995) or the need to address continually the interaction of personal factors, behavior factors, and the environment (Bandura, 1978). Providing a workshop on effective teaching behaviors for at-risk students will have little effect if the instructors are not encouraged to (a) reflect on the impact of their behaviors on a student's achievement, and (b) collaborate with peers to share concerns and solve problems. Furthermore, teachers must receive encouragement and support from administrators throughout the process. These components must be continually taken into consideration because each enhances the other two.

Teacher Efficacy and the Organization of Developmental Programs

To seriously address such issues as supportive environments and faculty development, a campus needs centralized developmental services. However, only about half of the programs in both four-year and two-year institutions have a centralized organizational structure (Boylan et al., 1994). Developmental administrators must continue to struggle for unity, recognition, and identity on their campuses. Research has shown that such departmental identity is critical not only for the well-being of faculty, but also for the well-being and achievement of students.

> Departmental influence on personal and educational changes is observable in those departments where faculty and students share common attitudes and values; where interpersonal exchanges are frequent, friendly, and not rigidly hierarchical; and where there is a departmental esprit de corps. (Pascarella & Terenzini, 1991, pp. 652-653)

Hodgkinson (1993), a long standing proponent for the development of a well-coordinated educational system of programs and services, noted that the top 20% of American high school graduates are comparable to the best in the world. The next 40% of our high school graduates are also capable of a college education, with some needing remediation, such as first-generation college students and those from low income backgrounds.

> We have colleges that serve a wide range of student abilities in the U. S., which explains the large American middle class. Having a wide range of undergraduate institutions that specialize in different kinds of students from different backgrounds is vital to success in a highly diverse nation. (Hodgkinson, 1993, p. 622)

An independent, visible, developmental education unit on campus is not an embarrassment, but rather a testimony to the philosophy of this country. By providing services for the at-risk college student, developmental educators give witness to equal educational opportunity, the existence of educational standards, and a belief in unbounded human potential: "We provide a second chance for students, an opportunity available in few other places in the world. Many of our students never had a first chance" (Darken, 1995, p. 23).

The Charge to the Developmental Educator

Educators selected for the developmental classroom must be carefully chosen and nurtured.

This is not a calling for the weak of heart. They must be capable of espousing the goals of developmental education. They must believe in the educability of each student. They must be optimistic. They must be "resolute strivers":

> Resolute strivers should be differentiated from wistful dreamers. Wistful optimists lack the efficacy strength and commitment to go through the uncertainties, disappointments, and drudgery that are part and parcel of high accomplishments. Resolute strivers believe so passionately in themselves that they are willing to expend extraordinary effort and suffer countless reversals in pursuit of their vision. They abide by objective realism when considering the normative reality but by subjective optimism when considering their personal chances of success. That is, they do not delude themselves about the tough odds of lofty attainments, but they believe they have what it takes to beat those odds. As long as subjective optimists believe that a desired attainment is probable, their belief will stand up against negative instances because such instances do not really show that the attainment is unachievable. (Bandura, 1997, pp. 74-75)

Developmental educators are protectors of an eternal flame who nurture, encourage, and instruct, always anticipating the opportunity to send forward another student to achieve and succeed. All students have the potential to carry the spark of motivation and learning inside their heads and hearts. It is the developmental educator, optimistic and efficacious, who must be ever vigilant for the opportunity to ignite that spark.

References

Alderman, M. K. (1990). Motivation for at-risk students. *Educational Leadership, 48,* 27-30.

Armor, D., Conry-Osequera, P., Cox, M., Kin, N., McDonnel, L., Pascal, A., Pauly, E., & Zellman, G. (1976). *Analysis of the school preferred reading programs in selected Los Angeles minority schools.* Santa Monica, CA: The Rand Corporation. (ERIC Document Reproduction Service No. ED 130 243)

Ashton, P. (1984). Teacher efficacy: A motivational paradigm for effective teacher education. *Journal of Teacher Education, 35,* 28-32.

Ashton, P. (1985). Motivation and the teachers' sense of efficacy. In C. Ames & R. Ames (Eds.), *Research on motivation in education: The classroom milieu* (pp. 141-171). New York: Academic Press.

Ashton, P. T., & Webb, R. B. (1986). *Making a difference: Teachers' sense of efficacy and student achievement.* New York: Longman.

Ashton, P. T., Webb, R., & Doda, N. (1983). *A study of teachers' sense of efficacy: Final report, executive summary.* Washington, DC: National Institute of Education. (ERIC Document Reproduction Service No. ED 231 833)

Astin, A. (1985). *Achieving educational excellence.* San Francisco: Jossey-Bass.

Bandura, A. (1978). The self system in reciprocal determinism. *American Psychologist, 33,* 344-358.

Bandura, A. (1986). *Social foundations of thought and action.* Englewood Cliffs, NJ: Prentice-Hall.

Bandura, A. (1993). Perceived self-efficacy in cognitive development and functioning. *Educational Psychologist, 28,* 117-148.

Bandura, A. (1997). *The exercise of control.* New York: W. H. Freeman.

Berman, P., McLaughlin, M., Bass, G., Pauly, E., & Zellman, G. (1977). *Federal programs supporting educational change. Vol. VII: Factors affecting implementation and continuation.* Santa Monica, CA: The Rand Corporation. (ERIC Document Reproduction Service No. ED 140 432)

Boyer, E. (1987). *College: The undergraduate experience in America.* New York: Harper & Row.

Boylan, H., Bonham, B., & Bliss, L. (1994). Who are the developmental students? *Research in Developmental Education, 11,* 1-4.

Darken, B. (1995). Standards for introductory college mathematics: A conversation with Marilyn Mays. *Journal of Developmental Education, 19,* 22-24, 26.

Denham, C. H., & Michael, J. J. (1981). Teacher sense of efficacy: A definition of the construct and a model for further research. *Educational Research Quarterly, 6,* 39-63.

Dweck, C. (1986). Motivational processes affecting learning. *American Psychologist, 41*, 1040-1048.

Dweck, C., & Henderson, V. (1989). *Theories of intelligence: Background and measures.* Unpublished manuscript, University of Illinois at Champaign-Urbana.

Dweck, C., & Leggett, E. (1988). A social-cognitive approach to motivation and personality. *Psychological Review, 95*, 256-273.

Enochs, L. G., Scharmann, L. C., & Riggs, I. M. (1995). The relationship of pupil control to preservice elementary science teacher self-efficacy and outcome expectancy. *Science Education, 79*, 63-75.

Fletcher, S. (1990, August). *The relation of the school environment to teacher efficacy.* Paper presented at the Annual Meeting of the American Psychological Association, Boston, MA. (ERIC Document Reproduction Service No. ED 329 551)

Fritz, J. J., Miller-Heyl, J., Kreutzer, J. C., & MacPhee, D. (1995). Fostering personal teaching efficacy through staff development and classroom activities. *The Journal of Educational Research, 88*, 200-208.

Fulk, B. J., & Mastropieri, M. A. (1990). Training positive attitudes: "I tried hard and did well!" *Intervention in School and Clinic, 26*, 79-83.

Fuller, B., Wood, K., Rapoport, T., & Dornbusch, S. M. (1982). The organizational context of individual efficacy. *Review of Educational Research, 52*, 7-30.

Gibson, S., & Dembo, M. H. (1984). Teacher efficacy: A construct validation. *Journal of Educational Psychology, 76*, 569-582.

Ginot, H. (1972). *Teacher and child.* New York: MacMillan.

Greenwood, G. E., Olejnik, S. F., & Parkay, F. W. (1990). Relationships between four teacher efficacy belief patterns and selected teacher characteristics. *Journal of Research and Development in Education, 23*, 102-106.

Guskey, T. R. (1988). Teacher efficacy, self-concept, and attitudes toward the implementation of instructional innovation. *Teaching and Teacher Education, 4*, 63-69.

Higbee, J. L., & Dwinell, P. L. (1994). Student evaluations of part-time and full-time faculty in a developmental education program. *Research and Teaching in Developmental Education, 10*(2), 109-117.

Hodgkinson, H. (1993). American education: The good, the bad, and the task. *Phi Delta Kappan, 74*, 619-623.

Hoy, W. K., & Woolfolk, A. E. (1993). Teachers' sense of efficacy and the organizational health of schools. *The Elementary School Journal, 93*, 355-372.

Klein, R. (1996). *Teacher efficacy and developmental math instructors at an urban university: An exploratory analysis of the relationships among personal factors, teacher behaviors, and perceptions of the environment.* Unpublished doctoral dissertation, University of Akron.

Lohman, D. F. (1989). Human intelligence: An introduction to advances in theory and research. *Review of Educational Research, 59*, 333-373.

Maxwell, M. (1988). *Improving student learning skills.* San Francisco: Jossey-Bass.

McDaniel, E. A., & DiBella-McCarthy, H. (1989). Enhancing teacher efficacy in special education. *Teaching Exceptional Children, 21*, 34-38.

Midgley, C., Feldlaufer, H., & Eccles, J. S. (1988). The transition to junior high school: Beliefs of pre- and post-transition teachers. *Journal of Youth and Adolescence, 17*, 543-562.

Midgley, C., Feldlaufer, H., & Eccles, J. S. (1989). Changes in teacher efficacy and student self- and task-related beliefs in mathematics during the transition to junior high school. *Journal of Educational Psychology, 81*, 247-258.

Miller, P. S. (1991). Increasing teacher efficacy with at-risk students. *Equity and Excellence, 25*, 30-35.

National Association for Developmental Education. (1996). *Developmental education goals & definition.* Carol Stream, IL: Author.

Pang, V. O., & Sablan, V. (1995, April). *Teacher efficacy: Do teachers believe they can be effective with African American students?* Paper presented at the Annual Meeting of the American Educational Research Association, San Francisco, CA.

Pascarella, E. T., & Terenzini, P. T. (1991). *How college affects students: Findings and insights from 20 years of research.* San Francisco: Jossey-Bass.

Raudenbush, S. W., Rowan, B., & Cheong, Y. F. (1992). Contextual effects on the self-perceived efficacy of high school teachers.

Sociology of Education, 65, 150-167.

Ross, J. A. (1995). Strategies for enhancing teachers' beliefs in their effectiveness: Research on a school improvement hypothesis. *Teachers College Record, 97,* 227-251.

Slate, J. R., Jones, C. H., & Charlesworth Jr., J. R. (1990). Relationship of conceptions of intelligence to preferred teaching behaviors. *Action in Teacher Education, 12,* 25-29.

Smylie, M. A. (1988). The enhancement function of staff development: Organizational and psychological antecedents to individual teacher change. *American Educational Research Journal, 25,* 1-30.

Swanson, H. L. (1990). Influence of metacognitive knowledge and aptitude on problem solving. *Journal of Educational Psychology, 82,* 306-314.

Tollefson, N., Melvin, J., Thippavajjala, C. (1990). Teachers' attributions for students' low achievement: A validation of Cooper and Good's attributional categories. *Psychology in the Schools, 27,* 75-83

Trentham, L., Silvern, S., & Brogdon, R. (1985). Teacher efficacy and teacher competency ratings. *Psychology in the Schools, 22,* 343-352.

Volkman, B. K., Scheffler, A. J., & Dana, M. E. (1992, November). *Enhancing preservice teachers' self-efficacy through a field-based program of reflective practice.* Paper presented at the 1992 meeting of the Mid-South Educational Research Association, Knoxville, TN. (ERIC Document Reproduction Service No. ED 354 232)

Vygotsky, L. S. (1978). *Mind in society: The development of higher mental processes.* Cambridge, MA: Harvard University Press.

Wax, A. S., & Dutton, M. M. (1991, April). *The relationship between teacher use of cooperative learning and teacher efficacy.* A paper presented at the Annual Meeting of the American Educational Research Association, Chicago, IL.

Weinstein, C., & Underwood, V. (1985). Learning strategies: The how of learning. In J. Segal, J. Chipman, & J. Glaser (Eds.), *Thinking and learning skills* (pp. 241-258). Hillsdale, NJ: Lawrence Erlbaum.

Woolfolk, A. E., & Hoy, W. K. (1990). Prospective teachers' sense of efficacy and beliefs about control. *Journal of Educational Psychology, 82,* 81-91.

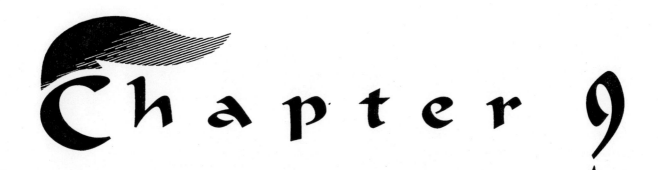

Chapter 9

The Impact of a Course in Strategic Learning on the Long-Term Retention of College Students

Claire E. Weinstein, Douglas Dierking, Jenefer Husman, Linda Roska, and Lorrie Powdrill

Developmental education, by definition, includes facilitating students' transition into higher education. The ultimate goal, however, is not only to help students prepare for college-level courses but also to facilitate (a) the transfer of what they are learning to other academic coursework, (b) their retention to graduation, and (c) the successful attainment of their academic goals. This chapter will describe a conceptual model of strategic learning, a one-semester course derived from this model, and some of the results of a five-year longitudinal study of freshman students who participated in this course in either the fall semester of 1990 or the spring semester of 1991. The tremendous long-term success of this course in strategic learning has strong implications for teaching strategies which help students learn how to learn. One of the major reasons for the success of this course is the consistent use of a model based on theories of strategic and self-regulated learning, in-class design and instruction.

Model of Strategic Learning

The Model of Strategic Learning (Weinstein, 1994; Weinstein, Husman, Dierking, & Powdrill, in press; Weinstein & McCombs, in press) that is used in the strategic learning course includes the following four components with elements (in parentheses) under each component: skill (e.g., cognitive learning strategies and study skills, reasoning skills); will (e.g., motivation, positive affect toward learning, self-efficacy for learning); self-regulation (e.g., time management, comprehension monitoring, strategic planning); and the academic environment (e.g., teachers' expectations and beliefs, plus available resources). The model, as depicted in Figure 1, emphasizes the direct effects and interactions among the elements across these components in specific academic environments and learning contexts.

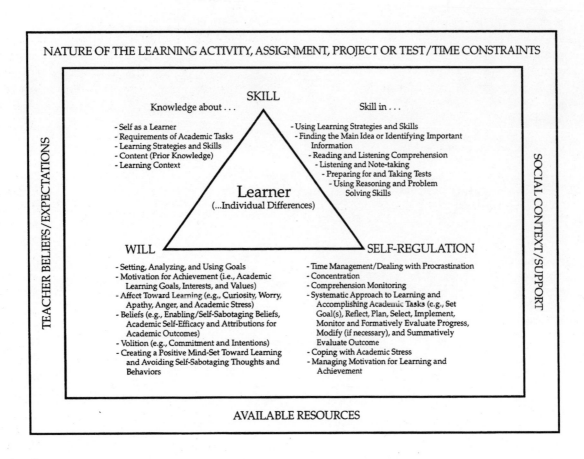

NATURE OF THE LEARNING ACTIVITY, ASSIGNMENT, PROJECT OR TEST/TIME CONSTRAINTS

TEACHER BELIEFS/EXPECTATIONS

SOCIAL CONTEXT/SUPPORT

SKILL

Knowledge about . . .

- Self as a Learner
- Requirements of Academic Tasks
- Learning Strategies and Skills
- Content (Prior Knowledge)
- Learning Context

Skill in . . .

- Using Learning Strategies and Skills
- Finding the Main Idea or Identifying Important Information
- Reading and Listening Comprehension
- Listening and Note-taking
- Preparing for and Taking Tests
- Using Reasoning and Problem Solving Skills

Learner
(...Individual Differences)

WILL

- Setting, Analyzing, and Using Goals
- Motivation for Achievement (i.e., Academic Learning Goals, Interests, and Values)
- Affect Toward Learning (e.g., Curiosity, Worry, Apathy, Anger, and Academic Stress)
- Beliefs (e.g., Enabling/Self-Sabotaging Beliefs, Academic Self-Efficacy and Attributions for Academic Outcomes)
- Volition (e.g., Commitment and Intentions)
- Creating a Positive Mind-Set Toward Learning and Avoiding Self-Sabotaging Thoughts and Behaviors

SELF-REGULATION

- Time Management/Dealing with Procrastination
- Concentration
- Comprehension Monitoring
- Systematic Approach to Learning and Accomplishing Academic Tasks (e.g., Set Goal(s), Reflect, Plan, Select, Implement, Monitor and Formatively Evaluate Progress, Modify (if necessary), and Summatively Evaluate Outcome
- Coping with Academic Stress
- Managing Motivation for Learning and Achievement

AVAILABLE RESOURCES

Figure 1. Weinstein's Model of Strategic Learning.

An underlying concept of the Model of Strategic Learning is that learners need to be aware of the elements from the four major components of the model: skill, will, self-regulation, and the academic environment. The interactions among these elements are crucial to strategic learning, transfer of learning, and ultimately, students' academic success, retention, and graduation.

Skill Component

There are a number of different elements within the skill component. All of these elements are important in and of themselves, but for students to be able to reach their academic goals they must also be aware of how these elements interact. For purposes of description, a number of these elements will be described individually.

Within the skill component five of the elements identify types of knowledge that students need to possess in order to become expert learners: 1. knowledge of self as a learner; 2. knowledge of different kinds of academic

tasks; 3. knowledge about strategies and skills; 4. knowledge about content often called prior knowledge; and 5. knowledge about the learning context. Each of these five essential types of knowledge are discussed below.

1. *Knowledge of self as a learner* is a key step toward metacognitive awareness (a critical feature of strategic learning) and the ability to think strategically about learning. This includes knowing one's strengths and weaknesses as a learner and one's attitude, motivation, and anxiety level towards learning. Knowledge of self as a learner provides crucial information to learners about areas where they may anticipate difficulties in a given learning context so that they may plan to avoid or minimize potential problems. For example, knowing that you do not like science courses and that you have had difficulty taking science exams can alert you to the potential benefits of participating in a study group or finding out about the availability of science tutors at the learning center. Students need to reflect and think about their answers to

a number of possible questions, such as: What are your preferences? What are your strengths? What are your weaknesses? What is the best time of day for you? The worst time? What are your interests and talents? What do you know about study habits and what are your current study habits and practices? Knowing about themselves as learners can help students orchestrate the resources they need to accomplish the studying and learning activities necessary for academic success. Management of resources includes both external resources (i.e., number of visits to the tutor) and internal resources (i.e., use of appropriate cognitive strategies, feelings, and study habits).

2. *Knowledge of the requirements of different academic tasks*. The student needs to understand what is required to complete successfully various academic tasks, such as writing a term paper, taking an essay test, taking notes, or giving an oral presentation. This knowledge includes the steps to be taken and the amount of time required for each step. This type of knowledge helps clarify the procedure that the learner needs to think about, plan for, and accomplish in order to reach a desired outcome.

3. *Knowledge about learning strategies and skills* is the third type of knowledge in the skill component of this model (Weinstein, 1994) and includes the acquisition, integration, reflection, and application of new learning. Learning and thinking strategies and skills are the tools students need to generate meaning, monitor learning progress, and store new information in ways that facilitate future recall or application.

Learning strategies can take a variety of forms ranging from simple paraphrasing to complex content analysis. The common factor underlying each of these forms is the active involvement of the student. Active cognitive involvement is crucial for meaningful learning. Students cannot be passive and expect to reach their learning

Knowing about themselves as learners can help students orchestrate the resources they need to accomplish the studying and learning activities necessary for academic success.

goals; they must build meaning and memories by actively engaging the material and by using learning strategies to help guide this active engagement. Strategic learners need a variety of strategies available in order to generate appropriate strategies for different learning goals and for different learning problems.

The simplest forms of learning strategies involve repetition or review, such as reading over a difficult section of text or repeating an equation or rule. A bit more complexity is added when students try to paraphrase or summarize in their own words the material they are studying. Other strategies focus on organizing the information by creating some type of scheme for the material. For example, creating an outline of the main events and characters in a story, making a time line for historical occurrences, classifying scientific phenomena, or separating foreign vocabulary into parts of speech are all organizational strategies. Some learning strategies involve elaborating on or analyzing new material to make it more meaningful and memorable. For example, using analogies to access relevant prior knowledge, comparing and contrasting the explanations offered by two competing scientific theories, and thinking about the implications of a policy proposal are examples of elaboration strategies.

There are two major reasons why students need a repertoire of learning strategies that they can use and adapt to a variety of academic as well as everyday learning situations. First, learners need to know about a variety of strategies and methods for learning before they can make mindful decisions about their preferences or the methods that seem to be most effective for them. Second, when students encounter different academic difficulties, they need a set of tools that they can use to resolve the various problems.

4. *Knowledge about content*, often referred to as prior knowledge, is the fourth type of essential knowledge. It is easier for individuals to learn

something new about a subject when they already know something about it. Part of the reason for this is that they already have an existing knowledge base that they can use to help organize, understand, and integrate the new information.

5. *Knowledge about the learning context* is the last type of knowledge under the skill component. Students need to know about present or future contexts in which they will need the new information they are currently trying to learn. In order to set realistic and challenging learning goals for themselves, students need to identify the importance or utility of the new information in meeting their personal, social, academic, or occupational goals (Lens & Rand, 1997). Students must value the outcomes of learning enough to translate their motivation into action (McCombs & Marzano, 1990).

The model is presented as a series of four components, each with its own sets of elements. The concept of strategic learning comes out of systems theory and Gestalt psychology. Strategic learners know that it is the interaction among the components and the elements within those components that is important. There are emergent properties of the system that only appear when it is operating as an interactive system; the whole is greater than the sum of the components or elements. For example, students' knowledge about themselves as learners helps them identify task characteristics that may be particularly problematic. Identifying these potential problems helps them think about which learning strategies and study skills will help address these particular problems. When students can think about information they have already acquired in an area, they can create more meaning for the new material in order to complete the task successfully.

Will Component

The second major component in the model is the will component. It is not enough for students to know how to study and learn new material, they must also want to do it. Motivation is a result of things we do or think, as well as things we do not do or think. Motivation has many elements and interacts with and results from

many factors (McCombs & Marzano, 1990; Pintrich & DeGroot, 1990; Pintrich, Marx, & Boyle, 1993; Pintrich & Schunk, 1996; Schunk, 1989). Goal-setting, analyzing, and using new information are central elements of motivation. The desire to reach learning goals becomes a driving force that can be used to help generate and maintain motivation, as well as the thoughts and behaviors necessary to accomplish the goals. Strategic learners set realistic, yet challenging, goals for their study and learning activities (Locke & Latham, 1990). Learning goals are both a standard to be met and a way to relate immediate task completion to long-term life and occupational goals. It is the usefulness or utility value of the learning goals for accomplishing present and future educational, personal, social, and occupational goals that helps to keep students on track (Raynor, 1981). Unrealistically high goals (often a symptom of students experiencing academic difficulty) can lead to frustration, feelings of helplessness, avoidance, and failure.

Motivation is also related to self-efficacy beliefs. Self-efficacy is defined as the degree to which students believe they can accomplish a task (Bandura, 1977, 1986). Self-efficacy beliefs affect both effort and persistence applied to a task: If students do not believe they can accomplish the task, then why should they try? Attributions (causal inferences) about learning also determine students' perceptions of whether or not their efforts will improve their grades (Weiner, 1986). To what do students attribute their successes? To what do they attribute their failures? If students do not attribute what happens to them in academic situations to their own efforts and abilities rather than to the system, the instructor, or the difficulty of the test, why would they ever try again? Students must have a sense of empowerment to believe that their efforts will make a difference.

Positive or negative emotions associated with learning goals and actions also will impact the behaviors students exhibit toward a task. Motivation is also related to a number of other variables such as interest, valuing, instrumentality, and a positive mind-set. Similar to the skill component elements, it is the interactive effects of these and other elements that ultimately results in what is called motivation.

Self-Regulation Component

The self-regulation of thoughts, beliefs, and actions in the model focuses on the self-management aspects of learning. Strategic learners manage both their skill and will factors through self-regulation. Essentially, self-regulation involves awareness and control of relevant factors in order to achieve a desired outcome. Strategic learners regulate on a macro level (such using time management and a systematic approach to studying) and on a micro level (such as focusing concentration, monitoring comprehension, and using coping strategies to manage academic stress).

Time management is one of the major macro elements of self-regulation and refers to the learner's use of time resources in the pursuit of learning tasks and goals. Self-regulation includes monitoring and controlling time management to help attain a desired learning outcome (Zimmerman, Greenberg, & Weinstein, 1994). Students need to balance the many demands on their time to help them meet their goals.

Another macro-level element of the self-regulation component is the use of a systematic approach to learning and accomplishing academic tasks. This systematic approach involves eight steps that are essential for self-regulated learning (Weinstein, 1988, 1994). These eight steps are discussed in some detail below and are shown in Figure 1 as elements in systematically approaching a learning task under the self-regulation component.

1. *Setting a goal.* This first step requires setting a goal for the desired outcome (for example, a specific grade in a course, a certain level of performance on an assessment instrument, or a level of proficiency in performing an academic task). To be most effective the goal needs to be specific, measurable, challenging, and realistic; in addition, an effective goal must have a specific completion date.

2. *Reflecting on the task.* In order to identify the requirements of a task, strategic learners must spend some time thinking about the task. During this reflection, they will consider task requirements in terms of their own levels of skill and will, and then determine how the task relates to their goals. Furthermore, strategic learners will reflect on relevant external contextual factors, such as the resources available to help them achieve the desired outcomes, the expectations of the instructor, and the social support upon which they can draw.

3. *Planning for achievement.* Having reflected on all the requirements involved in the task, the strategic learner moves to the third step, developing a plan. This planning step is best accomplished by brainstorming in order to identify several potential strategies. Mulling over these potential strategies leads to the next step.

4. *Selecting a plan.* From among the several plans considered, the strategic learner selects the most effective and efficient plan for achieving the desired outcome.

5. *Implementing the plan.* After selecting the best and most appropriate plan, a strategic learner then implements the plan.

6. *Monitoring and formatively evaluating progress.* At various stages during the implementation of the plan, the learner monitors and formatively evaluates the effectiveness of each strategy as it is being implemented. If the results are disappointing, the strategic learner will proceed to the next step.

7. *Modifying the plan.* If necessary, the self-regulated learner modifies the plan by replacing ineffective strategies with alternative strategies. These alternatives are then monitored and evaluated. If necessary, the learner may even decide to modify the learning goal itself.

8. *Evaluating outcome.* When the learning task has been completed successfully or unsuccessfully, the self-regulated learner performs the eighth and last step, which is summative evaluation, to measure the effectiveness and efficiency of the learning strategies applied and the outcome

achieved. The summative evaluation becomes a future reference when similar learning tasks arise. This final step contributes both to avoiding unsuccessful approaches in the future and also to increasing cognitive efficiency by helping the learner build up a set of useful approaches for similar future learning tasks.

On the micro level, strategic learners know ways to monitor and manage their level of stress, motivation, concentration, and personal comprehension. To monitor and manage their comprehension students need to know how to use self-assessment or self-testing to determine whether they are meeting their goals. There are many forms of self-assessment, which can be as simple as paraphrasing while reading or as complex as trying to teach new information or skills to someone else. Other forms of monitoring include trying to apply new knowledge, transforming it into another form (such as a diagram or outline), and summarizing it. Each of these activities is designed to help students determine how well they understand the new material. Often students believe that they understand, but they do not test themselves to confirm or refute this belief. When they are wrong, that is, when they have only the "illusion of knowing," students think that they have reached their achievement goals and do not realize that they have not.

On a micro level, strategic learners know ways to monitor and manage their level of stress, motivation, concentration, and personal comprehension.

Expert learners can also generate fix-up strategies when problems in their comprehension arise. Fix-up strategies are the approaches and methods that students use to help remedy a learning problem. These methods can range from very simple activities (such as rereading a confusing text section) to more complex activities (such as trying to reason through a problem-solving method, going to a tutor for help, or teaming up with someone else who is taking the same course in order to study diffi-

cult sections together). Each of these activities is designed to help solve a learning problem. Students need a repertoire of fix-up strategies so they can deal with a variety of academic problems that might occur.

Academic Environment Component

The Model of Strategic Learning also includes elements in the learning environment that are external to the learner. These are represented in the outside boundaries of the model (see Figure 1) and include: resources available to the learner; instructor expectations; nature of the learning activity, assignment, project, or test; time constraints; and social support. Each of these elements is discussed below.

Available resources refers to any materials or learning aids that the learner can use in acquiring knowledge, such as workbooks, reading materials, computers, reference materials, diagrams, examples, and case studies. Available resources also include campus resources such as labs, tutors, learning skills centers, teaching assistants, and advisors.

Teacher expectations refer to the expectations held by the instructor or course developer. These expectations could include the skill level of students, specific tasks the students should be able to perform, and appropriate teaching methods for the students. The extent to which the teacher's expectations match or do not match the learner's abilities and needs can have a major impact on the acquisition, retention, and transference of information. If the teacher's expectations exceed the learner's ability, the learner may not be able to acquire the information and may be less motivated to put forth the effort to learn or utilize the subject matter. If the teacher's expectations are below the learner's ability, the learner may become bored or place less value on the subject matter and subsequently experience less motivation to learn or utilize the subject matter.

The nature of the learning activity, assignment, project, or test refers to the specific task requirements the learner must complete in order to acquire the new information. This might include listening to a lecture, taking notes, role playing, demonstrating proficiency, writing a paper, or taking a timed test. The nature of a specific task assigned in a class interacts with the learner's level of skill and helps determine the degree of learning success. If the task calls for an activity for which a learner lacks skill or motivation, he or she may have difficulty in performing that activity or may seek to avoid it altogether.

Time constraints within which the course material is delivered, or other time constraints that may be impacting the learner (e.g., outside deadlines not related to the course), affect the learning outcomes. If the class time is limited, students may not be able to practice using the knowledge acquired in the program. Learners might also be overwhelmed if a large amount of information is presented in a short period of time, especially if their learning strategies and skills are limited.

Social support refers to the support learners receive from peers, fellow students, and family. Such support might include roommates and other students with whom the learner can study and share class experiences, and advice from siblings or parents. Beliefs of peers and family members, supportive or antagonistic, can also affect a student's motivation to learn course content and to participate in class discussions.

All of these external factors interact with the internal factors associated with the skill, will, and self-regulation components of the model. In this sense, the model is a dynamic system (i.e., change in one factor can produce changes in other factors). As in all systems, it is important to consider all factors. Strategic learners try to be aware of and control as many of these factors as possible so that new knowledge can be acquired, retained, integrated with existing knowledge, and ultimately transferred to new situations. This model seeks to emphasize the impact of changes in one factor on other strategic learning factors.

Strategic Learning Course

In 1977, Weinstein developed a semester-long course to determine the effects of teaching learning strategies to undergraduates at risk for low academic achievement or failure. The success of this experimental course resulted in its inclusion as a three-credit elective in the general educational psychology (EDP) undergraduate courses offered at the University of Texas at Austin. This course (EDP 310) has remained highly popular among student advisors and undergraduates with 16 sections filled to capacity each major semester. Two to three sections of the course are offered during each of the two summer sessions. Enrollment is limited to 28 students in each section. The course is taught by graduate students in the Educational Psychology doctoral program, primarily from the Learning, Cognition, and Instruction concentration. The course is highly structured; the course content, pacing, policies, testing, and assignments are the same across all 16 sections. The instructors receive extensive training in the Model of Strategic Learning, the specific topics covered during the course, and varied teaching and instructional methods.

The students enrolling in EDP 310 vary greatly in terms of academic standing, skill, motivation, and reason for taking the class. The majority of these students are freshmen or sophomores, frequently on scholastic probation (i.e., cumulative grade point averages less than 2.0 using a four-point system), or otherwise predicted to be at risk of leaving the university.

On other college campuses, many learning skills courses do not teach students how to select and evaluate appropriate study strategies for different learning tasks. As a result, these students have only a group of study techniques at their disposal with a limited understanding of the conditions under which these techniques will be most effective and what to do when the techniques do not work. Often students have learned a specific learning strategy in a highly contextualized manner. This is likely to limit their application of this strategy in other relevant situations that differ from the situation in which it was learned.

The EDP 310 course attempts to provide students with an awareness of the systems nature of strategic learning, the range of factors that influence learning, and the impact and interaction among factors. Students in this course receive instruction in both the theoretical underpinnings of the Model of Strategic Learning as well as practical applications of specific strategies, methods, and self-management techniques. With this awareness and knowledge, students should be better able to (a) strategically match their selection of learning strategies to task demands and their own learning goals, (b) identify problems and potential problems in the application of their strategies, and (c) generate alternative learning strategies when current strategies fail. By increasing awareness and knowledge about study skills, students will learn how to transfer these skills across tasks and courses.

Transfer

The ultimate goal of any learning strategies or study skills class is to facilitate transfer to other coursework and future learning. Salomon and Perkins' (1989) concept of high-road transfer—particularly forward-reaching high-road transfer—and their concept of "mindful abstraction" seem to fit quite well within the tenets of Weinstein's Model of Strategic Learning as well as other conceptions of self-regulated learning. In each of these conceptions the learner is metacognitively aware that the new information has potential current and future applications outside of the original learning context. The strategic learner goes forward from the learning-to-learn course in search of new contexts in which to apply what has been learned. Salomon and Perkins (1989) state that "the main distinction of the high-road to transfer is the mindful generation of an abstraction during learning and its later application to a new problem or situation from which basic elements are similarly abstracted" (p. 113).

The learning skills course, EDP 310, is based on Weinstein's Model of Strategic Learning as shown in Figure 1; but EDP 310 is also compatible with Sternberg and Frensch's (1993) model which posits four mechanisms that determine the successful transfer of knowledge. These four mechanisms are: encoding specificity, orga-

nization, discrimination, and set. Each of these mechanisms is discussed in more detail below.

The first mechanism is *encoding specificity*, in which the retrieval of information from memory is dependent upon the manner in which the information was encoded. Information that is encoded as context-specific is likely to be accessed only within that context. Students in the learning-to-learn course, EDP 310, complete assignments that require them to apply new information in a variety of contexts. Having students practice learning strategies on real coursework from other classes results in more natural strategy transfer (Stahl, Simpson, & Hayes, 1992). EDP 310 uses examples from a wide variety of academic settings to provide a "bottom-up" teaching approach as suggested by Bassock and Holyoak (1993). This should serve to generalize the encoding and enhance recall and subsequent transfer. Students who become strategic learners use many knowledge-acquisition strategies; for example, they are more likely to learn new information by applying it to themselves or their situation, making it meaningful within new settings. Therefore, the new information is embedded in several contexts and, hence, is more likely to be recalled in a wider range of situations.

The second mechanism is *organization* (Sternberg & Frensch, 1993), which refers to how the information is organized in memory. Organizing information within a clear framework and connecting it to prior knowledge improves the retrieval of the new information. The use of knowledge acquisition strategies and the ability to identify important information are also parts of Weinstein's Model. Learning strategies involve actively organizing information into a format that is meaningful to the learner and linking new information to the learner's prior knowledge. With a framework in mind, learners can identify which information is of primary importance (i.e., worthy of their focused attention) versus which information is of secondary importance (i.e., supporting details).

Sternberg and Frensch's (1993) third mechanism is *discrimination*, the ability to tag information as relevant or irrelevant to a novel situation. If students perceive new information to be useful in their coursework or occupation, they are likely to tag that information as relevant and plan ways to apply it. The ability to identify important information is also a critical factor in learning. The learner's perceived usefulness of new information determines what information will be tagged as important or relevant, and subsequently what information will be accessible in a transfer situation. Through the use of diagnostics, such as the Learning and Study Strategies Inventory (LASSI) (Weinstein, Schulte, & Palmer, 1987), class lectures, and exercises, students in the learning-to-learn course receive diagnostic and prescriptive feedback in order to enhance their ability to identify important information. In addition, exercises throughout the course encourage students to identify the relevant features of successful strategic learning situations, thus addressing Bassock and Holyoak's (1993) recommendations for a "top-down" approach to teaching for transfer.

The fourth mechanism in the model by Sternberg and Frensch (1993) is *set*, which indicates how the learner mentally approaches a problem or learning task (i.e., whether or not the learner is planning to transfer or use new material). This mechanism is also addressed in the Model of Strategic Learning by Weinstein. From the will component, motivation and attitude towards learning apply to *set*. If learners do not value the course or are not interested in actively participating, then they are not likely to have a *set* towards learning that is conducive to transfer of the study strategies to subsequent coursework. Within the self-regulation component, *set* is implied in the monitoring strategy in which the student checks to see if the material is being understood and can be applied at the desired level of performance. Knowledge of the learning context from the skill component of the model is also related to *set* (i.e., the more learners perceive the new information to be relevant to current or future coursework, the more likely they are to have a positive *set* towards the learning task). In other words, with a positive *set* towards the learning task, the student is more likely to demonstrate transfer.

In many cases transfer of learning strategies can not be directly observed, but must be inferred from other measures. In an academic setting there are two sources of information that are commonly used to indicate transfer of learning from academic assistance programs to future academic situations: grade-point average and retention/graduation rates (Simpson, Hynd, Nist, & Burrell, 1997).

The learning-to-learn course, EDP 310, addresses many of the issues that impact academic achievement, retention, and graduation rates. Weinstein's Model of Strategic Learning (as shown in Figure 1) is the foundation for this course; the model emphasizes the importance of being aware of and knowing how and when to use specific learning strategies as well as managing motivation, goals, and other self-regulatory factors. The model also addresses the environmental factors of social support (such as family and friends), available resources (such as money and computers), nature of the academic task (such as the size of classes and level of difficulty), and teacher beliefs and expectations (such as the amount of support provided by the teacher). These have all been identified as important factors that impact academic achievement, retention, and graduation rates.

Through learning about and using the Model of Strategic Learning, students in the learning-to-learn course develop three kinds of knowledge: (a) declarative knowledge which defines many different learning strategies, (b) procedural knowledge which explains ways to apply these strategies, and (c) conditional knowledge which examines appropriate conditions for application of specific strategies. The course provides direct instruction and practice in all three knowledge areas. Declarative, procedural, and conditional knowledge are all crucial in providing students with a systematic way of learning new material in any academic context. Not only are strategic learners fluent and flexible in that they possess a toolbox full of many different learning strategies, they are also able to choose which strategy to apply within a given situation to reach a desired outcome.

Simpson et al. (1997) indicate that learning-to-learn courses, such as the one which is being investigated in this study, should be one of the most effective types of academic assistance programs in producing a positive impact on

Table 1
Students Enrolled in EDP 310: Fall 1990 and Spring 1991

	First-Year Retention		Fifth-Year Retention	
	Freshmen Successful in EDP 310	All Other Freshmen	Freshmen Successful in EDP 310	All Other Freshmen
Dropped out—academic dismissal	1.9% *3*	6.9% *373*	0.6% *1*	12.7% *687*
Enrolled/Retained (continuing students)	92.3% *143*	84.9% *4576*	7.1% *11*	10.7% *577*
Graduated			71.4% *110*	55.3% *2981*
SAT—Verbal	458.3 *140*	512.5 *5180*	458.3 *140*	512.5 *5181*
SAT—Quantitative	523.1 *140*	586.3 *5180*	523.1 *140*	586.3 *5181*
Cumulative GPA	2.75 *155*	2.68 *5392*	2.72 *154*	2.58 *5392*
Course hours failed	.79 *155*	1.74 *5392*	2.55 *154*	4.91 *5392*
Course hours passed	29.23 *155*	31.00 *5392*	103.5 *154*	94.79 *5392*
Course hours undertaken	30.19 *155*	32.87 *5392*	106.5 *154*	100.2 *5392*

Note. Italicized numbers represent cell sizes.

follow-up measures such as grade point average, retention, and graduation rates. Learning-to-learn courses are based on theories of learning and cognition; such courses create strategic learners who possess a wide range of learning strategies and the ability to adapt those strategies to a variety of academic contexts and demands. Strategic learners, therefore, should demonstrate transfer of learning from the learning-to-learn course to other coursework through increased grade point average, retention, and graduation rates.

Results of a Five-Year Longitudinal Study of Freshmen

From semester evaluations of the pre- and post-data on the Nelson-Denny and LASSI scores, students showed highly significant gains on these measures. The research question for this study was: Did the course improve stu-

dents' subsequent GPAs and retention at the university. A summary of the data for students who entered the university in the 1990 fall semester is presented in Table 1.

The most dramatic data appear in the fifth-year follow-up statistics. Approximately 55% of the students who entered in 1990 and did not take the strategic learning course (EDP 310) graduated after five years; this statistic has remained the same for a number of years. However, despite significantly lower standardized test scores, approximately 71% of the students who successfully completed EDP 310 (i.e., did not drop out or fail due to excessive absences) graduated after five years. This 16-point difference is a dramatic finding that supports the long-term retention effects of an intervention in learning strategies. In addition, the cumulative GPAs for these students were higher than for the general population. These data offer strong support for the importance of developmental education for at-risk students.

Conclusion

At a time when developmental education is being attacked by policy makers, it is imperative to conduct research to demonstrate the achievements of our field. Developmental educators must remain open and susceptible to new learning theories being explored in other disciplines (i.e., instructional psychology, adult development, and cognitive and educational psychology). Ideas from these fields should be continually incorporated into theories from developmental educators to build more powerful models to describe how people learn. Also, additional research of this course and other developmental programs can provide a supportive database to strengthen further the field of developmental education. Such a database can be used by developmental educators, faculty, administrators, policy makers, and the voting public to make informed decisions about providing entry to and success in higher education for a broader range of our citizens. The research reported in this chapter documents an important fact: Developmental education makes a critical difference in the lives of many students.

References

Bandura, A. (1977). Self-efficacy: Toward a unifying theory of behavioral change. *Psychology Review, 84*(2), 191-215.

Bandura, A. (1986). *Social foundations of thought and action: A social cognitive theory.* Englewood Cliffs, NJ: Prentice-Hall.

Bassock, M., & Holyoak, K. J. (1993). Pragmatic knowledge and conceptual structure: Determinants of transfer between quantitative domains. In D. K. Detterman & R. J. Sternberg (Eds.), *Transfer on trial: Intelligence, cognition and instruction.* Norwood, NJ: Ablex.

Lens, W., & Rand, P. (1997). *Combining intrinsic goal orientations with professional instrumentality/utility in student motivation.* Unpublished manuscript.

Locke, E. A., & Latham, G. P. (1990). *A theory of goal setting and task performance.* Englewood Cliffs, NJ: Prentice-Hall.

McCombs, B. L., & Marzano, R. J. (1990). Putting the self in self-regulated learning: The self as agent in integrating will and skill. *Educational Psychologist, 25*(1), 51-69.

Pintrich, P. R., & DeGroot, E. V. (1990). Motivational and self-regulated learning components of classroom academic performance. *Journal of Educational Psychology, 82*(1), 33-40.

Pintrich, P. R., Marx, R. W., & Boyle, R. (1993). Beyond "cold" conceptual change: The role of motivational beliefs and classroom contextual factors in the process of conceptual change. *Review of Educational Research, 63,* 167-199.

Pintrich, P. R., & Schunk, D. H. (1996). *Motivation in education.* Columbus, OH: Prentice Hall.

Raynor, J. O. (1981). Future orientation and achievement motivation: Toward a theory of personality functioning and change. In G. D'Ydewalle & W. Lens (Eds.), *Cognition in human motivation and learning* (pp. 199-231). Hillsdale, NJ: Lawrence Erlbaum.

Salomon, G., & Perkins, D. N. (1989). Rocky roads to transfer: Rethinking mechanisms of a neglected phenomenon. *Educational Psychologist, 24*(2), 113-142.

Schunk, D. H., (1989). Social cognitive theory and self-regulated learning. In B. J. Zimmerman & D. H. Schunk (Eds.), *Self-regulated learning and academic achievement* (pp. 83-110). New York: Springer-Verlag.

Simpson, M. L., Hynd, D. R., Nist, S. L., & Burrell, K. I. (1997). College academic assistance programs and practices. *Educational Psychology Review, 9*(1), 39-87.

Stahl, N. A., Simpson, M. L., & Hayes, C. G. (1992). Ten recommendations from research for teaching high risk college students. *Journal of Developmental Education, 16*(1), 2-8.

Sternberg, R. J., & Frensch, P. A. (1993). Mechanisms of transfer. In D. K. Detterman & R. J. Sternberg (Eds.), *Transfer on trial: Intelligence, cognition and instruction.* Norwood, NJ: Ablex.

Weiner, B. (1986). *An attributional theory of motivation and emotion.* New York: Springer-Verlag.

Weinstein, C. E. (1988). Executive control processes in learning: Why knowing about how to learn is not enough. *Journal of College Reading and Learning, 21,* 48-56

Weinstein, C. E. (1994). Strategic learning/strategic teaching: Flip sides of a coin. In P. R. Pintrich, D. R. Brown, & C. E. Weinstein (Eds.),

Student motivation, cognition, and learning: Essays in honor of Wilbert J. McKeachie (pp. 257-273). Hillsdale, NJ: Lawrence Erlbaum.

Weinstein, C. E., Husman, J., Dierking, D., & Powdrill, L. (in press). Strategic learning. In C. E. Weinstein & B. L. McCombs (Eds.), *Strategic learning: The merging of skill, will and self-regulation.* Hillsdale, NJ: Lawrence Erlbaum.

Weinstein C. E., & McCombs, B. L. (Eds.). (in press). *Strategic learning: The merging of skill, will and self-regulation.* Hillsdale, NJ: Lawrence Erlbaum.

Weinstein, C. E., Schulte, A. C., & Palmer, D. R. (1987). *The learning and study strategies inventory (LASSI).* Clearwater, FL: H & H.

Zimmerman, B. J., Greenberg, D., & Weinstein, C. E. (1994). *Self-regulating academic study time: A strategy approach.* In D. H. Schunk & B. J. Zimmerman (Eds.), *Self-regulation of learning and performance* (pp. 181-199). Hillsdale, NJ: Lawrence Erlbaum.

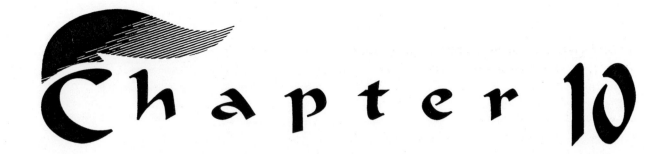

Chapter 10

Integrating Critical Thinking into the Developmental Curriculum

Linda Best

Over the past two decades, research on cognition has introduced theoretical insights on learning processes and how the contexts of learning can facilitate the transfer of knowledge and skills for use in other appropriate contexts. This research is important to developmental education in two ways: (a) by promoting students' acquisition of knowledge and skills in a way that ensures their application for success in other academic courses; and (b) by focusing on skills that do not become obsolete over time (e.g., decision making, analysis, problem solving, and self-reflection). These enduring skills enable individuals to understand their roles in the rapidly changing contexts surrounding them.

The Role of Critical Thinking

Critical thinking consists of a broad subset of skills, such as problem solving, comparing or contrasting, inferencing, organizing, and evaluating (Bransford, Sherwood, Vye, & Rieser, 1986). These skills enable individuals to utilize their knowledge in appropriate circumstances, to evaluate if and when they need to know more, and to detect how they might alter what is known (Brown, 1980). Learners connect new information to former knowledge; they select thinking strategies deliberately, and plan, monitor, and evaluate thinking processes (Kerka, 1992).

Unfortunately, while the informal learning of everyday activity has been found to offer a strong foundation for the development of thinking, the process of learning has been largely ignored by formal schooling, which emphasizes the transmission of information rather than focusing on problem solving and self-awareness (Chipman & Segal, 1985; Resnick, 1988). Knowledge and skills transfer well when individuals have firsthand experience of how the information they possess applies to other situations, relates to their own experiences, and suits their personal and academic needs, both at the moment and in the future (Potts, 1994).

Strategies and Skills of At-Level Versus Developmental Writers

The connection established between content knowledge and learning skills has been explored extensively in various studies (e.g., Bransford et al., 1986; Presseisen, 1987). Consistently, data illustrate the complex interaction of cognition and context. While dynamic and informative, these data often leave readers wondering about practical implications for instruction. A cognitive study examining the differences between developmental and at-level college writers gives insight into the patterns of strategies and content as they interact during learning (Best, 1996a). The data captured the delicate tension of cognition and content working together to facilitate the acquisition of knowledge and learning strategies. This study also examined the subprocesses of critical thinking that support the acquisition of knowledge and skills which in turn have implications for instruction. A review of the study follows, it includes in-depth discussion about two topics critical to this chapter: (a) the differences separating developmental writers and at-level college writers, and (b) the interaction of cognition and context (content) during the writing process.

In the early 1990s, I set out to examine developmental and at-level college students' varying strategies for and approaches to writing. I sought to compare the work of at-level college writers (those who demonstrated a writing ability that met or excelled the standards expected of college students) with that of developmental writers (students whose writing for whatever reasons falls short of these standards) in order to identify those strategies and skills developmental instruction should target. To date, no research on writing has sought to examine these differences; further, important cognitive studies on writing have heretofore been limited to studies of expert graduate-student writers (e.g., Flower & Hayes, 1981a, 1981b). While these studies have informed educational practice about the nature of the writing process by stressing writing, revising, and editing, they have not offered direction for the teaching of writing to students whose skills are weak.

I recruited a number of prospective participants and identified eight students—four developmental writers and four at-level college writers. In the tradition of cognitive research, the students talked aloud while writing the study's three prescribed tasks in individual writing sessions. Previously, through warm-up activities, the students demonstrated the ability to verbalize the steps in their writing process in accordance with the study's design. The students' verbal reports were rich.

The study's principal findings describe the qualitative differences separating the two types of writers. Those differences are explained in terms of the knowledge types Dillon (1986) describes:

♦ declarative knowledge (i.e., the knowledge of fixed information such as rules and facts);

♦ procedural knowledge (knowledge about how to use such fixed information);

♦ self-knowledge or metacognition (i.e., knowledge about one's own knowledge).

Metacognition pairs an understanding of what one knows with a personal awareness of the cognitive resources that support performance, such as the planning and monitoring that enables the selection of appropriate strategies, regulates performance, and measures outcomes (Wixson & Peters, 1987).

On the surface, all participants in this extensive study appeared to possess basic declarative knowledge about writing. A close examination of their verbalizations indicated, however, that the depth of their knowledge varied. The developmental writers' knowledge appeared limited and superficial; they often accessed a number of unrelated topics about writing and were unable to judge whether these were relevant to the task at hand. Clearly, their knowledge about writing was not organized in any manner. In general, the other group—the at-level college writers—exhibited a much more extensive and substantial knowledge base. Their knowledge of a given topic included multiple examples and information about the distinctions separating them. The at-level writers also accessed information related to topics they were using, whereas the developmental writers considered pieces of knowledge in isolation. In summary, the developmental writers handled information in a rote manner; they possessed clusters of decontextualized knowledge that made application difficult. In contrast, the at-level college writers processed information about writing at a higher level; they had constructed a coherent body of declarative knowledge.

Differences in procedural knowledge were also evident and most obvious in the students' treatment of punctuation. For the developmental students, punctuation surfaced as something abstract that they thought they needed to do but were not prepared to execute. They were curious about how to punctuate their work but did not or could not rely on a system for doing so. In the end, the developmental writers' efforts to punctuate were random acts that were not attentive to grammar and, therefore, resulted in a number of surface errors. The at-level college writers, on the other hand, employed systematic approaches for reviewing how they should use punctuation. They possessed both knowledge about the rules and a range of strategies for employing them. When checking punctuation, these writers analyzed structures to determine a need for punctuation; they spoke about phrases, clauses, and sentence types and then accessed appropriate examples for reference. Their work was methodical and, for the most part, correct.

The students' metacognitive skills followed the differences cited above, yet on a more global level. Whereas the at-level writers exerted control over the preparation of their texts from start to finish, the developmental writers adopted an add-on approach (after completing a paragraph, they wondered where they should go next). They searched for direction while their work was in progress, often starting something new in the middle of their essays. As a result, the texts they produced often incorporated irrelevant detail or drifted from the prescribed topic.

The at-level writers' data made explicit the aspects of thinking and learning that support successful performance. They possessed an organized knowledge base; they accessed information and understood connections between bodies of information related to the task; they selected appropriate strategies; they detected and responded to their weaknesses; and, finally, they monitored—as well as modified—their cognitive activity to ensure successful completion of the tasks. These acts were the very processes that the developmental writers could not perform.

The second critical finding in this research offers insights on the two forces—cognitive processes and content—that interact during writing, learning, and thinking. A certain pattern of cognitive activity was evident. More fluid, efficient, and sophisticated in the work of the at-level college writers, it involved the following critical process:

Whereas the at-level writers exerted control over the preparation of their texts from start to finish, the developmental writers adopted an add-on approach (after completing a paragraph, they wondered where they should go next).

♦ specific tasks accessed skills and influenced the selection of topics;

♦ skills then facilitated the focusing of information;

♦ information triggered the application of knowledge about writing.

A delicate tension, as well as forward and backward movement, existed as the following series of statements suggests:

1. *Topics triggered thinking.* In their initial verbalizations, the writers considered various topics and selected one.

2. *The writers' thinking was associative at first; ideas and concepts came to mind.* The verbalizations that followed the selection of

the topic exposed a string of associations. Focused on the word "loyalty," for example, one writer accessed ideas such as "personal experience," "in college now," "Terry last year," "age difference," and "distance."

3. *Knowledge about writing was accessed and interacted with the topic on a general level, sharpening its focus.* After advancing their ideas, the writers shifted to thinking about strategies for writing. For example, they talked about providing background information or defining terms to get started. The writers began to envision their essays.

4. *The thinking began to focus on the particular topic for writing.* Having initially thought about what to do in their introductory paragraphs, the writers proceeded to develop their ideas around topics to write about in those paragraphs.

5. *Specific knowledge about writing was evident.* The students demonstrated their understanding of the thesis statement, the need to avoid repetition when writing, and the need to avoid drifting from the topic. This knowledge interacted with ideas about the topic, bringing the texts produced closer to the conventions for writing.

6. *The writing topic became clear.* Examples and points began to stand out. In their verbalizations, the writers showed how they began to balance the processes of advancing and writing ideas. They qualified and stated supporting details.

7. *Knowledge of and strategies for writing interacted with the topic.* Embedded in the advance ideas or writing episode were occasional references to knowledge about and strategies for writing. One writer, for example, evaluated the point of view she adopted and the topic she selected.

8. *The students' thoughts were transformed beyond personal or private to something coherent and understandable to someone unfamiliar with the students' experiences or perspective.*

One writer discovered a connection between two friendships and transformed her details into a message about friendships in general. She elevated her discussion of a personal story to a broad theme.

The writers appeared to cross over and return to the activities and processes described above, experiencing a sense of illumination as they discovered their texts. Subprocesses of critical thinking, such as planning and anticipating, analyzing, making judgments, evaluating, making connections, and problem-solving characterized the writers' work. The cognitive processes they employed pushed me to explore how instruction might support this cognitive activity, how the need exists to employ methods interweaving "essential thinking processes into complex content knowledge in a pedagogical manner that enhances meaningful thought" (Arrendondo & Block, 1990, p. 8).

Theory in Practice: Integrating Critical Thinking into Curricula

The literature offers compelling descriptions of thinking activity. The following concepts explain the nature of thinking and establish a foundation and strategies for teaching critical thinking skills:

1. *Even though explanations and descriptions of the development of thinking vary, the understanding that it progresses over time remains constant.* In fact, research on the topic is quite specific about this progression, pointing to the concrete operations associated with early childhood and the abstract, formal operations characterizing adolescent thought. Individuals' skills are influenced by individual interests and aptitudes as well as external factors, and, therefore, are likely to progress at different rates. Thus, information about the stages of thinking guides educators at each level to understand the skills students might possess and those they might attain (Damon, 1983).

2. *While thinking progresses over time, some of its subprocesses, such as the ability to compare items or concepts, are apparent across time.*

Their nature and depth undergo changes, often corresponding to or emerging with the subject matter on which mental activity is focused (Nickerson, 1986).

3. *Thinking involves multiple cognitions.* These are oriented to factors or conditions both within and outside the individual. These cognitions include perceptions of self and the environment and reflect the interaction of external forces and internal processes (Connell, 1991). Programs targeting cognitive skills focus on individuals. Instruction, in turn, becomes sensitive to the social and motivational factors that may affect an individual student's cognitive skills (Snow, 1986).

4. *Thinking reflects the interaction of cognitive processes.* Although these components might appear cohesive in this interaction, they serve distinct roles. Content triggers mental functions, moving thought from specific information to concepts. General skills, on the other hand, incorporate content, synthesizing and integrating it within a conceptual framework (Arrendondo & Block, 1990).

5. *Thinking is a process.* References to thinking describe the mental activity and response of individuals. Applied to formal attempts to teach thinking, this insight suggests a focus on individuals and active learning. Critical to the teaching of thinking are student engagement with content and the learning activities that help its promotion (Brown, Collins, & Duguid, 1989).

A curriculum anchored by critical thinking accounts for the aforementioned principles. Curriculum has two purposes: to have students acquire certain knowledge and skills, and to engage students in critical thinking which will enhance cognitive development and ensure the retention and application of information studied. Instruction in this environment accounts for individual learners, stresses the use of knowledge, and engages them in meaningful learning activities. Opportunities exist to examine, reflect,

redo, and evaluate. Learning is active rather than passive. Critical thinking plays a complex role—it serves as both a means for, and an outcome of, teaching.

Applying Theory: Program Practices and Class Activities

Introducing theory-based curriculum in the classroom necessitates a transition from the direct teaching of declarative knowledge to teaching and learning that are anchored in both procedural knowledge and metacognition. While all three types of knowledge (i.e., declarative, procedural, metacognitive) are essential for the completion of tasks, procedural knowledge plays a distinct role. Procedural knowledge focuses on what learners do with what they know and is most often associated with strategies and skills. Procedural knowledge offers students opportunities to measure the effectiveness of what they know and do. Especially effective are structured opportunities such as peer groups, tutorials, or student and teacher conferences, which guide students to reflect on the way in which they approach their work. These strategies assist students in the following: identifying their strengths and weaknesses, determining how to improve performance, and comparing their work to that of others. Through these types of activities, students use knowledge and come to know how they use it. They discover what they do well and where they need help.

Integrating critical thinking skills into the curriculum transforms the classroom experience, allowing students to play an active rather than passive role and teachers to assume the role of facilitators rather than transmitters of information. Suitable instruction offers students opportunities to access higher-order thinking skills such as analysis and inference. Such higher-order thinking skills allow students to process information, to develop knowledge, to understand self-knowledge, and to grasp the applications of knowledge studied.

The Program Level

Integrating critical thinking into the developmental curriculum is a large-scale effort that involves measures on both the program and classroom levels. Its broad aim attempts to counteract the trends that threaten the efficacy of developmental programs and the promising students they serve; these trends include early failure in developmental courses, risk and eventual failure in advanced courses, and high attrition. The key to addressing such topics of concern is an effort to make explicit, through program practices and classroom practices, fundamental concepts associated with critical thinking, such as the organization of knowledge and information, the connections between bodies of knowledge, and ways to facilitate information processing.

Developmental education programs that are anchored in critical thinking play the important role of making explicit the connections between developmental courses and the broader college curriculum. In addition to reminding students that developmental courses serve as prerequisites for college-level courses, such programs inform students through orientation sessions and promotional materials about the specific skills they will acquire in their developmental courses and how these skills will benefit them in advanced required courses, as well as courses in their majors. More importantly, information presented to students orients them to the type of learning environment which they will experience and the responsibilities they have as active learners.

Integrating critical thinking skills into the curriculum transforms the classroom experience, allowing students to play an active rather than passive role and teachers to assume the role of facilitators rather than transmitters of information.

Establishing Connections with Other Programs

Developmental education programs can establish connections with other programs to make these principles for learning more explicit. New student seminars, for example, can guide students to understand their role in the context of higher education. Instructors may serve as the new students' advisors for the full year, guiding them through the curriculum and their individual programs of study. Interaction between developmental studies program staff and staff who organize the new student seminars

strengthens connections for students, making them feel part of the college experience. All too often, students who test into developmental courses lack the preparation for—and orientation to—college studies. They may also be part of a special admissions program, and either or both of these circumstances make them feel isolated or without purpose. Feelings of isolation and purposelessness may lead to lack of motivation and may interfere with progress. When developmental education administrators interact with other programs serving new students, they make explicit the connectedness between developmental courses and the broader academic context.

Linked Courses

Other efforts to establish connections between developmental education and the institution include the pairing of developmental courses and appropriate content courses (Blinn & Sisco, 1997; Wilcox, delMas, Stewart, Johnson, & Ghere, 1997). With this arrangement, each developmental reading or writing course is linked with a companion course—an introductory course such as Introduction to Psychology or Introduction to Sociology. Students are required to register for both courses. The instructors who teach the sections collaborate to offer a content-based approach to skills development. Material in the content area, along with other related assignments, is the anchor for critical thought and skills acquisition in the developmental course. The focus on critical thinking in the developmental course guides students to interact with the material presented in the content course. They read to understand, to connect content to other relevant matter, to respond, and to determine how they will use the content in the other courses they take.

At some institutions today, the desire to connect developmental education to the broader curriculum has resulted in the development of packaged courses. Similar in format to block scheduling, packaged courses offer a great deal more than a convenient, workable schedule. They represent a deliberate effort to offer students a module of courses with objectives, required skills, workload, and assignments that are connected and balanced carefully by a team of professors who collaborate to provide an integrated educational experience. Packaged courses often follow a particular theme, such as the 20th century, global problems, women's issues, or diversity. Skills and knowledge are context-bound in an effort to facilitate development and to transfer for long-term academic success.

Establishing Connections within the Developmental Program

While it is essential for developmental programs to establish connections to the broader curricula, it is also important to establish connections among the different areas of developmental education programs. These connections are established through:

♦ a coherent institutional mission statement about developmental education that governs all skill areas for which instruction exists and sets forth the instructional strategies for fulfilling this mission;

♦ materials for faculty and advisors that articulate the mission statement and provide information about grading, attendance, and other practices so that developmental courses are consistent and demonstrate students' participation in a program of study rather than individual, unrelated courses;

♦ faculty training that orients instructors to the thinking skills common to the different developmental skills areas and guides them to build upon each other's work in the classroom;

♦ training and orientation for tutors, academic center staff, and Supplemental Instruction facilitators that aims to integrate services with students who need to enhance study skills.

In addition to making connections among the developmental skills areas, programs anchored in critical thinking attend to individual students' needs and rates of progress. An ongoing concern, as a result, focuses on the delivery of program services and the exploration of creative ways to structure courses. The recent renewed interest in "express" developmental courses at Kean University offers an authentic example of the topic at hand. The intensive three-week express developmental courses offered during summer sessions and winter breaks appeal to and meet the needs of students who wish to immerse themselves in the skills course or those who need nothing more than a skills refresher. The courses, which follow the standards and demands of the traditional semester courses, are successful; more importantly, they illustrate that traditional courses shaped by the academic calendar and course periods may not be the only means for facilitating the skills of developmental students.

Programs must be based in theory to establish a framework for developmental courses. This framework guides instruction and sets forth consistent aims across skill areas.

The Classroom Level

Integrating critical thinking skills into the developmental curriculum alters the classroom experience, making teachers facilitators of learning rather than transmitters of information. Instruction which integrates critical thinking skills with course content offers students opportunities to connect new information to former knowledge, to select strategies deliberately, and to plan, monitor, and evaluate thinking processes (Kerka, 1992). A sampling of suitable activities follows:

Cognitive Monitoring. Cognitive monitoring is a key tool for learning. Designed by teachers or contained in textbooks and consisting of a series of task-oriented questions, cognitive monitoring guides students to inventory their skills and understand the processes and outcomes of learning. Students carefully and deliberately respond to certain questions and probes, recording answers so that they might review and evaluate their work further at another time or so that others, such as teachers or tutors, might monitor their knowledge and rates of progress. The responses students provide often indicate where, in the presence of deficiencies, a breakdown in processing may exist. Cognitive monitoring is not a lesson; it is a process that suits different proficiency levels, academic skills, and content areas.

Cognitive monitoring takes place before, during, or after learning activity, depending on the goals and objectives of the lesson at hand. For example, students in a math class, who engage in cognitive monitoring as they set out to review a particular unit respond to questions or probes like these:

♦ Scan the problems in the review section and jot down the knowledge you have that will help you solve these problems.

♦ Identify the problems that may give you difficulty and explain why this is the case.

♦ Identify the problems you can complete without difficulty.

♦ Describe the skills you will use to solve the problems.

Instruction which integrates critical thinking skills with course content offers students opportunities to connect new information to former knowledge, to select strategies deliberately, and to plan, monitor, and evaluate thinking processes (Kerka, 1992).

♦ Which problems are similar to one another?

♦ How are these problems similar?

♦ How do the similarities help you?

These questions and probes foster analytical thinking. None elicit a binary response of yes or no; these questions expose skills. Students consciously go through the process of making connections, accessing information, selecting strategies, and recognizing what they can and cannot do.

Developmental writing students have the opportunity to engage in cognitive monitoring as do students in reading courses. In the writing

course, students may engage in cognitive monitoring to plan an essay or assess one already written. As a prewriting activity, cognitive monitoring guides students' selection of a topic and vision of a plan through questions and probes like these:

♦ What do you know about these topic choices?

♦ Which one(s) must you eliminate? Why?

♦ What topic do you think you will choose? Why?

♦ Explain your knowledge about this topic.

♦ What message do you want to convey in an essay about this topic?

♦ Who might be interested in this topic? Why?

Questions and probes continue along this line. They trigger thinking, putting writers in touch with their knowledge about the subject; then writers examine their actions, provide a rationale for the actions they take, and discover the knowledge and skills that will enable them to complete the task. The number of items to include in a particular monitoring exercise will depend on many factors: the assignment, the amount of time available for the monitoring activity, and the conditions under which the cognitive monitoring will take place (e.g., in class, in peer groups, or as an out-of-class assignment).

Cognitive Monitoring and Peer Group Work. Cognitive monitoring promotes critical thought in a measured, focused way. The probes and questions to which students might respond independently also work effectively in peer groups. Peer group activities introduce the creative tension of several individuals thinking together and providing feedback for one another. By discussing questions and probes like those listed above, the members of a group learn about different perspectives and strategies, which then broaden their understanding of the management of academic tasks. In groups, students consider how their course content relates to the cognitive monitoring activities. They might offer individual reports or lessons about different topics, prepare or present projects, review assignments, and compare class notes. Peer groups serve multiple purposes in the classroom. While the social benefits are a plus, the reasons for working together are more deeply tied to learning and development. Peer work offers opportunities to benefit intellectually from others. Peer group activities must be carefully designed to rehearse, model, or supplement cognitive monitoring skills; such activities guide students in peer groups to formulate and present ideas, to explain insights, and to anticipate and respond to reactions.

Self-Evaluation. The skills and processes students employ through cognitive monitoring and related learning strategies enable them to handle another important class activity: self-evaluation. Over the last decade, a focus on process learning and individualized instruction has prompted faculty across the disciplines and levels of education to ask students to appraise their work periodically. In a writing course, for instance, after accumulating papers through the course of a semester, students prepare and submit portfolios of their work for a final grade. They select representative pieces, arrange them, and write about them, providing descriptions of their personal strategies, skills, and growth as part of the process. This practice is common in many skill and content areas; routinely, students describe the nature and progress of their knowledge and skills at the beginning, middle, and end of the term. They present the conclusions they formulate in a number of formats, namely written work, conferences with instructors, and tutorials.

When asked to complete such tasks, many students, especially developmental students, feel lost early and throughout the term if clear guidelines for performing this type of task do not exist. The students may not be certain about the strategies and skills they employ; they may not be able to speak about or describe the knowledge they possess; and they may not have an accurate understanding of their progress in the course. Their class work has been graded, yet they remain uncertain about how or why they received these grades. They may speak about external factors that impede their learning rather than looking to themselves and their involvement in the course and interaction with its content. Exercises like cognitive monitoring place developmental students on a deliberate, carefully designed course of self-discovery that makes self-evaluation possible. Questions and probes guide students to dig into and examine their work at a high level of specificity. Students become the agents of their learning; the act of self-evaluating in an academic context becomes a welcome, legitimate task.

Modeling. Modeling is the act of verbalizing cognitive monitoring skills. Individuals proficient in a certain field model knowledge and skills in use. Models start with a task and through oral presentation or demonstration analyze it, break it down into its parts and cite the knowledge essential for completing the task successfully. The individuals modeling a task perform the task. They talk about what they are doing, exposing the strategies and skills they select from a number of options. They explain the reasons supporting their selections, such as the conditions surrounding the task and other important rationale.

A number of individuals can model learning activity: teachers, tutors, students who have completed a certain course, outside experts, and others competent in the field. In a math class, for example, an individual might model the processes of reading, interpreting, and analyzing problems, selecting formulas, and performing calculations. Someone modeling activity in a writing course may demonstrate how to analyze a rhetorical task and start shaping an introductory paragraph. In a reading course, a model can demonstrate how to identify levels of information in a chapter or how to outline the chapter. Modeling expresses cognitive activity. The personal touch it offers may attract students' attention. Most importantly, the modeling of how skills, strategies, and knowledge interact to complete a particular task shows that a given task is, indeed, doable.

Writing Activity. Over the last decade, research on writing has introduced critical insights about the skill, exposing its nature as a mode of thinking (Best, 1996b; Odell, 1993). Involving the explicit selection of information, use of strategies, translation of ideas into words, and recursive thought, writing can serve as a tool for learning. Engaged in suitable content-based writing activities, students get firsthand experiences with the content they study. Writing accesses knowledge about content areas and make gaps in the knowledge base visible. Through routine writing activities such as learning logs, journals, and individual study guides, students recall and rehearse their course information. Since the purpose of writing is to encourage students to produce and explore knowledge, emphasis rests with the production of ideas rather than the conventions for writing. Students who engage in writing activity in a specific discipline write for several reasons: to practice writing, to read what they write, and to learn content through writing. Discipline-based instructors typically monitor the content the students produce rather than their proficiency as writers (i.e., their writing skills *per se*).

Writing can be incorporated into developmental courses in a number of ways. Students might prepare summaries of what occurred during different classes and share these for discussion as class sessions open or close. The requirement to complete summaries requires students to rehearse the content of the course and keeps instructors informed about how their students are grasping its content. Exams and quizzes can include open-ended questions that ask students to describe their test-taking strategies, to assess their performance on the test, or to explain the degree of difficulty they experienced with the different test items. Brief freewriting episodes can also take place in class. Prior to starting class work, major assignments, or peer group work, students can write to guide their thoughts about the task at hand. The writing experience will tap knowledge and expose students' perceived ability to complete assigned tasks successfully.

All too often, unbeknownst to a teacher, students begin a task or exercise with no or little understanding of its purpose, their relationship to it, or its relationship to the course and other broad objectives. Students who are not in touch with what they are doing in a course (or those who rarely have something to say) can benefit from freewriting which gives them the time and the mechanism to try to express their ideas. The information they generate, whether shared orally in class, self-recognized only, or submitted for the teacher's review, offers critical insights into a student's comprehension of the content and process of the tasks at hand.

Dialogue Journals and Electronic Mail. An increasingly popular writing activity is the dialogue journal—a writing exercise in which teachers and students (or students and students) regularly exchange ideas about the course, the material, their progress, or their concerns. The journal may be a weekly requirement. Certain parameters shape it. Entries must focus on specific aspects of a course. Students write about any of these, referencing grades or class notes to supplement what they have to say. They work with the material of the course, using the language and terminology associated with it. Students write the journal for their instructors, knowing that they will respond to the material presented. Instructors read what the students write, acquiring novel insights on their thinking and knowledge. Instructors also respond, offering individual guidance especially helpful to those whose knowledge and skills lag behind that of others. Exchanges between students and teachers continue through the course of a semester, thereby heightening students' awareness of their work in the course and informing instructors of their students' growth and progress.

A new form of communication, electronic mail (email), has introduced even greater potential for this type of communication about course work between student and teacher, among classmates, or both. Email offers rapid feedback and response. By communicating with teachers and classmates electronically, students can seek guidance about their studies and outside assignments without being constrained by class meeting days or the need to be on campus. Instructors may require communication through email from students during periods when critical work on new or complex topics is underway. Students provide updates on their progress and receive feedback or guidance that directs their learning further. Informed about individual students' progress between class meetings, instructors can plan subsequent class meetings, scaling activity to match students' learning curves and anticipating the need for intervention, such as tutoring, for those students well below the perceived class level. Ongoing communication outside class time, as provided through email, enables instructors to pace a class according to the strategies and skills their students demonstrate. Students get the added benefits of strengthening both their communications skills and their technical skills.

Technology. Email is one of many technological applications that benefits developmental students. Advancements in software design have introduced materials for reading, writing, and mathematics that adapt to individual students' knowledge and skills. As students use the software to solve problems, to read passages, or to revise texts, the software application monitors their proficiency level and navigates them through exercises offering suitable practice at a comfortable level, and then eases them towards a new level of proficiency. Hands-on work with technological tools offers students more autonomy as learners than traditional materials do. Options exist, and students make choices. Feedback comes readily, and students develop self-awareness and the ability to monitor their work. Technology can transform classrooms into laboratories, making students true active learners who progress through customized supplemental lessons for their individual skill development (Best, 1997).

Class materials involving technology are not limited to the costly packages vendors might provide; a vast amount of information and scores of teaching materials are available on the Internet. Much of what is available supports

All too often, unbeknownst to a teacher, students begin a task or exercise with no or little understanding of its purpose, their relationship to it, or its relationship to the course and other broad objectives.

course work in novel ways. Students will find study guides, exercises, learning style inventories, critical thinking exercises, student exchanges, reading material, and tests to assess their skills. These teaching/learning aids can both inform them about and provide exercise to practice skills in reading, writing, and mathematics. Structured opportunities to use these materials guide students to analyze their course material, search for related information, select and review what is available, and connect it to what they know. Such technological opportunities fold into and supplement the agenda of developmental education courses; these courses offer students innovative, interactive means for working with course content.

The activities described in this section are adaptable for use in all the skills areas comprising developmental education. Anchored in cognitive activity, they guide students to reflect on what they know and do. While the activities adopt a singular focus and aim, they direct students toward this aim in different ways. Some activities focus on the student working independently. Others expose a communicative intent, an interactive nature, or a technological component. The activities are representative of a wide range of student-centered, cognition-rich options from which instructors can choose to integrate critical thinking into the curriculum.

Conclusion

When critical thinking becomes an integral part of the developmental curriculum, students play an active role in their learning by assuming responsibility for engaging in self-discovery and by monitoring the curriculum prescribes. Working with their course content, students are expected to explore, to participate, to interact, to analyze, to communicate, to respond, to connect, and to reflect. While the curriculum may present expectations different from those that students have been conditioned to anticipate, its benefits are many and far-reaching. The shift to an active role is liberating, exhilarating, and appropriate. Students assume responsibility for their learning during a period which mirrors their newfound independence and self-sufficiency. Skill development becomes the outcome of deliberate learning, rather than a random discovery by chance. Analyzed, connected, and applied through different learning activities, the necessary knowledge and skills are acquired and retained to ensure success in the developmental course and beyond.

Ultimately the success of this curriculum rests with its development and implementation. The theories and practical insights described here provide direction to shape course material and use teaching methods that will guide student learning. Most importantly, the chapter stresses the significance of the institutional and programmatic practices that support the classroom experience. These enrich the curriculum and establish connections, giving developmental courses their proper place in the broader academic context.

References

Arrendondo, D., & Block, J. (1990). Recognizing the connections between thinking skills and mastery learning. *Educational Leadership, 47,* 4-10.

Best, L. (1996a). The nature of developmental writing: A cognitive explanation with practical implications. *Research and Teaching in Developmental Education, 13*(1), 5-18.

Best, L. (1996b). The nature of reflection during composing: A series of cognitive studies and their application in the classroom. *The Journal of Teaching and Learning 1*(1), 24-28.

Best, L. (1997). The nature of teaching and learning in the laboratory classroom: Process, activity, problem-solving, engagement. *Proceedings of the Mid-South Instructional Technology Conference '97,* 183-200.

Blinn, S., & Sisco, O. (1997). Linking developmental reading and biology. *Selected Conference Papers, 2,* 8-9.

Bransford, R., Sherwood, R., Vye, N., & Rieser, J. (1986). Teaching thinking and problem solving: Research foundations. *American Psychologist, 41,* 1078-1089.

Brown, A. L. (1980). Metacognitive development in writing and reading. In R. J. Spiro, B. C. Bruce, & W. F. Brewer (Eds.), *Theoretical issues in reading and comprehension* (pp. 453-482). Hillsdale, NJ: Lawrence Erlbaum.

Brown, J. S., Collins, A., & Duguid, P. (1989). Situated cognition and the culture of learning. *Educational Researcher, 18,* 32-42.

Chipman, S., & Segal, J. (1985). Higher cognitive goals for education: An introduction. In S. Chipman, J. Segal, & R. Glaser (Eds.), *Thinking and learning skills: Research and open questions* (Vol 2, pp. 1-18). Hillsdale, NJ: Lawrence Erlbaum.

Connell, J. (1991) Context, self, and action: A motivational analysis of self-systems processes across the life span. In D. Cicchetti & M. Beeghly (Eds.), *The self in transition: Infancy to childhood.* Chicago: University Press.

Damon, W. (1983). *Social and personality development.* New York: W. W. Norton and Co.

Dillon, R. F. (1986). Issues in cognitive psychology and instruction. In R. Dillon & R. Sternberg (Eds.), *Cognition and instruction* (pp. 1-12). New York: Academic Press.

Flower, L., & Hayes, J. R. (1981a). A cognitive process theory of writing. *College Composition and Communication, 4,* 365-387.

Flower, L., & Hayes, J. R. (1981b). The pregnant pause: An inquiry into the nature of planning. *Research in the Teaching of English, 15,* 229-244.

Kerka, S. (1992). *Higher order thinking skills in vocational education.* Office of Educational Research and Improvement, Washington, DC (ERIC Documentation Reproduction Service No. ED 350 487).

Nickerson, R. (1986). Reasoning. In R. Dillon & R. J. Sternberg (Eds.), *Cognition and instruction* (pp. 343-382). New York: Academic Press.

Odell, L. (Ed.). (1993). *Theory and practice in the teaching of writing: Re-thinking the discipline.* Carbondale, IL: Southern Illinois University Press.

Potts, B. (1994). *Strategies for teaching critical thinking.* Washington, DC: ERIC/AE Digest. (ERIC Documentation Reproduction Service No. ED 385 606).

Presseisen, B. A. (1987). *Thinking skills throughout the curriculum.* Bloomington, IN: Pi Lambda Theta, Inc.

Resnick, L. (1988). Learning in school and out.

Educational Researcher, 16, 13-20.

Snow, R. (1986) Individual differences and the design of educational programs. *American Psychologist, 41,* 1029-1039.

Wilcox, K., delMas, R., Stewart, B., Johnson, A., & Ghere, D. (1997). The package course experience and developmental education. *Journal of Developmental Education, 20,* 3, 18-20, 22, 24, 26.

Wixson, K. K., & Peters, C. W. (1987). Comprehension assessment: Implementing an interactive view of reading. *Educational Psychologist, 22,* 333-356.

Chapter 11

Metacognition: Facilitating Academic Success

Cynthia M. Craig

Although study skills courses have been included in college curricula since the early 1920s, the programs created to assist at-risk students overcome academic deficiencies and prepare for college-level course work traditionally focus on the basic content skills of reading, writing, and mathematics. Vital elements of meaning-making, information processing and monitoring, and information retrieval and memory are frequently sacrificed in order to maximize content coverage. In addition to being deficient in the content areas, students requiring developmental education are frequently deficient in the skills necessary to become active and effective participants in the teaching and learning process.

In behaviorism, learning usually requires an external motivator or reward, and application is regarded as the transfer of training to problems that share common elements. The teacher directs the learning process and is the primary actor while the student is the passive receiver of information (*Cognito: The Cognitive Paradigm*, 1997).

However, since the 1970s advances in educational and cognitive psychology have reconceptualized the role of learners and their responsibilities in the teaching and learning process. Rather than portraying the learner as a passive recipient who assimilates knowledge in a mechanical, robotic manner, the learner is characterized as an active information processor, interpreter, and synthesizer. In this new educational paradigm, the student is an "active meaning maker" (*Cognito: The Cognitive Paradigm*, 1997, p. 6). This view of education revamps the role of the teacher from that of the primary actor and director of instruction to that of a facilitator of student learning. The student then becomes the prime actor involved in setting educational and personal goals, acquiring and building new information into appropriate cognitive structures, and applying new knowledge and ideas in a variety of problems and settings.

In this "cognitive paradigm," the following principles apply:

♦ Learning becomes an active process in which students explore and choose between various response patterns.

♦ Learning itself is intrinsically rewarding.

♦ Knowledge is the acquisition of new information while understanding is the creation of patterns.

♦ Application requires that the learners see relationships between problem situations.

♦ The students direct their own learning (*Cognito: The Cognitive Paradigm*, 1997).

"Students who know how to use effective strategies to organize and monitor learning, memory, and information retrieval can take greater responsibility for their own learning and become instrumental in adapting the learning environment to fit their individual needs and goals" (Weinstein, 1988, p. 6).

The ultimate goal of developmental education programs is to equip the students with the skills necessary to be successful.

The ultimate goal of developmental education programs is to equip the students with the skills necessary to be successful. In addition to the content area deficiencies, developmental education students seem to be particularly deficient in the metacognitive skills and strategies that are necessary not only for academic success, but also for success in the workplace. Therefore, as educators, administrators, and curriculum planners and developers, we must include both direct and indirect instruction of these skills and strategies in the instructional programs in order to facilitate greater student success at all levels.

Metacognition Defined

Metacognition spans many subareas in psychology and education and seems to mean different things to different people. Broadly defined, metacognition is the study of how people think

and control their thought processes. This can be further categorized as metacognitive monitoring and metacognitive control. Blakey and Spence (1990) define metacognition as thinking about thinking—as knowing what we know and what we don't know. They offer the analogy, "Just as an executive's job is management of an organization, a thinker's job is management of thinking" (Blakey & Spence, 1990, p. 1). This involves the metacognitive strategies of connecting new information to former knowledge, selecting thinking strategies deliberately, and planning, monitoring, and evaluating thinking processes. The concept of metacognition can be further refined by defining its various aspects, including metamemory (the knowledge about and regulation of one's memory processes), metacomprehension (the self-monitoring for comprehension), and meta-attention (the regulation and control of one's attention).

Schoenfeld (1987) notes that many of the attempts to translate metacognition into everyday language result in imprecise ballpark definitions that are not really useful in the educational arena. He suggests a working definition of metacognition should focus on three related yet distinct categories of intellectual behavior:

1. Your knowledge about your own thought processes. How accurate are you in describing your own thinking?

2. Control, or self-regulation. How well do you keep track of what you're doing when (for example) you're solving problems, and how well (if at all) do you use the input from those observations to guide your problem-solving activities?

3. Beliefs and intuitions. What ideas about mathematics do you bring to your work in mathematics, and how does that shape the way that you do mathematics? (Schoenfeld, 1987, p. 190)

Although Schoenfeld addresses mathematics specifically, these behaviors can be extended to any subject area.

Metacognition is perhaps best described by John Flavell (1976), the person most responsible for bringing the concept and its significance to the attention of educators and psychologists:

> Metacognition refers to one's knowledge concerning one's own cognitive processes and products or anything related to them, e.g., the learning-relevant properties of information or data. . . . Metacognition refers, among other things, to the active monitoring and consequent regulation and orchestration of these processes in relation to the cognitive objects on which they bear, usually in the service of some concrete goal or objective. (p. 232)

Marzano, Brandt, Hughes, Jones, Presseisen, Rankin, and Suhor (1988) put it in simpler terms, "Metacognition is being aware of our thinking as we perform specific tasks and then using this awareness to control what we are doing" (p. 9).

This description of metacognition contains two definably distinct, yet related, elements of the metacognitive processes—knowledge of one's own cognition and the regulation of one's cognitive processes. These two elements also coincide with the first two intellectual behaviors identified by Schoenfeld (1987) in his discussion of metacognition and also by Marzano et al. (1988).

Knowledge Concerning One's Cognition

The knowledge element of metacognition can be differentiated into two distinct classes: metacognitive knowledge and metacognitive experience. In addition, distinctions can be made between metacognitive and cognitive strategies (Flavell, 1981).

Metacognitive Knowledge

According to Flavell (1979), metacognitive knowledge "consists primarily of knowledge or beliefs about what factors or variables act and interact in what ways to affect the course and outcome of cognitive enterprises" (p. 907). In other words, it is what individuals know or believe (sometimes incorrectly) about their own strengths, weaknesses, and processes involved in the execution of particular cognitive tasks (i.e., "I can correctly factor any factorable quadratic expression if given enough time, because I am aware of procedures to factor such expressions" Garofalo, 1986, p. 35). Metacognitive knowledge can be further subdivided according to involvement and influence of person, task, or strategy factors on the performance of a cognitive task (Flavell & Wellman, 1977).

Metacognitive Person-Knowledge

Metacognitive person-knowledge refers to what individuals know or believe about themselves as cognitive beings (grammarian, mathematician, educator, parent, student, etc.). For example, such statements as the following are indicative of potential personal beliefs:

(a) I am sloppy in note taking; I make a lot of careless mistakes in spelling; I am better at fill-in-the-blank questions than I am at true or false questions.

(b) I am not as proficient as my classmates in analogical reasoning; I am better than most of my peers in computations.

(c) Material that I need to understand thoroughly and remember needs to be read more slowly and carefully than material I want to read strictly for enjoyment.

These types of statements would be categorized by Flavell (1981) as (a) intra-individual differences, (b) inter-individual differences, and (c) universals, respectively.

Metacognitive Task-Knowledge

This knowledge category refers to knowledge or beliefs about the parameters, relative difficulty level, conditions, and requirements of specific tasks. Knowledge concerning a particular task and predicted performance on that task are generally related to the relative difficulty level. Examples of metacognitive task-knowledge include the following statements: Some mathematics problems have more than one solution; I have more difficulty solving application types of problems than computational problems; new material on topics I am familiar with is always easier to understand than material on topics I have never studied; concise topic sentences assist me in getting the gist of the passage that I am reading; when a story is arranged in the traditional order, I can remember the order of events more accurately.

Metacognitive Strategy-Knowledge

This area not only concerns the specific content, heuristics, and control strategies necessary, but also requires knowing when and where to apply them. Such judgments require the utilization of "criteria of effectiveness" (Gall, Gall, Jacobsen, & Bullock, 1990, p. 22) to determine how well a particular learning strategy is really working. Examples of this knowledge include the following statements: When I orally rehearse and elaborate material in my own words, it aids in information processing, helps me better store material in long-term memory, and makes retrieval of information easier when I need it; utilizing the SQ4R reading method makes it easier to comprehend and remember new material; if I am having difficulty solving a problem, it sometimes helps if I first solve a simpler version of the problem; do I understand what I am reading, hearing, seeing, or doing? The responses to these types of ideas determine the effectiveness of the strategy and whether or not to continue with the selected strategy or employ an alternative approach. Unfortunately, students with a limited repertoire of study skills and learning strategies frequently continue to employ ineffective strategies because of the lack of alternatives.

It is appropriate here to mention two significant aspects of metacognitive knowledge. First of all, the previously mentioned categories are not discrete but rather are highly interactive (as can be

Unfortunately, students with a limited repertoire of study skills and learning strategies frequently continue to employ ineffective strategies because of the lack of alternatives.

seen in the above examples). The majority of metacognitive knowledge cannot be easily categorized into person-, task-, or strategy-knowledge because the interplay of two (or all three) of the categories is involved. This knowledge about cognition is prior, relatively stable, can be verbalized, is stored in long-term memory and, therefore, available for the individual to apply to the task at hand. Rather than a collection of facts, metacognitive knowledge is "an intricately interwoven system of knowledge" (Wellman, 1983, p. 32). Garner (1987) demonstrates the complexity of the fabric in the following examples:

> If I know, for instance, that inventing a topic sentence when one is not provided by the author assists me in completing a summation task, I have *task* x *strategy* [task times strategy] information. If I know that I tend to read with a global processing approach, and if I expect that the criterion task for understanding a text chapter will be a detailed-oriented test, I might decide that a note-taking or underlining strategy (emphasizing details) is in order to prepare for the test. This latter case demonstrated *person* x *task* x *strategy* information. (p. 18)

Metacognitive Experiences

On the other hand, metacognitive experiences differ from metacognitive knowledge in that they are fleeting thoughts, insights, realizations, and feelings that occur while tackling a specific cognitive task. These experiences usually concern progress toward the successful completion of the goal and are related to the student's preparation, understanding, and evaluation of the activity involved. Such metacognitive experiences occur during working memory and are generally momentary. Garofalo (1986) provides the following examples: "I don't understand what this problem is asking. I've seen problems like this before. I don't know what I am doing. This method is not helping me solve this problem" (p. 36). Although these thoughts are a separate phenomena, there is significant interplay between metacognitive knowledge and metacognitive experience. An individual's metacognitive experiences are sometimes dependent upon metacognitive knowledge, which in turn can be modified by metacognitive experiences. Garner (1987) clarifies this interaction in the following scenario:

> Assuming that [a] particular learner has some of the metacognitive person, task, and strategy variables . . . already discussed, metacognitive experiences might occur along these lines. Before beginning the reading, the learner might experience relief that the next day's class will bring a fill-in format quiz on the material, a format with which he or she is relatively comfortable. While reading, the learner might realize that verbally rehearsing dates . . . might assist in retrieval for the quiz . . . After reading the chapter, the learner might become aware of the boldface topic sentences which will make further prequiz studying fairly easy. (pp. 18-19)

In the above scenario, Garner notes that

> The before-reading knowledge tapped relates to a personal strength, the during-reading information is strategy-knowledge, and the after-reading knowledge utilized is task information. In all three cases, metacognitive knowledge has served as a base for metacognitive experiences that are perhaps best described as awarenesses, realizations, [or] 'ahas.' (p. 19)

Frequently, metacognitive experiences come into play when cognition is unsuccessful. The failure of the cognitive activity may produce a fleeting or sometimes prolonged state of confusion. Garner (1987) and Markman (1981) note that the questions "Do I understand?" or "Am I doing this correctly?" do not need to be explicitly posed in order for metacognitive experiences to occur. During the process of thinking through a task, information is gained about how successfully the process is proceeding. How the student reacts to the feelings of confusion and the direction taken in proceeding with the task are, in turn, partially de-

pendent upon the individual metacognitive knowledge base.

The Regulation of One's Cognitive Processing

According to Miner and Reder (1994), metacognitive control can be defined as the volitional direction by individuals of their own thoughts and memory retrieval. Both metacognitive knowledge and metacognitive experiences affect the way students prepare for, approach, and perform cognitive activities. Obviously, metacognitive strategy-knowledge significantly influences performance. Yet the interplay between metacognitive person-, task-, and strategy-knowledge and metacognitive experiences is much more sophisticated and complex than it may first appear. The interactions between these dimensions affect the whole of the metacognitive and cognitive processes—the decisions made in examining the following conditions of a specific task:

♦ understanding what is required,

♦ establishing an action plan to accomplish the task,

♦ selecting and organizing appropriate strategies to implement the plan,

♦ determining the amount of time to be allocated for the completion of the task,

♦ monitoring actions and progress,

♦ checking the appropriateness of results and outcomes,

♦ evaluating the effectiveness of strategies and plans,

♦ revising ineffective/inefficient plans and strategies (or perhaps abandoning them entirely to begin anew),

♦ reflecting upon decisions made and plans implemented while trying to reach a cognitive goal (Garofalo, 1986).

These actions are generally referred to as metacognitive processes; however, they are best thought of as cognitive processes enacted for metacognitive reasons (i.e., reasons derived from metacognitive knowledge, metacognitive experiences, or both).

Implication for the Classroom and Instruction: The Metacurriculum

There are many ways that awareness of metacognitive knowledge, metacognitive processes, and metacognitive experiences can increase teacher effectiveness with at-risk students who require developmental education or learning support services. The first and most inclusive is for the teacher to incorporate instruction that facilitates the development of a rich and accurate fund of metacognitive person-, task-, and strategy-knowledge. This requires the implementation of a variety of instructional strategies within the classroom. For example, questions and assignments could be devised that require the student to reflect upon personal abilities, limitations, and procedures. What do you do and what can you do to help yourself learn procedures more effectively? What are your weaknesses in this area? What do you think you can do to correct them? Questions such as these encourage students to articulate what knowledge and beliefs they do have about the task or problem at hand. In this instance the teacher would serve as a reactor and provide constructive feedback to the student (Garofalo, 1986). Following this approach, *Cognito: The Cognitive Paradigm* (1997) advocates the following teacher behaviors to promote student thinking:

♦ asking questions that demand "why" and "how" responses,

♦ emphasizing "metacognition". . .
  • identifying particular problem-solving strategies,
  • reflecting with students about their strategies,
  • reminding students to apply strategies in context,

♦ setting appropriate "disposition" for thinking in class by establishing an accepting tone during discussion,

♦ allowing students time to think and respond,

♦ seeking/encouraging multiple answers to questions,

♦ promoting inductive thinking (moving from specific data to general principles),

♦ providing summaries for students,

♦ using different "modalities" for learning,

♦ requiring/encouraging students to elaborate and refine important ideas (and make them more precise),

♦ setting expectations that all students can and will improve their cognitive functioning. (p. 8)

These suggestions are particularly cogent in light of the special needs and limited academic experience of the "typical" (if such a definition can be derived) developmental education student. In addition, the teacher should facilitate the development of metacognitive knowledge and processes through illustrating various aspects of the nature of the discipline and the tasks that affect performance on the present cognitive activity. Within mathematics, Garofalo (1986) offers such examples as: (a) mathematical procedures have rationales, and knowing the rationales can enhance student performance; and (b) not all mathematics problems can be solved by direct application of a standard procedure. Such examples illustrate the integration of explicit instruction in metacognitive skills (such as study strategies) within the context of a specific discipline. These examples negate the argument that the amount of content to be covered precludes the inclusion of such "extras." Within this framework, the instructor or facilitator should assist the student in building a repertoire of disciplinary and interdisciplinary procedures, heuristics, and control strategies in conjunction with a knowledge of their value and usefulness and with information concerning how and when to implement them.

In order to do this, the instructor needs to provide direct instruction in the utilization of such strategies, model the selection and implementation, and provide opportunities for application and practice. To ensure that students understand the metacognitive aspects of these strategies, assignments should be structured that require students to articulate the usefulness of an individual strategy, compare and contrast various strategies and their appropriateness to specific situations, explore alternative approaches to specific conditions and situations, and create questions from the text about procedures. The teacher should also provide students with guidelines and rationales for regulating and controlling their behavior during the cognitive exercises. Perhaps most importantly, the teacher should model these behaviors and strategies during actual problem solving.

A metacognitive perspective can also assist the teacher in diagnosis and intervention. Many of the learning problems and difficulties experienced by at-risk students are associated with deficiencies in metacognitive knowledge or with insufficient metacognitive processing (or both). A thorough understanding of metacognition and metacognitive skills, procedures, and processes and their influence on performance can assist the teacher in examining student errors, difficulties, and failures in a more profound way and with an eye for intervention at the root of the problem.

Many of the learning problems and difficulties experienced by at-risk students are associated with deficiencies in metacognitive knowledge or with insignificant metacognitive processing (or both).

Learning to Learn Competencies

Among the primary goals of developmental education programs is to assist students in becoming more autonomous, self-directed learners who can assume greater responsibility for their own learning. This transition from passive receptor to active participant in the teaching and learning process is fundamental to academic success in college-level course work. When compared to the traditional high school environment, a significantly greater portion of learning transpires autonomously at the college level while interacting with instructional media and resources, collaborating with peers, participating in out-of-class discussion and study groups, and engaging in individual re-

search. Passage from a teacher-directed to a student-directed learning environment is frequently traumatic for at-risk students (including nontraditional students who have been out of the formal educational environment for several years), and this passage necessitates direct intervention within developmental education and learning support programs in order to maximize student success and retention.

Weinstein (1982) identifies several basic competencies needed for effective learning (separate from content-specific competencies) which she classifies as learning-to-learn competencies. These competencies include cognitive information-processing, active study, and self-management (also known as executive control).

Information-processing. Information-processing includes techniques for organizing and elaborating incoming information into a meaningful construct. Such strategies facilitate knowledge acquisition, retention, and retrieval for later application. These techniques involve the following: relating new information to previous knowledge, creating mental images, identifying logical relationships, creating analogies, making inferences, drawing conclusions, revising schema, and relating parts to the whole. As with all instructional and learning strategies and education in general, the ultimate goal is to encourage the student to become an active participant in the learning process. The need for active involvement in the learning process is graphically illustrated by Wong (1997) in the Information Processing Model. The six components of the model (sensory input, short-term memory, rehearsal, feedback loop, long-term memory, and long-term memory retrieval) have distinctive functions in processing information; yet the components do not operate independently. Wong (1997) describes the Information Processing Model as follows:

♦ Our senses take in information, or sensory input.

♦ Our short-term memory receives the information and holds it briefly.

♦ We rehearse the information we want to learn.

♦ If we aren't retaining what we rehearse, that information goes through the feedback loop for more rehearsal.

♦ Information that is adequately rehearsed moves into our long-term memory, where it is stored more permanently.

♦ Information stored in long-term memory is accessed through long-term retrieval, and the output shows that we have learned. (p. 83)

Garner (1987) notes that typical information-processing approaches share a common emphasis on "input into and output from the human (typically adult) cognitive system" (p. 21). It is between the input and output stages of information-processing that cognitive processes act upon information. The similarity between information-processing and a computer is not coincidental. Hovland (1960) observed, "The analogy between the high speed computer and human thinking has long been noted. We frequently see the Univac, Johniacs, Illiacs referred to in the popular press as 'giant brains' or 'thinking machines'" (p. 687). In 1987 Garner noted, "computer programs that simulate human cognitive processing of complex tasks have been written as theories of the mind" (p. 21).

Active study strategies. Active study strategies involve using information-processing strategies as an integral part of an organized system of study. As has been previously noted, study skills courses are not new to the college curriculum, but have been included since the early 1920s. Because reading is a dominant activity in school, the majority of study skills courses concentrate on reading comprehension and related study strategies, such as annotating the text, note taking, outlining, and reading systems such as "Survey, Question, Read, Recite, and Review"

(SQ3R, which has now been expanded by addition of a "Record" phase to SQ4R). Associated topics frequently include time-management procedures, test-taking skills, concentration management, and vocabulary development.

Unfortunately many of these programs frequently focus on organization of the study environment and study procedures without taking into account the interactive nature of information-processing strategies with study procedures. It is important to combine information-processing strategies with traditional study procedures to create an active study strategy system. For example, an active note-taking system used in reading a text might include embellishing the notes with other information or analogies that make the content material more easily understood. While using the SQ4R reading system, the learner might elaborate and create questions for monitoring comprehension. Text marking could become an active study strategy by adding margin notes that explain the materials and integrating these with a note-taking system such as the Cornell method. By using such strategies, students become more actively involved in the learning process, activate more portals of sensory input, and rehearse new and expanded information as it is processed and organized. Emphasis on making learning meaningful is critical—the more meaningful the information, the more retrievable, durable, and generalizable it becomes. As is also indicated by the Information Processing Model (Wong, 1997), information that is processed deeply, rehearsed, and embedded in long-term memory is more retrievable than information that is only shallowly processed. Learning improves as the depth of information-processing increases. In addition, learning improves further as the relevance of the information to the instructional task increases. Learning is further improved and retrieval is facilitated when learner-generated elaborations based on personal prior knowledge and experience are associated with the incoming information. After all, learning *is* dependent on the integration of new information with prior knowledge.

Self-management/Executive control. Strategies for self-management (also known as executive control) include strategies aimed at controlling anxiety, managing time and resources, improving concentration, and boosting motivation. Executive control, according to Weinstein (1988), "refers to our capability to plan, implement, monitor, evaluate, and, if necessary, modify a cognitive course of action" (p. 4). Although many variables can and do affect student learning, the role of learners in creating and managing their own cognitive and emotional environment cannot be overemphasized.

Test anxiety (performance or evaluative anxiety), for example, is frequently defined as a behavioral reaction to stresses in the environment outside of the control of the individual learner that requires the learner to make an adjustment in behavior (Gall et al., 1990). Such stress manifests itself in the form of physical responses such as increased blood pressure, rapid heart rate, butterflies in the stomach, hyperventilation, and sweaty palms. However, this robotic view of human responses ignores the role of human cognition and thought processing in determining behavior. Usually it is not the environmental event, but the individual's perception of that event, that produces stress. Stress is increased by the perceived demand or threat in a specific situation, especially when individuals are unsure of their capacity to respond appropriately to the situation. The physical manifestations of stress, except in the most extreme cases, do not interfere with student performance on a task. The difficulty lies in the diversion of attention from studying or performing the task to dwell on the potential of failure or repercussions of poor performance (Gall et al., 1990; Weinstein, 1982, 1988; Wong, 1997). Frequently students who worry about performance on tests turn their attention inward, focusing on self-criticism, feelings of incompetence, and expectations of failure. This impedes concentration and can subsequently produce a spiral effect in which poor performance reinforces feelings of incompetence, thus intensifying anxiety and creating an unending circle and self-fulfilling prophesy of failure.

Teachers have many opportunities to teach learning competencies while simultaneously teaching the knowledge, skills, and attitudes of the content area.

Learners can implement a variety of techniques to control their own cognitive processes and redirect attention away from fears toward more positive and productive means of information processing and performance. One such activity is positive self-talk. Instead of concentrating on past failures with such comments as "I have never been able to do this; I'm too old to learn anything like this; I'll never be able to pass," a learner can monitor these thoughts and refocus attention on the task at hand through positive self-talk that puts the task and performance into proper perspective. These types of attention-directing strategies combined with information-processing and active study strategies help the learner remain focused on the task and thereby break the cycle of poor performance and confirmation of incompetence.

Time management, another element of self-management and executive control, seems to be especially difficult for at-risk student populations. Strategies for effective time management become increasingly important as a student moves from the teacher-directed to the student-directed learning environment of college courses. Students must frequently balance family and employment commitments along with those of school. Wong (1997) suggests that students strive for balance in three primary areas: school, work, and leisure. "School" includes such categories to schedule as attending class, doing homework, making study tools, and preparing for tests. "Work" involves full- or part-time employment, active parenting, household duties, and errands. (Not included in this area by Wong, but relevant in light of national emphasis on "volunteerism," is community service.) It is also appropriate to note at this point that "working" is not limited to those types of activities from which income is derived, but also includes all activities associated with managing a household and caring for a family. "Leisure" includes spending quality time with family and friends, hobbies, recreational activities, and personal time. Although

Wong (1997) advocates balance, she does not suggest that an equal amount of time will or should be spent in each area. "It is not likely (or desirable) that your 'life's pie' will be divided into three equal sections. How the pie is 'sliced' will differ from one person to another" (p. 30). Division of an individual's personal "pie" is dependent upon the goals, requirements, and interests. A proper balancing act will result in feelings of confidence, satisfaction, fulfillment, happiness, and control (Wong, 1997).

Implementing the Metacurriculum

The challenge at this point for all educators, but especially for those involved with at-risk students, is to include both direct and indirect instruction in these strategies and competencies. Because these can be thought of as prerequisites for academic success, inclusion in the curriculum is not only justified but imperative in order to meet the goals of the educational process. According to Weinstein (1982), converting teaching strategies to include a metacurriculum of learning strategies involves making effective teaching procedures more explicit and incorporating discussions and examples of learning competencies not previously included. Teachers have many opportunities to teach learning competencies while simultaneously teaching the knowledge, skills, and attitudes of the content area. In fact, it is virtually impossible to separate effective teaching strategies from effective learning strategies in a didactic interaction, since many teaching strategies are the flip-side of learning strategies.

> By using instructional methods that demonstrate, cue, and reinforce the use of learning strategies, college teachers can implement a learning strategies curriculum. It is a metacurriculum in the sense that it requires an analysis of the regular course curriculum and the learning demands it places on students. (Weinstein, 1982, p. 92)

The instructor who offers a variety of examples of a particular principle to a class is trying to connect with the students' various experiential backgrounds. The instructor who creates an analogy that relates the topic under study to an everyday phenomenon is facilitating the integration of new information with established cognitive constructs. The topics of scheduling, goal setting, and time management could easily be introduced by an instructor when giving a long-term assignment. Test anxiety and the effects of the fear of failure on performance and how to control and overcome these could be introduced when the first class examination is announced. Such teaching and learning devices can be easily included in the metacurriculum by simply making the techniques explicit. Instead of merely presenting a technique and then continuing with the content topic, the teacher can make the instruction explicit by drawing attention to the method, why it is effective in learning new information, and how the technique can be used individually or in conjunction with other strategies and methods while studying. A single experience clearly would be insufficient for most students to develop competence in a particular learning strategy. However, repeated exposure to a strategy in a variety of contexts and in conjunction with prompting and corrective feedback would facilitate development of the technique as an effective learning tool (Weinstein, 1982). These are but a few illustrations of the innumerable opportunities in the classroom for teaching learning competencies while presenting content material and explaining course requirements.

A Final Note

At-risk students are predictably deficient in metacognitive skills and strategies, and therefore benefit significantly from both informal and formal instruction in this area. Resistance by instructional faculty to the imposition of additional curricular demands, such as the inclusion of learning competencies metacurriculum, is often based on their perceptions of the time such additional requirements take away from the regular course content. Although it may appear initially that the inclusion of metacurriculum strategies in an explicit teaching situation is time consuming at both the planning and instructional stages, it should be recognized that not all such instruction needs to be formally planned. In most instructional situations, a significant portion of class time is spent in discussion and in responding to student questions. Such natural didactic interactions can be effectively (and painlessly) used to introduce, elaborate, and reinforce metacognitive strategies. Because it is presented in conjunction with the subject area material under study, the actual class time dedicated to the explicit instruction of metacognitive skills and strategies is virtually imperceptible. Although it is true that a portion of the instructional time will be diverted from content-based instruction, it is also true that the teaching of metacognitive competencies will improve students' abilities to benefit from all instruction. Therefore, the time spent to present the learning competencies metacurriculum is a general educational investment that can yield increased learning effectiveness and efficiency throughout the educational process.

References

Blakey, E., & Spence, S. (1990). *Developing metacognition*. [On-line]. Available: metacog.dig@www.valdosta.peachnet.edu.

Cognito: The cognitive paradigm. (1997). [On-line]. Available: http://www.edu.drake.ed.../cognitive_paradigm.html.

Flavell, J. H. (1976). Metacognitive aspects of problem solving. In L. Resnick (Ed.), *The nature of intelligence* (pp. 231-236). Hillsdale, NJ: Lawrence Erlbaum.

Flavell, J. H. (1979). Metacognition and cognitive monitoring: A new area of cognitive-developmental-inquiry. *American Psychologist, 34*, 906-911.

Flavell, J. H. (1981). Cognitive monitoring. In W. P. Dickson (Ed.), *Children's oral communication skills* (pp. 35-60). New York: Academic Press.

Flavell, J. H., & Wellman, H. M. (1977). Metamemory. In R. V. Kail & J. W. Hagen (Eds.), *Perspectives on the development of memory and cognition* (pp. 3-33). Hillsdale, NJ: Lawrence Erlbaum.

Gall, M. D., Gall, J. P., Jacobsen, D. R., & Bullock, T. L. (1990). *Tools for learning*. Alexandria, VA: Association for Supervision and Curriculum Development.

Garner, R. (1987). *Metacognition and reading comprehension*. Norwood, NJ: Ablex.

Garofalo, J. (1986). Metacognitive knowledge and metacognitive process: Important influences on mathematical performance. *Research & Teaching in Developmental Education, 2*(2), 34-39.

Hovland, C. I. (1960). Computer simulation of thinking. *American Psychologist, 15,* 687-693.

Markman, E. M. (1981). Comprehension monitoring. In W. P. Dickson (Ed.), *Children's oral communication skills* (pp. 61-84). New York: Academic Press.

Marzano, R. J., Brandt, R. S., Hughes, C. S., Jones, B. F., Presseisen, B. Z., Rankin, S. C., & Suhor, C. (1988). *Dimensions of thinking: A framework for curriculum and instruction*. Alexandria, VA: Association for Supervision and Curriculum Development.

Miner, A. C., & Reder, L. M. (1994). A new look at feeling of knowing: Its metacognitive role in regulating question answering. In J. Metcalfe & A. P. Shimamura (Eds.), *Metacognition: Knowing about knowing*. Cambridge, MA: MIT Press.

Schoenfeld, A. H. (1987). What's all the fuss about metacognition? In A. H. Schoenfeld (Ed.), *Cognitive science and mathematics education* (pp. 189-215). Hillsdale, NJ: Lawrence Erlbaum.

Weinstein, C. E. (1982). A metacurriculum for remediating deficits in learning strategies of academically underprepared students. In L. Noel & R. Levitz (Eds.), *How to succeed with academically underprepared students: A catalog of successful practices* (pp. 91-93). Iowa City, IA: The American College Testing Program.

Weinstein, C. E. (1988). Executive control process in learning: Why knowing about how to learn is not enough. *Journal of Developmental Education, 12*(2), 1-4.

Wellman, H. M. (1983). Metamemory revisited. In M. T. H. Chi (Ed.), *Trends in memory development research* (pp. 31-51). Basel, Switzerland: Karger.

Wong, L. (1997). *Essential study skills*. Princeton, NJ: Houghton Mifflin.

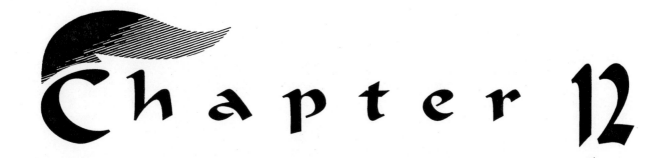

Chapter 12

STUDENT BELIEFS, LEARNING THEORIES, AND DEVELOPMENTAL MATHEMATICS: NEW CHALLENGES IN PREPARING SUCCESSFUL COLLEGE STUDENTS

Irene Mary Duranczyk and Joanne Caniglia

Traditional-age students entering developmental mathematics come with exposure to reform-based mathematics, and more specifically, approaches following the standards given by the National Council of Teachers of Mathematics (1989). Non-traditional-age students (i.e., those who do not enter college right out of high school) begin developmental mathematics with a history of using one or more of the following curricular methods: modern math, spiral learning, mastery-based learning, or "Back-to-Basics." Upon completing developmental mathematics, many college students encounter reform-based mathematics (standards set by the American Mathematics Association of Two-Year Colleges and by the Mathematics Association of America exemplified by the Harvard series). Can a traditional-age classroom or lab-based developmental program adequately prepare students for the challenges they will face? Can students from such diverse backgrounds become successful at college mathematics?

Research on the goals of reform mathematics (Simon, 1995), theories of teaching (Clements & Battista, 1990; Koch, 1992; Narode, 1989; Selden & Selden, 1990), and developmental mathematics students' beliefs about mathematics (e.g., Schoenfeld, 1989; Zahorik, 1995) form the foundation for the current study. In these findings there are areas of compatibility and seamless transition. Some of these findings, however, create new challenges for developmental educators.

123

What are the implications for curriculum development based on students' beliefs and learning theories? What types of programs provide the best transition and take students from being developmental learners to successful college students?

Preparing successful college mathematics students embodies two major goals. First, students need to develop mathematical structures that are more complex, abstract, and powerful than the ones they already possess so that they are increasingly capable of solving a wide variety of meaningful problems. Second, students need to become autonomous and self-motivated in their mathematical activity (Cobb, 1988). Within this framework, developmental students can be successful in college programs involving mathematics and in real-life experiences beyond the classroom.

Review of the Literature

Schoenfeld (1989) found that students' beliefs about mathematics as well as their beliefs about the learning and teaching process play a significant role in shaping their behavior. Evidence that this is an important research finding can be found in four empirical sources: studies of student belief systems on learning and success, tenets of major learning theories, designs of developmental mathematics programs, and reform mathematics initiatives.

Impact of Student Belief Systems on Learning and Success

Although the topic of student participation in developmental mathematics has received attention in higher education research, few studies examine the phenomena of learning theories and student beliefs. Much of the groundbreaking research on student beliefs has been with kindergarten through 12th-grade (K-12) students and has been done in relationship to student success, with exit grades providing the measure of achievement. Recent studies in de-

velopmental mathematics education (Elliott, 1990; Hackett, 1985; Mau, 1991; McLeod, 1992; Nickson, 1992; Stage & Kloosterman, 1995; Stage & McCafferty, 1992) address the unique needs of adult learners. These studies examine issues of gender, beliefs, classroom environment, and their effect on achievement. Unfortunately, an analysis of the relationship between developmental students' beliefs and operative learning theories or instructional design has not been attempted.

Randall and Silver (1988) noted that "beliefs about mathematics" were an underrepresented theme in research on how students learn mathematical problem solving. Since then, the topic of beliefs has become a familiar area of research. Researchers hypothesized that beliefs might explain gender differences in mathematics achievement because beliefs appear to have a substantial impact on behaviors of students as well as teachers. Exploratory studies of the relationship between remedial college-level students' beliefs and achievement found that men and women did not differ significantly in their beliefs, but that beliefs were more strongly linked to course grades for women than they were for men (Randall & Silver, 1988).

Schoenfeld (1989) found that students' beliefs about mathematics as well as their beliefs about the learning process play a significant role in shaping their behavior.

Tenets of Major Learning Theories

Fifty-seven percent of developmental students have learned mathematics over a span of 15 to 20 years (Institute, 1993). Consequently, these students have been exposed to radical changes in mathematics education. This suggests the potential for wide variations in developmental students' experiences and views of mathematics. By examining the tenets of behaviorism and constructivism and the part they play in mathematics education, potential differences in students' beliefs will become more clear. Characteristics of these theories are summarized in Appendix A.

Behaviorism was the dominant learning theory for the first part of the 20th century. School mathematics was seen as a hierarchy of skills that required students to compute with accuracy and speed (Resnick & Ford, 1981). Teachers were perceived as transmitters of information who sought correct answers to validate student learning. Curriculum often was presented in isolated parts. Lower level skills were emphasized before more complex problems were introduced.

While behaviorism emphasized the learning of isolated facts and procedures, the New Math movement of the 1960s stressed a different approach. In response to post-Sputnik concern, university mathematicians reorganized the content of school mathematics into interconnected structures. Rigor was essential in understanding the logic of mathematics for students of all ages. The New Math was not only a disappointment to teachers but also to a public that demanded greater accountability, a desire which inspired renewed interest in measuring specific learning outcomes. The Back-to-Basics movement of the 1970s was in large part responsible for states mandating competency or proficiency testing. The demise of the movement was due in large part to reports from the National Assessment of Educational Progress (Carpenter, Kouba, Brown, Linquist, Silver, & Swafford, 1988) documenting students' poor performance in problem solving.

Interconnections among mathematical sciences and the pervasive presence of technology have changed mathematics education once again. Constructivist learning theory helps learners focus on what they currently know, be receptive to new information, and fit the new information into their current knowledge structures (Zahorik, 1995). Within this theory, mathematics is viewed as a human construction based on observation and reflection (National Council of Teachers of Mathematics, 1989).

Designs of Developmental Mathematics Programs

Twenty-four percent of all entering college freshmen need developmental mathematics before they can successfully complete a college-level mathematics course or a college-level course that demands mathematical reasoning or computation (Lewis & Farris, 1996). Studies

have shown that after completing up to one year of developmental mathematics, college persistence rates for developmental students approach those of all college students (Lewis & Farris, 1996).

The Institute for Research on Higher Education (1993) reports that only 43% of all undergraduates at four-year colleges attending full-time are young adults (under age 25). This percentage is even lower at two-year institutions. Women now make up at least 55% of undergraduate students. Older students, part-timers, and two-year collegians are higher education's new majority.

Schroeder (1993) identified learning characteristics of this new college student majority. Sixty percent of entering students preferred the sensing mode of perceiving information compared to 40% who prefer the intuitive mode.

> In general, students who prefer sensing learning patterns prefer the concrete, the practical, and the immediate. These students lack confidence in their intellectual abilities and are uncomfortable with abstract ideas. They have difficulty with complex concepts and low tolerance for ambiguity. Furthermore, they are often less independent in thought and judgment and more dependent on the ideas of those in authority. They are also more dependent on immediate gratification. (Schroeder, 1993, p. 22, 24)

Developmental mathematics programs offer two major delivery systems: direct classroom instruction and individualized instruction in learning or tutorial centers. Many programs combine instructional strategies within these frameworks. In Michigan, a study of two-year college developmental programs indicates that 69% use individualized instruction (Michigan State Board of Education, 1990). National statistics indicate that 70% of all higher education institutions offer remedial courses through the mathematics departments (Lewis & Farris, 1996).

Reform Mathematics Initiatives

Constructivism has not only affected K-12 teaching and learning, but under a National Science

Foundation grant, faculty at Harvard and other higher education institutions have redesigned calculus courses emphasizing a balanced approach to the teaching of new topics. One of the guiding principles is the "Rule of Three," (Hughes-Hallett, Gleason, Flath, Gordon, Lomen, Lovelock, McCallum, Osgood, Pasquale, Tecoksy-Feldman, Thrash, Tucker, & Bretscher, 1994) which states that wherever possible topics should be approached graphically, numerically, and analytically. Conceptual understanding underlying such a curriculum is difficult for students to grasp, especially if their background has exclusively emphasized procedural skills (Hughes-Hallett et al., 1994). The significant shift in approach emphasizes the interpretation of results as well as computational skill in order to engage students in thinking about what they are actually doing.

Research Questions

Are developmental students' backgrounds and their belief systems related? Which learning theories are compatible with developmental students' belief systems? What are the curricular implications for linking developmental students' beliefs with learning theories and college-level reform mathematics? These questions have guided this research. As developmental mathematics faculty and staff come to understand the beliefs and attitudes of students, higher education practitioners can make significant changes to enhance the learning experiences of at-risk students and end the cycle of underprepared college students.

Method

Sample

This study was conducted at a multipurpose public university in the Midwest, serving both full-time and part-time students representative of the national trend of older adults returning to complete their college education. Women comprised almost 60% of the student body.

This study surveyed all students who enrolled in a pre-algebra course during the winter, spring, or summer sessions, a population of 164 students (seven sections). From this group 112 students participated and 109 surveys were usable. The population generally reflected the university profile with 68.5% female students ($n = 75$) and 65.1% traditional-age students (under 24 years old) ($n = 71$).

Course

The pre-algebra course carried no credit but was required for these students because of their deficiencies determined by a computerized placement test. Topics of the course included a review of basic arithmetic skills and geometry in a pre-algebra format. Each class section contained approximately 25 students and was taught by a full-time faculty member with at least a master's degree and three years of developmental teaching experience. The syllabi, texts, tests, and grading were uniform across all sections.

Procedures

After a brief description of the purpose of this research, a six-page survey form was distributed to each student in all sections of developmental pre-algebra. Students were told that their involvement was optional, but greatly appreciated. Surveys turned in without signed consent forms were excluded from the study. Most surveys were filled out in class and returned immediately, taking approximately 20 minutes. Students were allowed to take the forms home, fill them out, and return them the next day. After coding the consent forms and survey forms, the consent forms were detached.

Instrumentation

The survey containing 52 closed (four-point Likert Scale) and nine open-ended questions was adapted from a questionnaire created by Schoenfeld (1989). Multiple-choice questions referred to attributions of success or failure, students' perceptions of mathematics, their views of teaching and learning processes, as well as personal performance and motivation. The open-ended questions were designed to give students the opportunity to clarify their beliefs.

Analysis

The initial analysis consisted of grouping 45 of the 52 items into four categories: causal attribution (nine items), beliefs about mathematics teaching (two items), beliefs about mathematics learning (26 items), and perceived usefulness of mathematics (eight items). Answers consistent with constructivist beliefs were recoded high on all items before analyzing the group data. To determine group differences in developmental students' perceptions of mathematics, a two-way analysis of variance (ANOVA) was performed on students by age and gender using the Statistical Package for the Social Sciences (SPSS) (1996) computer program. The data analyzed were nonparametric due to the limited range of responses (only four discrete choices) in the Likert Scale. Therefore, the Kruskal-Wallis ANOVA method was used. Because of multiple conditions of interaction between the groups, a Kruskal-Wallis one-way ANOVA was then performed with independent group categories: traditional-age male, traditional-age female, nontraditional-age male (24 years old or older), and nontraditional-age female. A Kruskal-Wallis one-way ANOVA and, when applicable, subsequent multiple comparison tests were performed on each of the 45 questions and the four groupings of questions as identified above.

Results

Causal Attribution

Table 1 shows the means for three survey questions on attributions of success/failure in math. Table 2 shows the Analysis of Variance (ANOVA) of these data by age and sex. As Table 1 shows, most students in the survey attribute success or failure to effort as indicated by the responses to A.1 and B.6 (Table 1). Only when looking at question 17 (Table 1) does one see a different attribution—innate ability—which is consistent with Stevenson, Lee, and Stigler's (1986) and Schoenfeld's (1989) finding that American students attribute success to native ability (as compared to Asian students).

Kruskal-Wallis one-way ANOVA results (Table 2) indicate no statistically significant difference

Table 1
Mean Scores for the Three Survey Questions on Casual Attribution

Items	Mean	Standard Deviation
Range: 1 = very true, 2 = sort of true, 3 = not very true, and 4 = not at all true		
A. When I get a good grade in math . . .		
1) . . . it's because I work hard.	1.28*	.51
2) . . . it's because the teacher likes me.	3.43	.74
3) . . . it's just a matter of luck.	3.28	.84
4) . . . I never know how it happens.	3.44	.86
5) . . . it's because I am always good at math.	3.17	.85
B. When I get a bad grade in math . . .		
6) . . . it's because I don't study hard enough.	1.86*	.96
7) . . . it's because the teacher doesn't like me.	3.69	.56
8) . . . it's just bad luck.	3.53	.74
Range: 1 = strongly agree, 2 = agree, 3 = disagree, and 4 = strongly disagree		
Item #17. Some people are good at math and some are not.	1.58	.66

*Items recoded during the next phase of analysis so that a rating of "4" would be consistent with constructivist beliefs.

Table 2

One-Way ANOVA Scores for the Compilation of the Three Survey Questions on Casual Attribution

| | Mean Rank | |
	Nontraditional-Age	Traditional-Age
Female	63.04	53.58
Male	60.05	42.02

Note. Kruskal-Wallis one-way ANOVA $\chi^2(3, N = 107) = 6.08$, not significant.

between Mean Ranks on the compilation of questions regarding causal attribution. The Kruskal-Wallis test uses a chi-square analysis to determine significant differences between the expected versus the actual Mean Ranks (i.e., not between the actual group means.) Therefore, a chi square of 6.08 with three degrees of freedom and a population of 107 as shown in Table 2 is not significant.

Examining the individual questionnaire items in Table 3, there is a significant difference between nontraditional-age females and each of the other groups for the item that asks "When I get a good grade in math it's because the teacher likes me." As indicated in Table 3, traditional-age males attribute good grades to "it's because the teacher likes me" more than any other group.

Beliefs about Mathematics Teaching

Two items in the survey highlight students' opinions about the role of a good instructor in mathematics (see Table 4). Students' responses,

as indicated in Table 4, seem contradictory. Students tend to agree strongly that good mathematics teachers show students many different ways to look at the same question. Although students may not strongly agree, they do at least tend to agree that good mathematics teachers show the exact way to answer the mathematics test questions.

Viewing the same data by traditional-age, nontraditional-age male and female groupings, as shown in Table 5, reveals a statistically significant difference between nontraditional-age males and traditional-age females, and also between nontraditional-age males and nontraditional-age females. Both traditional-age and nontraditional-age females' beliefs are more consistent with constructivist tenets.

See Table 6 for the Kruskal-Wallis one-way ANOVA results by individual items: Item #19 shows a significant difference between nontraditional-age females' beliefs in good mathematics teachers showing "many ways to look at the

Table 3

One-Way ANOVA Results for Individual Survey Questions: Casual Attribution

Item #A2: When I get a good grade in math . . . it's because the teacher likes me.		
Range: 1 = very true, 2 = sort of true, 3 = not very true, 4 = not at all true		
	Mean Rank	
	Nontraditional-Age	Traditional-Age
Female	69.93	52.96
Male	49.60	41.74

Note. There is a significant difference between nontraditional-age females and each of the other groups (nontraditional-age males, traditional-age females, and traditional-age males). Kruskal-Wallis one-way ANOVA $\chi^2(3, N = 107) = 10.73$, $p < .01$

Table 4

Mean Scores for Beliefs about Mathematics Teaching Survey Questions

Items	Mean	Standard Deviation
Range: 1 = strongly agree, 2 = agree, 3 = disagree, and 4 = strongly disagree		
Item #19. Good mathematics teachers show students many different ways to look at the same question.	1.44*	.57
Item #20. Good mathematics teachers show you the exact way to answer the math questions on which you'll be tested.	2.18	.81

*Item recoded during the next phase of analysis so that a rating of "4" would be consistent with constructivist beliefs.

same question" and traditional-age students; Item #20 shows a significant difference between traditional-age females' beliefs about good mathematics teachers not showing "you the exact way to answer the math questions you'll be tested on" and each of the other groups—nontraditional-age males, traditional-age males, and nontraditional-age females.

Beliefs about Mathematics Learning

In the cluster of responses about mathematics learning, the quantitative and qualitative data are consistent. Qualitative data were obtained through open-ended Items #53 through #59 listed in Appendix B. Each of these questions required students to reflect on: (a) processes that mathematicians use to solve problems, (b) connections among mathematics courses, (c) purposes of memorization, (d) steps students take during an impasse in problem solving, and (e) operations of metacognition. Students believe that mathematics is best learned in groups, by memorizing formulas and rules with little inte-

gration to other subjects and real life. They believe that mathematics must be presented before it is understood, with answers that are either correct or incorrect and "checked" against external references. Qualitative analysis not only highlights students responses but adds clarity to quantitative data in Table 7. Although the compiled quantitative data in Table 8 do not show significant differences between the groups, Item #28 ("Real math problems can be solved by common sense instead of math rules you learn in class") in Table 9 indicates a significant difference between traditional-age males and the following groups: nontraditional-age females and traditional-age females.

Working cooperatively. The responses to "Do you think mathematicians work alone on problems or together?" point not only to the processes of learning mathematics, but also to students' motivation. Over 50% of each student group believes that mathematicians work together (see Figure 1); yet a significant number of students viewed small group work primarily as a means

Table 5

One-Way ANOVA Scores for the Compilation of Belief about Mathematics Teaching Survey Questions

	Mean Rank	
	Nontraditional-Age	Traditional-Age
Female	59.28	59.38
Male	42.50	41.02

Note. There is a significant difference between nontraditional-age males and each of the following groups: nontraditional-age females and traditional-age females. Kruskal-Wallis one-way ANOVA $\chi^2(3, N = 107) = 8.17, p < .05$

of checking their answers. Nontraditional-age females most frequently state that their motivation for working together was to gain multiple perspectives in problem solving.

Memorization and creativity. Overall the majority of students believe that memorization is essential to knowing mathematics. Many of these students seem to envision a dualistic notion toward memorization. While some realize that memorization is important, conceptual understanding is also essential. Another group (approximately 75%) insists that memorization will help on tests and in future life. Student responses to the value of memorization seem contradictory when compared with their beliefs that mathematics is a creative process. The contradiction becomes less obvious if one considers that the students' level of creativity refers to everyday mathematics. One can create mathematics in the real world. The following statements

reflect the majority of students' beliefs about whether mathematics can be discovered or must be shown: "Students can discover mathematics on their own in everyday life, like with their checkbook, buying different products, etc." and "Yes, math can be discovered by using it in cooking, converting recipes, banking, making a budget." Examining the quantitative data gives further evidence of students' beliefs that school mathematics is different from real-life mathematics. Table 9 highlights significant differences between the groups for "Real math problems can be solved by common sense instead of math rules you learn in class." Traditional-age males tend to be more behavioral in their response than any of the other groupings.

Connections. A major difference exists between traditional-age and nontraditional-age students in how they view mathematics coursework. Traditional-age students see mathematics

Table 6
One-Way ANOVA Results for Individual Survey Questions: Beliefs about Mathematics Teaching

Item #19. Good mathematics teachers show students many different ways to look at the same question.

Range: 1 = strongly disagree, 2 = disagree, 3 = agree, and 4 = strongly agree

	Mean Rank	
	Nontraditional-Age	Traditional-Age
Female	65.95	52.07
Male	47.60	46.43

Note. There is a significant difference between nontraditional-age females and each of the following groups: traditional-age females and traditional-age males. Kruskal-Wallis one-way ANOVA $\chi^2(3, N = 107) = 8.04$, $p < .05$

∙∙

Item #20. Good mathematics teachers show you the exact way to answer the math questions you'll be tested on.

Range: 1 = strongly agree, 2 = agree, 3 = disagree, and 4 = strongly disagree

	Mean Rank	
	Nontraditional-Age	Traditional-Age
Female	53.76	63.03
Male	43.60	42.30

Note. There is a significant difference between traditional-age females and each of the other groups (nontraditional-age males, traditional-age males, and nontraditional-age females) using the Kruskal-Wallis one-way ANOVA $\chi^2(3, N = 108) = 9.53$, $p < .05$.

Table 7
Mean Scores for Survey Items on Beliefs about Learning Mathematics

Items	Mean	Standard Deviation
Range: 1 = very true, 2 = sort of true, 3 = not very true, and 4 = not at all true		
C. The math that I learn in school is . . .		
10) . . . mostly facts and procedures that have to be memorized.	1.96	.83
11) . . . thought provoking.	2.08*	.86
12) . . . just a way of thinking about space, numbers, and problems.	2.23*	.71
Range: 1 = always, 2 = usually, 3 = occasionally, and 4 = never		
13) You have to remember the right answer to answer it correctly.	2.49	.96
14) There are many possible right answers you might give.	2.66*	.76
15) You have to think very hard to answer it.	2.37*	.76
16) Students who understand only need a few seconds to answer correctly.	2.04	.80
Range: 1 = strongly agree, 2 = agree, 3 = disagree, 4 = strongly disagree		
18) In mathematics something is either right or it's wrong.	1.83	.70
25) Everything important about math is already known by mathematicians.	2.77	.88
26) In mathematics you can be creative and discover things by yourself.	2.20*	.83
27) Math problems can be done correctly in only one way.	3.03	.77
28) Real math problems can be solved by common sense instead of math rules you learn in class.	2.67*	.88
29) The best way to do well in math is to memorize all the formulas.	2.40	.90
30) To solve math problems you have to be taught the right procedure, or you can't do anything.	2.06	.82
E. When you get the wrong answer to a math problem . . .		
31) . . . it is absolutely wrong. There's no room for argument.	2.50	.78
32) . . . you only find out when it's different from the book's answer or when the teacher tells you.	2.36	.77

*Item recoded during the next phase of analysis so that a rating of "4" would be consistent with constructivist beliefs.

Table 8
One-Way ANOVA Scores for the Compilation of Survey Items on Beliefs about Learning Mathematics

	Mean Rank	
	Nontraditional-Age	Traditional-Age
Female	50.67	53.45
Male	48.85	51.95

Note. Kruskal-Wallis one-way ANOVA $\chi^2(3, N = 103) = .2736$ finds no significant difference between groups.

courses as connected while nontraditional-age students cite their time away from school as the primary reason for seeing no relationships among topics. Although many traditional-age students found relationships among classes, they see mathematics as a series of building blocks. To many students, mathematics is like a "road race in stages, from preschool to university." Comments also indicated that students define mathematics as numbers, variables, or formulas and rules. The fewer the number of courses in the students' background, the narrower the view of mathematics.

Autonomy. Two questions referred to students' level of autonomy and level of confidence. The first asked what students do when they get "stuck." Students across all categories ask someone for help or depend on the textbook when they are confused. These results coincide with the responses to the second question pertaining to autonomy, "How do you know you are correct?" In a cross match, students who re-

ported they would seek assistance or who dropped the problem (not to come back) were the same students using external measures to insure that they knew they were correct. Students who utilized problem-solving strategies also used internal measures to determine their level of understanding.

Perceived Usefulness of Mathematics

Students believe most strongly that the primary reasons to learn mathematics are: It is required for their program, and they want to do well in the course. These two answers in Table 10 represent a continuum of responses between external and internal motivation. As indicated in Table 10, students did not strongly agree with the response, "to help me think more clearly," another internal motivation question.

No significant difference exists between the groups with respect to the cluster of questions

Table 9
One-Way ANOVA Results for Individual Survey Item on Beliefs about Learning Mathematics

Item #28: Real math problems can be solved by common sense instead of math rules you learn in class.

Range: 1 = strongly disagree, 2 = disagree, 3 = agree, 4 = strongly agree

	Mean Rank	
	Nontraditional-Age	Traditional-Age
Female	61.75	68.70
Male	56.61	35.39

Note. There is a significant difference between traditional-age males and the following: nontraditional-age females and traditional-age females. Kruskal-Wallis one-way ANOVA $\chi^2(3, N = 108) = 14.40, p < .01$

measuring the perceived usefulness of mathematics. The group that seems to deviate the most in Table 11 is nontraditional-age females, but this finding is not significantly different. It is only when looking at the one-way ANOVA results of the individual questions that a significant difference between the groups arose. Nontraditional-age females in Table 12 significantly differ from traditional-age females on Item #37, "The reason I try to learn mathematics is . . . it's interesting." On Item #41, "The reason I try to learn mathematics is . . . to make the teacher think I'm a good student," nontraditional-age females differ from each of the other groups.

Discussion

The data presented in the previous sections reveal some general conclusions regarding developmental students' beliefs toward mathematics and how these beliefs interrelate with reform-based college classes. Both data sources, survey and open-ended questions, suggest commonalties that enable fairly definitive statements regarding the beliefs of developmental mathematics students. These commonalties became clear through grouping students into four categories: nontraditional-age females, nontraditional-age males, traditional-age females, and traditional-age males.

Students in general attribute success and failure in mathematics to internal factors such as effort and hard work. They do not believe that failure is "just bad luck" nor do they base their failure on teachers' likes or dislikes. Although most students believe that mathematicians work together, they also believe that cooperative learning's primary function is to correct one another's mistakes. Beyond these statements, student responses adhere to behaviorist theories of learning (see Appendix A).

According to developmental mathematics students in this study, memorization of formulas, rules, and procedures is a necessary ingredient to understanding. They consider instruction effective when it is clear and direct. Although it may be essential to offer explanations, students believe teachers are disseminators of content. They consider answers in mathematics as either right or wrong. Evidence that students depend on external validation is found in their beliefs that when they are stuck (while working on a problem), they most frequently ask for help and rely on tests and grades to determine if they

Table 10
Mean Scores for Items about Perceived Usefulness of Mathematics Survey

Items	Mean	Standard Deviation
Range: 1 = strongly agree, 2 = agree, 3 = disagree, and 4 = strongly disagree		
F. The reason I try to learn mathematics is . . .		
34) . . . to help me think more clearly.	2.70*	.86
35) . . . it's required for my program.	1.58	.74
36) . . . I want to do well in the course.	1.49	.57
37) . . . it's interesting.	2.42*	1.00
38) . . . I'll get in trouble if I don't.	3.04	.97
39) . . . I feel stupid if I don't understand something.	2.33	.95
40) . . . I don't want to look dumb.	2.44	.98
41) . . . to make the teacher think I'm a good student.	3.06	.83

*Items recoded during the next phase of analysis so that a rating of "4" would be consistent with constructivist beliefs.

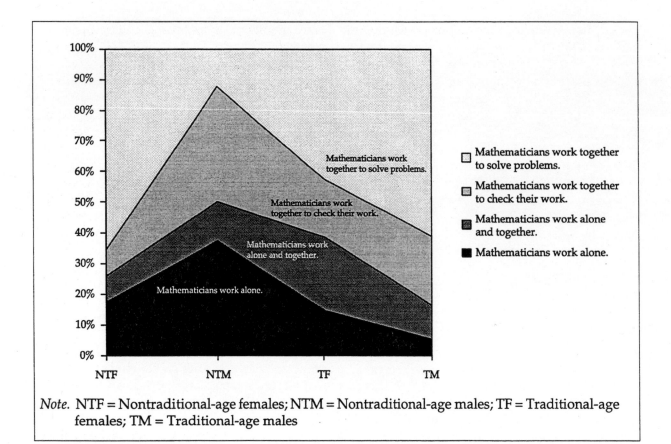

Note. NTF = Nontraditional-age females; NTM = Nontraditional-age males; TF = Traditional-age females; TM = Traditional-age males

Figure 1. Example matrix for summarizing student responses: Do you think mathematicians work alone on problems or together?

know mathematics. These findings are consistent with Schoenfeld's (1989) work with high school geometry students.

In addition to these more general conclusions, the results of this study indicate that categorizing students by gender and age offers helpful information. Nontraditional-age female students' beliefs are most often consistent with constructivist theory. They realize the impor-

tance of understanding and making connections in learning. Small group work for these students provides opportunities for sharing different facets of problem solving versus "checking for mistakes." The following response from a nontraditional-age female student illustrates this point:

> I imagine they (mathematicians) would work together because maybe another

Table 11
One-Way ANOVA Scores for Items on Perceived Usefulness of Mathematics Survey

	Mean Rank	
	Nontraditional-Age	Traditional-Age
Female	64.81	49.53
Male	48.25	55.48

Note. Kruskal-Wallis one-way ANOVA $\chi^2(3, N = 108) = 4.59$

person could bring out another aspect of the problem. A different way to solve it might be presented and dissected by several people. Putting thoughts together leads to better solutions and problem solving.

In other questions as well, nontraditional-age female students respond in ways that express interdependence and creativity in formulating solutions. Finding connections between mathematics courses was difficult for this group because of the years away from academic course work. Nontraditional-age male students were also consistent; they adhere to behaviorist views as shown in Appendix A. They believe that (a) working alone is more beneficial than together, (b) seeking assistance from authority is better than using problem-solving strategies, (c) showing solutions is better than constructing knowledge, and (d) using procedural knowledge (memorization) to the exclusion of concepts is essential.

While, overall, nontraditional-age female and male students were consistent in their beliefs,

other clusters of students espoused dualistic viewpoints. Traditional-age males envisioned that understanding was important (versus memorization) and found many interconnections within mathematics courses, yet they believed that mathematics must be shown (versus created). Female traditional-age students often comment on mathematics as two separate disciplines. There is the mathematics that can be used in everyday life and another mathematics that is taught in the classroom: "Learning math will not help me in my career. I only need it for my basic studies requirement. I will use very little of this knowledge."

The qualitative data of this study reveal that developmental students' difficulties are attributed to histories of negative mathematical experiences with poorly qualified teachers. These teachers fail to instill in their students a proper conceptual understanding of the benefits of mathematics. Many developmental students will choose to become teachers themselves and further perpetuate this negative cycle. Ball's (1990) findings confirm that prospective teachers

Table 12
One-Way ANOVA Results for Individual Survey Item on Perceived Usefulness of Mathematics

F37. The reason I try to learn mathematics is . . . it's interesting.

Range: 1 = strongly disagree, 2 = disagree, 3 = agree, 4 = strongly agree

	Mean Rank	
	Nontraditional-Age	Traditional-Age
Female	66.37	45.48
Male	58.35	57.72

Note. There is a significant difference between traditional-age females and each of the other three groups. Kruskal-Wallis one-way ANOVA $\chi^2(3, N = 108) = 9.05, p < .05$

F41. The reason I try to learn mathematics is . . . to make the teacher think I'm a good student.

Range: 1 = strongly agree, 2 = agree, 3 = disagree, 4 = strongly disagree

	Mean Rank	
	Nontraditional-Age	Traditional-Age
Female	67.81	41.95
Male	52.27	48.98

Note. There is a significant difference between nontraditional-age females and each of the other groups. Kruskal-Wallis one-way ANOVA $\chi^2(3, N = 108) = 8.68, p < .05$

bring to teacher education an understanding of math that is weak and rule-bound; it is unlikely that their students will acquire an appropriate view of mathematics as a result of content courses. The beliefs of preservice teachers are likely to shape not only the way in which they will teach mathematics, but also the way in which they approach learning to teach mathematics (Ball, 1990).

Overall, student beliefs seem to contradict reform-based calculus curricula, which reestablishes thinking as an essential part of learning mathematics (Hughes-Hallett et al., 1994).

> Getting students to think has to be our top priority. Thinking means being able to look at problems from several points of view.... Unfortunately, it seems that we have led them to believe that "real mathematics" consists entirely of the skillful manipulation of X's. (p. 124)

Even more discouraging is the statistical profile of developmental mathematics programs nationwide (Lewis & Farris, 1996). With the majority of developmental mathematics programs conducting programmed learning or individual learning stations, not only is the risk of misconceptions increased, but the benefits of group work are also curtailed.

Because many students in developmental programs will eventually take mathematics, the following instructional and programmatic implications based on this study emerge:

1. Developmental mathematics courses should engage students in meaningful mathematics by addressing inadequate conceptual understanding, instead of focusing on drill and practice. Research in mathematics education offers guidance concerning the kinds of misconceptions and errors that students display in various domains (Wilson, 1993).

2. Learning theory recommends mathematical discourse by emphasizing the importance of group interaction to facilitate conceptual understanding (Forman, 1988). Within social relationships all students benefit from the verbalization of problem-solving processes.

According to Slavin (1988), cooperative learning environments lead to improved student achievement given: (a) the presence of cognitive conflict, (b) the exposure of inadequate reasoning, and (c) the resolution of dissonance. Through the interaction of these elements, critical learning follows. Too often developmental students in this study did not fully capture these benefits. They perceived the usefulness of cooperative learning as a means of "checking their work."

3. Many countries (England, Japan, Bulgaria, Sweden, Israel, and Hungary) have a core curriculum similar to the one proposed by the National Council of Teachers of Mathematics (1989). Instead of the present curriculum of paper and pencil computation, students would experience the full range of topics in algebra, geometry, trigonometry, probability, statistics, and discrete mathematics. Although the approach in developmental mathematics would be more concrete, with informal symbolism, and less complex applications, students would experience the interconnectedness and rich relationships in mathematics. The only connection students in the study recognized among their previous and present coursework was remediation.

4. Four-year programs that understand the experiences and beliefs of students entering their classes. Often these are in conflict with instructors' beliefs or with the philosophy behind the curriculum.

Increasingly, mathematics departments must ask how well their programs, services, and schedules meet the needs of a growing number of students who do not consider mathematics as a necessary part of the total educational experience but only as a way to acquire particular skills and knowledge necessary to compete in today's society (Institute for Research on Higher Education, 1993).

References

Ball, D. L. (1990). The mathematical understanding that prospective teachers bring to teacher education. *The Elementary School Journal, 90*(4), 449-467.

Carpenter, T. P., Kouba, V. L., Brown, C. A., Lindquist, M. M., Silver, E. A., & Swafford, J. O. (1988). Results of the fourth NAEP Assessment of mathematics: Trends and conclusions. *Arithmetic Teacher, 36*(4), 38-41.

Clements, D. H., & Battista, M. T. (1990). Constructivist learning and teaching. *Arithmetic Teacher, 38*(1), 34-35.

Cobb, P. (1988). The tension between theories of learning and instruction in mathematics education. *Educational Psychologist, 23,* 87-103.

Elliott, J. C. (1990). Affect and mathematics achievement of nontraditional college students. *Journal for Research in Mathematics Education, 21*(2), 160-165.

Forman, E. A. (1988). Learning through peer instruction: A Vygotskian prespective. *The Genetic Epistemologist, 15*(2), 7-15.

Glaser, B., & Strauss, A. (1967). *Discovery of grounded theory.* Chicago: Aldine.

Hackett, G. (1985). Role of mathematics self-efficacy in the choice of math-related majors of college women and men: A path analysis. *Journal of Counseling Psychology, 32*(1), 47-56.

Hughes-Hallett, D., Gleason, A. M., Flath, D. E., Gordon, S. P., Lomen, D. O., Lovelock, D., McCallum, W. G., Osgood, B. G., Pasquale, A., Tecosky-Feldman, J., Thrash, K. R., Tucker, T. W., & Bretscher, O. K. (1994). *Calculus.* New York: John Wiley & Sons.

Institute for Research on Higher Education. (1993). Landscape: The changing faces of the American college campus. *Change, 25*(4), 57-60.

Kagan, D. M., & Tippins, D. J. (1991). Helping student teachers attend to student cues. *The Elementary School Journal, 91*(4), 343-354.

Koch, L .C. (1992). Revisiting mathematics. *Journal of Developmental Education, 16*(1), 12-14, 16, 18.

Lewis, L., & Farris, E. (1996). *Remedial education at higher education institutions in fall 1995* (NCES 97-584). Washington, DC: U. S. Department of Education, National Center for Education Statistics.

Mau, S. (1991, April). *Beliefs of college-level remedial mathematics students.* Paper presented at the annual meeting of the American Educational Research Association, Chicago.

McLeod, D. A. (1992). Research of affect in mathematics education: A reconceptualization. In D. A. Grouws (Ed.), *Handbook of research on mathematics teaching and learning* (pp. 575-596). New York: MacMillan.

Michigan State Board of Education. (1990). *A survey of student assessment and developmental education in Michigan's public community colleges.*

Narode, R. (1989). *A constructivist program for college remedial mathematics at the University of Massachusetts, Amherst.* (ERIC Document Reproduction Service No. ED 309 988).

National Council of Teachers of Mathematics. (1989). *Curriculum and evaluation standards for school mathematics.* Reston, VA: Author.

Nickson, M. (1992). The culture of the mathematics classroom: An unknown quantity. In D. A. Grouws (Ed.), *Handbook of research on mathematics teaching and learning* (pp. 101-114). New York: MacMillan.

Randall, C. I., & Silver, A. (Eds.). (1988). *The teaching and assessing of mathematics problem solving. Research agenda for mathematics education* (Vol. 3). Reston, Va: National Council of Teachers of Mathematics.

Resnick, L. B., & Ford, W. W. (1981). *The psychology of mathematics for instruction.* Hillsdale, NJ: Lawrence Erlbaum.

Schroeder, C. C. (1993). New students—New learning styles. *Change, 25*(4), 21-26.

Schoenfeld, A. H. (1989). Explorations of students' mathematical beliefs and behavior. *Journal for Research in Mathematics Education, 20*(4), 338-55.

Selden, A., & Selden, J. (1990). Constructivism in mathematics education: A view of how people learn. *UME Trends, 2*(1), 88.

Simon, M. A. (1995). Reconstructing mathematics pedagogy from a constructivist perspective. *Journal for Research in Mathematics Education, 26*(2), 114-145.

Slavin, R. E. (1988). Developmental and motivational perspectives on cooperative learning: A reconciliation. *The Genetic Epistemologist, 15*(2), 17-28.

Stage, F. K., & Kloosterman, P. (1995). Gender, beliefs, and achievement in remedial college-level mathematics. *Journal of Higher Education, 66*(3), 294-311.

Stage, F. K., & McCafferty, P. L. (1992). Nontraditional and traditional students in the college mathematics classroom. *NASPA Journal, 29*(2), 101-106.

Statistical Package for the Social Sciences. [Computer software]. (1996). Chicago: SPSS Inc.

Stevenson, H.W., Lee, S. Y., & Stigler, J. W. (1986). Mathematics achievement of Chinese,

Japanese, and American children. *Science, 231,* 693-698.

Wilson, P. S. (Ed.). (1993). *Research ideas for the classroom.* New York: Macmillan.

Zahorik, J. A. (1995). Constructivist teaching. *Fastback, 309.* Bloomington, IN: Phi Delta Kappa Educational Foundation.

Appendix A

Characteristics of Behaviorism Versus Constructivism

Behaviorism	Constructivism
Mathematics is a set of facts, concepts, or rules waiting to be revealed.	Mathematics is a creative process. The Learner attempts to bring meaning to a situation.
Knowledge exists independent of the knower.	Learning is always based on previous knowledge.
Focus is on isolated bits of information.	Focus is on the "whole."
Ladder metaphor can be used.	Scaffolding metaphor can be used.
Teacher disseminates information for students.	Teacher mediates environment for students.
Students primarily work alone.	Students primarily work in groups.
Assessment of student learning is viewed as separate from teaching and occurs almost entirely through testing.	Assessment of student learning is interwoven with teaching and occurs through teacher observations of students at work and through student exhibitions and portfolios.

Appendix B

Open-Ended Survey Items

53. What math courses have you enrolled in? Which ones have you completed and why? What math courses are you enrolled in now?

54. Do you think mathematicians work alone on problems or together? Which do you think is better and why?

55. Are the different mathematics courses you've taken in high school or college related to each other in any way? If so, how?

56. How important is memorizing in learning mathematics? If anything else is important, please explain how.

57. What do you do if you get stuck while doing a math problem?

58. Do you think that students can discover mathematics on their own, or does all mathematics have to be shown to them? Please explain.

59. How can you know whether you understand something in math? What do you do to measure yourself?

Chapter 13

MAINSTREAMING BASIC WRITERS: CHRONICLING THE DEBATE

Mary P. Deming

At a recent conference of English teachers a panel of college instructors discussed the transition from high school English classes to college composition courses. Included on this panel were the chair of a university English department, two university English faculty members, and two college basic writing instructors. Just as the session was ending, a member of the audience raised her hand and asked two perennial questions debated in postsecondary education circles today: "Why do we have to have remedial English classes anyway?" and "Why don't students learn what they need to know in high school?" These questions were greeted with enthusiastic applause from the high school teachers in the audience and were answered by the members of the college instructors' panel in as much detail as time allowed. This scenario was not surprising. Since the earliest days of instruction of basic writers, these same questions have been posed by various sectors of society: college administrators, English faculty members, parents, taxpayers, and legislators to name only a few. All ponder the question of what to do with students who come to college underprepared.

To put this dilemma into an historical context, it is somewhat comforting to know that educators have worried about college students of all types and their lack of writing abilities since the earliest days of American college education. For example, by 1883-1884 Harvard College had instituted a requirement that "literature was to be studied, not for itself or even for philology, but as a subject for composition" (Applebee, 1974, p. 30). Harvard College also required its first entrance examination in written English in 1874, and it was failed by more than half of the students (Connors, 1987; Rose, 1985). In the late 1880s, our national education system was criticized for its poor preparation of high school students, and colleges as prestigious as Harvard were critical of the skills of students entering their institutions; so much so, many implemented entrance examination compositions. The Harvard Board of

Overseers in 1891 appointed a committee of laymen to study students' difficulty with composition. This committee reported that 20% of Harvard's 1892 entrance exam students failed the exam; another 47% passed conditionally or less than satisfactorily (Lunsford, 1987a, p. 247).

Nationally, in the late 1800s, students' lack of literacy skills in general was discussed widely. Consequently, The National Education Association appointed a "Committee of Ten" to investigate public secondary schools' curriculum (Applebee, 1974; Lunsford, 1987a). The Conference on English, one of the nine commissions of the Committee, made a number of recommendations, including the infusion of literature instruction at the secondary level. In regards to composition instruction in high schools, the Conference on English suggested that literature instruction and composition instruction be united and that students should write more in high school. The Conference on English also recommended that remedial courses belonged in high schools (Lunsford, 1987a).

Despite raised college entrance requirements in the 1890s, ill-prepared students still entered college. As a result, some Ivy League and Seven Sisters institutions (like Harvard, Yale, and Wellesley), offered special courses to help students with academic deficiencies (Lunsford, 1987a). At Yale in the early 19th century, students met in "awkward squads" to study grammar, punctuation, and spelling (Lunsford, 1987a, p. 249). Lunsford notes:

> the courses offered no college credit and were clearly punitive in nature. They emphasized mechanical correctness and relied heavily on drills and exercises; ill-prepared students were often thought of as either lazy or stupid—or both. . . . Finally, the courses were taught by teachers either totally or largely unprepared to teach writing and uninterested in doing so when they could be lecturing on moral excellence or on a favorite work of literature. (p. 249)

Remedial College English Courses

Remedial college English classes in various guises have continued on many campuses from previous decades to the present. In some cases, students enrolled in special classes, tutorial sessions, "how-to-study classes," remedial reading classes, and open-admission community college classes (Lunsford, 1987a, p. 250). Underprepared students continued to come to college for a number of reasons. In the late 1940s and 1950s, soldiers returning from World War II attended college on the GI Bill, and many of them were underprepared. As a result, numbers of remedial courses were increased to help this new breed of students. By 1950, most colleges offered remedial courses that reviewed the basics of English grammar and usage (Kitzhaber, 1963).

The open-admissions programs of the 1960s and 1970s greatly impacted the institutions of higher learning at the time. These "new students," as they were referred to by Patricia Cross (1971), included housewives, technical workers, students seeking new careers and needing basic skills, and students setting vocational rather than academic goals. Shaughnessy (1977) noted that these students lacked fluency, and what they did write was error-filled. Troyka (1987b) described this new class of students as older and nontraditional, perhaps the first generation in their families to go to college. Many of these nontraditional students were parents, either married or single, who had jobs yet lacked strong literacy skills. Some of these students barely graduated from high school or earned General Educational Development diplomas (GEDs) years after high school. Many nontraditional students were older women or foreign-born students.

As a result of the influx of these "new" students, "by the late 1960s, practically, every two-year institution was making some institutional effort to provide redemption for the increasing numbers of students who enrolled without the basic rudiments of a high school education" (Roueche & Snow, 1977, p. 7). Lunsford (1977) reported that by 1976, 90% of the institutions that she surveyed had established or planned to establish remedial English programs.

Trimmer (1987) described this heyday period of remedial education, recalling:

> The most recent history of remediation begins in the 1960s with the growth of

community colleges and the advent of open admissions and reaches its first flowering in the mid-1970s with the creation of comprehensive remedial programs, the formation of the National Association of Developmental Education (1976), and the publication of the work of Mina Shaughnessy. (p. 3)

Shaughnessy (1977) noted in the introduction to her landmark book, *Errors and Expectations*:

> In the Spring of 1970, the City University of New York adopted an open-admissions policy that guaranteed to every city resident with a high school diploma a place in one of its 18 tuition-free colleges . . . (enrollment was to jump from 174,000 in 1969 to 266,000 in 1975). (p. 1)

City University of New York (CUNY) students at that time were required to write a placement essay and take a reading test. Laurence (1993) remembered those early days at CUNY when open admissions was "initiated in 1970 because of student takeovers and the shutting down of the campus, including the barring of gates and the burning of rooms . . . and buildings. Open admissions began on the campus of City College with a virtual revolution" (p. 23).

Troyka (1987b) coined the 1980s the "Decade of the Non-Traditional Student" (p. 16), and the term "basic writing" became well known because of the writings of Mina Shaughnessy (Troyka, 1987a). Also, a survey of 1,500 schools during the 1980s revealed that open admissions was the policy at 34% of schools surveyed, including both two-year (75%) and four-year colleges (25%) (Troyka, 1987b). Trimmer's survey (1987) confirmed that programs in basic writing were prevalent in record numbers in the late 1980s as well. Eighty-two percent of the schools surveyed had some form of basic writing program.

Harris (1995) described the teaching of basic writing during the last 20 years in terms of three metaphors: growth, initiation, and conflict.

Origins of Mainstreaming

Throughout the history of basic writing, discussion has occurred among basic writing theorists concerning the best way to prepare students for regular freshman composition classes. However, from the days of Shaughnessy's pioneering work (1977) to the early 1990s, theorists have been concerned primarily about the content of the courses. The debate concerning whether or not basic writing classes even belong in institutions of higher learning (Bartholomae, 1983; Shaughnessy, 1977) has been undertaken primarily by college administrators and state and national legislators. Basic writing theorists (Rose, 1985; Troyka, 1987b) have focused their work on identifying the characteristics that define the "basic writer," a difficulty that still exists today (Gray-Rosendale, 1996; Stygall, 1994; Troyka, 1987a). Theorists also have explored the relationship between basic writing and the demands of academic discourse (Bizzell, 1978, 1982; Rose, 1983), and others have studied the composing processes of basic writers (Perl, 1979; Sommers, 1980). Shaughnessy (1977) examined students' error patterns in over 4,000 placement essays composed by college freshmen at CUNY from 1970 to 1974. Based on her research, Shaughnessy contended "that BW [basic writing] students write the way they do, not because they are slow or non-verbal, indifferent or incapable of academic excellence, but because they are beginners and must, like all beginners, learn by making mistakes" (p. 5).

Enos's (1987) seminal work, A *Sourcebook for Basic Writing Teachers*, provided a rich reservoir for many of the discussions of the 1980s related to the pedagogical and philosophical concerns of basic writing instructors. This edited volume described a context for basic writing, relevant theories, and strategies for basic writing teachers. Articles included those written by such leaders in the field as Bartholomae, Bizzell, Bruffee, Greenberg, Hull, Lunsford, Perl, Rose, Shaughnessy, Troyka, and a host of others.

In a more recent article, Harris (1995) described the teaching of basic writing during the last 20 years in terms of three metaphors: growth, initiation, and conflict. Basic writing instruction in the 1970s and 1980s is best understood through the use of the metaphor of growth to discuss the difficulties faced by basic writers. Basic writers were considered immature or inexperienced writers, and the job of basic writing teachers was then to help students develop as users of language (Lunsford, 1987b). "Their writing was seen as 'concrete operational' rather than 'formal,' or 'egocentric' rather than 'reader-based,' or 'dualistic' rather than 'relativistic'" (Harris, 1995, p. 29). On the other hand, other compositionists (Bartholomae, 1986; Bizzell, 1978; Kogen, 1986; Rose, 1983, 1985), represented the "initiation" model of basic writing. Harris (1995), summarizing Bizzell's beliefs, writes:

> the academy formed a kind of "discourse community" with its own distinctive ways of using language . . . the task of teachers was not to help students grow into more complex users of language but to "initiate them" into the peculiar ways in which texts get read and written at a university. (p. 30)

In the late 1980s and early 1990s, some compositionists began to see basic writing classes as a place where "the conflicts between our own discourses, those of the university, and those which our students bring with them to class are made visible" (Harris, 1995, p. 31). Mary Louise Pratt (1991) coined the term "contact zones" as "spaces where cultures meet, clash, and grapple with each other, often in contexts of highly asymmetrical relations of power, such as colonialism, slavery, or their aftermaths as they are lived out in the world today" (p. 34).

Many basic writing theorists and instructors place the official beginning of the debate over the mainstreaming of basic writers at the 1992 Maryland Basic Writing Conference. However, it is difficult to pinpoint exactly when a movement is born. Perhaps stirrings of discontent were brewing earlier in private conversations, Conference on College Composition and Communication Conference (CCCC) presentations, Conference on Basic Writing (CBW) meetings, or intimated in various articles (Bartholomae, 1986; Elbow, 1991; Lu, 1991, 1992; Rose, 1985; Shor, 1980) published in the 1980s and 1990s. "The national debate on this movement was, if not initiated, certainly brought to the fore at the 1992 National Conference on Basic Writing, in presentations by Peter Dow Adams and David Bartholomae" (Gunner, 1997, p. 4). The discussion, both theoretical and pedagogical, has continued ever since.

Along with the ongoing theoretical discussions, national political influences have made the mainstreaming of basic writers a reality for many students. The term "mainstreaming" has its roots in special education and has stood to mean the instructional integration of students with "normal" peers in a regular classroom (Hallahan & Kauffman, 1982). Hence, mainstreaming is the opposite of tracking, or homogeneous grouping.

Presently around the country, both federal and state leaders are reluctant to fund remedial education at the postsecondary level.

Presently around the country, both federal and state leaders are reluctant to fund remedial education at the postsecondary level. After all, why pay twice for information that students were supposed to learn in high school? Many students who might normally attend four-year colleges or universities are now required to take their developmental courses at two-year colleges. States including Alabama, Colorado, Florida, Georgia, Missouri, Nevada, New York, Ohio, South Carolina, and Virginia are shifting—or are considering shifting—developmental classes from the four-year colleges and universities to the two-year colleges. Consequently, students who might have been admitted provisionally into four-year colleges or universities are now granted regular admission into two-year colleges, enforcing a type of mainstreaming. Other students may be denied admission at any institution due to increased admissions requirements. Legislators cite shrinking funds as the reason for reducing or abolishing developmental programs (Arendale, 1997). With public opinion and political realities hitting home, it is becoming increasingly difficult for basic writing proponents to justify their programs, and perhaps this pressure, subtle or not, has influenced the mainstreaming movement on all levels of postsecondary education.

The Fourth National Basic Writing Conference was held in College Park, Maryland, October 8-10, 1992, with the theme "Critical Issues in Basic Writing: 1992." David Bartholomae, the Director of Composition at the University of Pittsburgh, delivered the keynote address. This address and other papers from the conference were published in subsequent issues of the *Journal of Basic Writing*. In his speech, "The Tidy House: Basic Writing in the American Curriculum," Bartholomae (1993) described basic writing as a way of naming and thus producing a course of study or a type of writing that mirrors the liberal world view represented in colleges and universities:

> I think basic writing programs have become expressions of our desire to produce basic writers, to maintain the course, the argument, and the slot in the university community; to maintain the distinction (basic/normal) we have learned to think through and by. The basic writing program, then, can be seen simultaneously as an attempt to bridge AND preserve cultural difference, to enable students to enter the "normal" but to insure, at the same time, that there are basic writers. (p. 8)

Bartholomae suggested that basic writing classes exist because of our desire as liberals who design courses that emphasize a commonness among students by making their differences superficial and surface-level. He noted that we design courses that try to erase these differences, but in doing so we maintain them. Instead, Bartholomae recommended that we adopt the type of curriculum envisioned by

Mary Louise Pratt in which students can engage differences in the "contact zones." Pratt asks that we

> Imagine a curricular program designed not to hide differences (by sorting bodies) but to highlight them, to make them not only the subject of the writing curriculum, but the source of its goals and values (at least one of the versions of writing one can learn at the university). (Bartholomae, 1993, p. 13)

Bartholomae (1993) agreed with Pratt and even suggested that "we could offer classes with a variety of supports for those who need them. These might be composition classes where the differences in students' writing become the subject of the course" (p. 14).

While restating his argument that basic writing is a reiteration of the liberal projects of the past that produce "others" of our students and construct a curriculum and a career for teachers, Bartholomae (1993), in his concluding remarks, acknowledged the good work of basic writing instructors. He asked the profession to think beyond the either/or formula or reductionistic position. In sum, Bartholomae (1993) asked us to reexamine our position on separate classes for basic writers: "I think it would be useful, if only as an exercise, to imagine a way of talking that called the term 'basic writing' into question (even, as an exercise, to treat it as suspect)" (p. 20).

Adams (1993) contributed to the debate by questioning the value of separating basic writers by adding another salient point: How successful are basic writing programs? He began his article reiterating the dangers of tracking or homogeneous grouping—namely that students in lower groups are stigmatized by others, are demoralized by the experience, lack proficient role models, and receive less weighty material. In addition, Adams reminded his audience that many basic writing classes lack college credit, and hence, negatively affect students even more. Adams also noted that what is taught in basic writing classes is not significantly different from other writing courses, but the level of performance expected may be less. While Adams did not wholeheartedly support eliminating basic writing classes and mainstreaming underprepared students into regular freshman composition classes, he did suggest that we begin to question seriously whether segregated basic writing classrooms are the best environments for helping basic writers develop into proficient college-level writers. To answer this question, Adams recommended collecting data evaluating our programs, reexamining regular freshman classes to see if they will be able to accommodate a wider range of student abilities, offering other types of support, and considering options for students who fail freshman composition courses in their first attempt. Finally, Adams suggested that we "initiate pilot programs or experiments, which are rigorously evaluated, in which volunteer basic writers are mainstreamed into freshman English classes" (p. 25).

In her article, "The Politics of Basic Writing," in the same issue of the *Journal of Basic Writing* (*JBW*), Greenberg (1993) presented an argument for the opposite side of the debate, disagreeing with Bartholomae's (1993) assertion that basic writing classes are "obstacles rather than opportunities" and arguing that "many basic writing programs *are* sorting students into 'useful and thoughtful' courses that have helped thousands of inexperienced writers persevere and succeed in college" (Greenberg, 1993, p. 65). Agreeing with Adams, Greenberg emphasized that basic writing teachers need to design effective assessment measures to evaluate the effectiveness of their programs and classes. She was against the "sink or swim" model proposed by some basic writing theorists and politicians. She also recommended matching more of current theory with the curriculum, as many institutions still adhere to the remedial or skills model of basic writing instruction. Instead, she suggested programs that "integrate the learning of language and literacy with the development of higher level cognitive abilities" (p. 68). Such programs rely on a good placement that identifies students' strengths and areas in need of improvement. At Hunter College, where Greenberg teaches, she noted that students do well in their basic writing classes with a class pass rate ranging from 80-93%, and a graduation rate of approximately 55% (after eight years of enrollment).

In a later *JBW* article, Sheridan-Rabideau and Brossell (1995) argued that basic writing classes offer the most efficient support for at-risk students and their writing. They also reiterated that courses in basic writing are not an anomaly because other disciplines (such as mathematics, languages, and science) offer courses to help prepare students for the rigors of these disciplines. The advantages of many basic writing classes are that they meet for more hours and have fewer students. Basic writing teachers can offer more feedback in a warm, supportive space. "Whatever we call it, the practical yet safe environment that offers underprepared students the writing experiences they need is one to be honored. That environment remains, in our view, the basic writing classroom" (Sheridan-Rabideau & Brossell, 1995, p. 26). Analyzing opponents' arguments, Sheridan-Rabideau and Brossell stated, "Though we recognize the valuing of diversity and attending to the needs of individual writers are not mutually exclusive, we remain convinced that the primary goal of basic writing is the practical improvement of student writing" (p. 25). They also pointed out that neophyte English graduate teaching assistants may not be trained to meet the needs of basic writers enrolled in regular freshman composition classes, and unless basic writers tell others that they are enrolled in these courses, there is no way to determine just who is in basic writing classes.

Finally, in their *JBW* Editors' Column, Greenberg and Smoke (1995) summarized the mainstreaming debate when they wrote:

> We have listened carefully (and uncomfortably) to our colleagues' critiques of basic writing. Within the past two years, colleagues whom we respect and admire have spoken at various conferences about the need to reenvision basic writing. Some have characterized basic writing programs as tracking systems which serve to preserve the idea of non-traditional students as being different. Several scholars have asserted that basic writing courses ghettoize students, prevent them from joining the mainstream of college-level courses, and often serve as obstacles rather than opportunities.

Other have challenged our profession to provide evidence that basic writing courses work. (p. 2)

Alternative Programs for Basic Writers

Although many states now relegate basic writers to community college developmental studies classes, some institutions mainstream these students into regular freshman composition courses. However, many institutions that mainstream their basic writers offer some additional support or different types of program configurations.

Mainstreaming Plus Support Model

University of Pittsburgh students diagnosed as basic writers based on the results of a summer diagnostic essay are placed in general writing sections with other students who have been diagnosed as "general writers." Basic writers, however, are required to enroll in a one-credit add-on course titled "General Writing Intensive" (GWI). This class consists of tutoring groups with five students assigned to a tutor from the writing center who is trained to work with individual writing problems. Typically in these tutorial sessions, GWI students bring their compositions with their writing teacher's comments on them to be used in group discussion. In order to pass the course, GWI students must receive a passing grade from both their writing instructor and from their tutor (P. Smith, personal communication, July 21, 1997).

California State University, Chico, has mainstreamed its basic writers in an attempt to meet the diverse needs of students. (Rodby, 1996, p. 108). All students, regardless of nationality, race, and socioeconomic class, are mainstreamed into a regular freshman writing course that emphasizes academic writing, in particular writing about ideas requiring research. Students with low placement scores take an additional no-credit adjunct workshop with their regular freshman composition class. This workshop is comprised of 10 students who meet twice a week for 50 minutes each session. Generally, students from a variety of freshman composition classes take part in a workshop where they draft and revise their essays and work on other writing and research assignments. One variation of this course is the case in which the workshop leader attends the regular composition class and holds workshops with students from that class alone.

In South Carolina, the Commission of Higher Education requires that universities no longer offer remedial courses. The University of South Carolina at Aiken has phased out its developmental courses and instead mainstreams all of its basic writers. To support these students, it has lowered its class size to 18, built up its writing center by hiring a new director and increasing center space, trained peer tutors, and started a Writing Across the Curriculum (WAC) program. The institution has also proposed a junior-level portfolio project to help students with their writing skills (L. Rhodes, personal communication, July 7, 1997).

At the main campus of the University of South Carolina at Columbia, incoming freshman composition students submit a portfolio of previous writings to their English 101 instructors and write two diagnostic writings, one in class and one at home. Based on these essays, students may be exempted from one or two freshman composition classes or be required to participate in the Studio Program along with their freshman composition class. Students who sign up for a Studio session (a writing support group) meet one hour weekly in addition to their regular English 101 class. During the Studio sessions, students share drafts of their essays with one another and with their Studio leader, and they also work on other class assignments. The Studio sessions are graded pass/fail based on attendance. If students perform exceptionally well, they receive a "pass with distinction." Students and Studio leaders meet in the writing studio—a large, comfortable room equipped with computers. Studio leaders as a group meet weekly—a meeting which plays an integral part in understanding their students and their assignments. Studio leaders also communicate weekly with students' English 101 instructors through "Dialogue Sheets." Instructors are encouraged to respond to the Studio leaders (Grego & Thompson, 1996).

The Stretch Model

Arizona State University (ASU) also mainstreams its basic writers into regular freshman composition classes, but does it over two semesters, hence the name of their program—The Stretch Program. The underlying theory of the Stretch Program is that basic writers need more time to think, write, and revise their papers, so assignments for English 101 are completed over two semesters rather than one. Students write three multiple-draft essays each semester, use the same textbook as regular freshman composition students, and have their work evaluated using portfolios.

At Arizona State, students are placed in different composition courses based on their American College Testing (ACT) or Scholastic Aptitude Test (SAT) scores. If they are placed in the Stretch Program, they are required to enroll their first semester in Writing Across the Curriculum (WAC) 101 and their second semester in English 101. WAC 101 counts as three hours of elective credit toward graduation and is a pass/fail course. Although students do not receive a letter grade for WAC 101, the grades they earn in this class count as 50% of their final English 101 grade. Teachers remain with the group for both courses—WAC 101 and English 101—and each semester's work counts as one half of each student's final English 101 grade. This combined grade is awarded at the end of the English 101 semester. If students should fail WAC 101, they receive a failing grade (in this case an E grade) which lowers their overall GPA (Glau, 1996). Latest figures seem to document the Stretch Program's success: The average pass rate for all English 101 students between 1991 and 1996 was approximately 85%; whereas the average pass rate for English 101 Stretch students between 1994 and 1996 was approximately 91%. Prior to the introduction of the Stretch Program, many ASU students enrolled in English 071, which was a basic skills class. Only 66% of those in English 071 passed English 101 the last

> *The underlying theory of the Stretch Program is that basic writers need more time to think, write, and revise their papers.*

five years this class was offered; whereas 87% of those in WAC 101 passed English 101 in the fall of 1994 through the spring of 1997 (G. Glau, personal communication, July 7, 1997).

At the City College of New York (CCNY), Barbara Gleason and Mary Soliday secured a grant from the Foundation for the Improvement of Post-Secondary Education (FIPSE) to support a three-year mainstreaming project titled "An Enrichment Approach to Language and Literacy." This six-semester credit hour, two-course sequence, was designed to replace the two remedial courses and one college-level course required at City College. Instead, students worked together for a full year with a classroom instructor and a well-trained classroom tutor. The course curriculum began with:

> the language variety and cultural differences that City College students bring to the classroom. By foregrounding students' language experience and the everyday use of language in social contexts as resources for teaching writing ... we try to enhance students' awareness of the complexity of their spoken language and its relationship to written language. (Soliday, 1996, p. 87)

The first-semester course was designed to introduce students to language concepts and theories, including dialects, registers, and code-switching. Students investigated their own use of language and the language of others through self-reflective writings, research reports, autobiographies, and ethnographies (which describe the literacy activities of those in their community). Students read literacy narratives and watched films related to language. In the second semester course, students examined teacher-chosen themes that emerged from the first-semester course and would most likely re-emerge in the core curriculum. In the second course, the emphasis was on writing from sources and research. Portfolio assessment was used to evaluate students' growth as writers in both courses, and teachers were encouraged to use a variety of instructional methods and technology (M. Soliday, personal communication, December 6, 1995; Soliday, 1996).

Recent project evaluation results indicate that students enrolled in the pilot program were judged by CCNY English faculty readers to be competitive with students placed into regular college freshman composition classes. In addition, most of the students in a 22-student sample achieved satisfactory or higher on their writing portfolios as reviewed by five outside readers. Student self-report surveys revealed that students were extremely satisfied with their own learning in the pilot project. For remedial students and for students who had previously enrolled in one English as a Second Language (ESL) class, there were positive correlations between pilot course participation and student progress and achievement. Furthermore, an outside evaluator praised the program and recommended that it be immediately adopted (M. Soliday, personal communication, September 16, 1997).

Washington State University (WSU) has designed a multilevel model of composition instruction for its incoming freshman students. All first-year students take the Writing Placement Examination, a two-hour timed writing assignment in which they are asked to write an analytical or argumentative essay and one piece of reflective writing. The results of these placement essays determine whether students are placed in English 100, English 101, or English 101 plus English 102. In English 100, the first part of a two-hour "stretch" course, students do the same kinds of writing as their counterparts in English 101, but in smaller classes with more individualized attention. English 100 students enroll in English 101 the next semester and complete their freshman composition requirement in two semesters.

Many students, including a large number of volunteers, enroll in English 101 plus English 102 (a one-hour credit course that is provided free to full-time students). In this configuration, five students and a peer-tutor facilitator are connected to an English 101 course. These small groups meet weekly for 10 weeks and work in groups to write and revise their essays. The course is extremely popular, having served over 850 students including 500 volunteers in 1996 and 1997 (W. Condon, personal communication, August 1, 1997). Other students enroll in the regular freshman composition course—English 101—by itself (WSU Writing Program: On-line Brochure, 1997).

The Intensive Model

Quinnipiac College, a private four-year college in Connecticut, after an extensive review of its basic writing program, decided to implement an Intensive Model in which developmental students enroll in a regular college-level English 101 composition course that meets for additional class time in specially designed "Intensive" sections of the course. These "Intensive Sections" meet for five hours of instructional time, rather than the three hours of instructional time for regular English 101 classes. Students receive regular college credit for the Intensive Model course, and when completing it, move on to English 102, the next course in the composition sequence. Instructors use the five hours to meet individual student's needs, offering workshops, conducting conferences, and giving whole group instruction. Administrative benefits include the advantages of using the same text in both courses combined with easier and more flexible staffing, as well as an increase in overall student satisfaction. In addition, because of this new program, students also seem more motivated, pleased that they do not have to go to summer school to catch up, and happy that they do not have to pay for noncredit courses. Time and effort are spent training faculty members who teach these courses, and faculty share sample syllabi and ideas while practicing holistic scoring procedures. Time spent on instructor training results in maintaining standards (Segall, 1995).

Another version of the Intensive Model is found at Ohio's Bowling Green State University where the General Studies Writing Program consists of three courses: English 110, Developmental Writing; English 111, Introductory Writing; and English 112, Varieties of Writing, which is the only course required by the university. Students are put into one of these courses based on a placement essay; most students place in English 111 and then are required to enroll in English 112.

English 110 is a credit-bearing five-hour intensive course, as opposed to the three-hour English 111 and 112 classes. In English 110, students use the same textbooks and complete the same types of writing assignments; they also utilize a supplemental text reviewing mechanics and sentence structure. During the extra two hours of class a week, English 110 students meet as a class to write drafts of their essays alone and in groups, while continuously working on sentence structure and mechanics activities. Teacher-student conferences are an important part of the course, and class size is kept at 18 or fewer students. At the end of the term, students in the two different classes turn in a portfolio for evaluation. This evaluation determines whether English 110 students, like English 111 students, may go on to English 112. Passing criteria for English 110 and English 111 are the same. Students who pass English 110 skip English 111 and enroll directly in English 112. The extra class hours spent in English 110 seem to bring students up to the passing level of their classmates in other classes (D. Nelson-Beene, personal communication, July 30, 1997).

John Jay College of Criminal Justice, a four-year liberal arts college which is part of the City University of New York (CUNY) system, has piloted an Intensive Writing program. Based on placement scores, students who are normally placed in one of two remedial courses are instead enrolled into the next higher level course. In other words, students with the lowest scores are placed in English 100, the second level, one-hour, credit-bearing course. Students with higher scores are placed in English 101, a regular college composition course, worth three credit hours. Intensive Writing sections meet four times a week and are taught by two different adjunct instructors who teach on alternate days. Each Intensive Writing course shares a common syllabus around a particular theme such as "Discovering the Self" or "Trials." Themes are woven into class reading and writing assignments, films, and other class activities (P. Licklider, personal communication, August 21, 1997).

For a short period of time, writing instructors at Ohio State University paired an honors class with a basic writing class. Classes met in adjoining computer classrooms and were team taught using a common syllabus. Students worked collaboratively in group-processing essays. The curriculum was rigorous for both classes (S. Duffey, personal communication, July 23, 1997; Duffey, 1996).

The Supplemental Instruction Model

Point Loma College, a college with a student body of 1,800 located in San Diego, California, is a rigorous, private liberal arts college that mainstreams its freshman composition students. At Point Loma, Supplemental Instruction (SI) is supplied for high-risk classes like science and history. For these classes, SI leaders attend class, take notes on lectures, and complete assignments in the course in order to assist students in the SI group (S. Bejko personal communication, August 12, 1997). In the past, Supplemental Instruction was also used to help freshman composition students. As with other SI configurations, SI leaders attended the composition class, took notes, and completed assignments. The SI leaders also helped with in-class writing assignments and worked with professors to individualize instruction for students whose native language was not English. Supplemental Instruction leaders also scheduled a minimum of two hours a week in the Writing Center to tutor students or to hold group workshops (McMillin, 1993).

Supplemental Instruction has been offered for composition courses at the University of Missouri-Kansas City where SI first began. In fact, more than half the students served by the Writing Lab are enrolled in composition courses. Supplemental Instruction takes the form of small group sessions, workshops, and individual tutoring. Supplemental groups and workshops focus on basic English skills, while small writing groups might meet twice a week to work on sentence-level skills and other composition topics. Lab staff members keep in close contact with faculty members concerning course assignments, students' progress, and new avenues of service. The Lab has been particularly successful with high-risk students in freshman composition. Studies have indicated that over 60% of these high-risk students were able to earn a C if they participated in the Lab as few as two times. Students who attended Lab sessions on a regular basis increased their chances of earning a C or better. This supports the idea that "the degree and rapidity of the student's improvement is in direct proportion to his/her participation in the Lab" (McCormick, 1997, p. 5).

The Support Course Model

Georgia State University offers a three-hour, noncredit course to support its regular freshman composition course, English 111. Students enroll in both courses during the same quarter. The population of these classes is derived from a variety of sources: students who have passed the lower level of the basic writing sequence [i.e., Learning Support Programs (LSP 080)] with a B average and have passed the department's exit essay; students who have failed English 111 and who want support the second time in the class; and others who want to bolster their work in English 111.

This support course, LSP 082, while focusing on the individual writing needs of the students in the class, addresses various rhetorical patterns, conventions of academic discourse, and the idiosyncracies of the varying language values of the university that become apparent during the term. Quite often the students in this co-course are enrolled in 10 to 15 different sections of composition classes with perhaps that many composition instructors. Needless to say, this type of setting encourages the class to become a community of learners who strive to discover more about the language required by the university, especially the demands of communicating with different audiences. Members of this learning community work closely to support each other in freshman composition (M. Singer, personal communication, August 6, 1997).

The Writing Across the Curriculum (WAC) Model

The University of Minnesota's General College has experimented with a Writing Across the Curriculum (WAC) approach for basic writers. A group of basic writers were part of a learning community that participated in an integrated package of credit-bearing, writing-intensive courses in environmental science, history, and composition. Writing assignments in all three classes were analogous and incrementally designed in levels of difficulty. With this package, writing was used as tool for learning, and writing assignments were carefully designed to provide success for students as they moved from narrative to other areas, including process, writing about reading, description, and analysis. Students had the opportunity to write multiple drafts. Designers of the program said their objectives were "to develop a workable paradigm of active learning and cross-disciplinary instruction and to identify the outcomes of such an approach for those developmental, rather than 'mainstream,' students who participated" (Miller, Brothen, Hatch, & Moen, 1988, p. 6). Students in the WAC package scored higher in subsequent freshman composition courses than did a control group, and after three quarters of academic work, outperformed the control group in terms of attaining the needed 2.5 grade point average (GPA) to transfer to regular baccalaureate programs. Student persistence was higher for the students enrolled in the learning package approach.

The Summer Bridge Model

Essex Community College in Baltimore offers a three-week summer program for selected developmental students before they are mainstreamed in regular composition classes in the fall. Students are placed in this three-week version of basic writing based on their Nelson-Denny reading scores and on their Test of Standard Written English (TSWE) results. Students who meet the placement requirements are then invited to attend the "Summer Institute" (a noncredit class). The Summer Institute is held the last three weeks in August, and meets every day for three-hour sessions that cover the content of the college's upper-level basic writing course. The class is taught in a computer classroom where students can easily revise their papers and communicate with their instructors through the local computer network. The content of the course concentrates on in-class reading and writing, but students also work in the college writing center. Early results indicate that the freshman composition pass rate for students enrolled in this intensive summer program has been much higher than those who take the semester-long, upper-level basic writing class (D. George, personal communication, July 24, 1997).

The Self-Placement or Directed Self-Placement Model

One of the latest variations of mainstreaming programs is student "self-placement" or "directed self-placement." At Grand Valley State University, incoming freshmen decide for themselves the English class in which they want to enroll rather than being placed in classes based on their test scores. They decide whether to enroll in English 098, a noncredit preparatory class, or English 150, a four-hour credit class focusing on academic discourse and research-based writing. Of the 2,200 freshmen in last year's class, approximately 22% chose to enroll in the noncredit developmental class.

At orientation sessions for incoming freshmen, English faculty members use a brochure entitled "English 098 or 150? A Guide to Placing Yourself in the Freshman Course that is Right for You" to help students decide which course is best for them. The course brochure provides a rubric to aid students with this important decision. Generally, it is appropriate for students to register for regular freshman composition (i.e., English 150) if they can answer affirmatively many of the statements on the following checklist:

- I read newspapers and magazines regularly.

- In the past year, I have read books for my own enjoyment.

- In high school, I wrote several essays per year.

- My high school GPA placed me in the top third of my class.

- I have used computers for drafting and revising essays.

- My ACT-English score was above 20.

- I consider myself a good reader and writer. (Royer & Gilles, 1997, p. 4)

If students do not see themselves in most of those statements, or do not consider themselves as strong readers and writers, they might consider enrolling in English 098, where they will work on fluency and on addressing specific audiences with the help of Writing Center tutors. Students who can answer affirmatively to most of the following statements should consider enrolling in English 098, the noncredit developmental course:

- Generally, I don't read when I don't have to.

- In high school, I did not do much writing.

- My high school GPA was about average.

- I'm unsure about the rules of writing (i.e., commas, apostrophes, and so forth).

- I've used computers, but not often for writing and revising.

- My English ACT score was below 20.

- I don't think of myself as a strong writer. (Royer & Gilles, 1997, p. 5)

Programs for basic writers should be designed to meet each institution's particular needs and to help each specific student population.

Instructors explain that English 098 is designed to help students develop and clarify their writing and to write for a college-level audience. Grades are given in English 098 and count in the students' GPA, but do not count towards graduation.

Students who have difficulty deciding which is the appropriate course for them can meet with English faculty members or the chair of the department who will be glad to talk with them and review their writing. In addition, during the first week of class, students may switch courses based on a recommendation from their teachers (D. Royer, personal communication, July 6, 1997; Royer & Gilles, 1997).

Conclusion

The debate over whether to mainstream basic writers into regular college composition classes or to maintain separate basic writing classes is ongoing. Perhaps this debate will continue as long as:

> American education is subject to two contrasting underlying motifs: egalitarianism, the argument that everyone should have opportunities for success, and elitism, the restriction of opportunities to the most "deserving" which often means to those from a relatively privileged home. (White, 1995, p. 75)

No matter what are the contributing factors fueling this debate, writing program administrators and compositions theorists and faculty are heeding Bartholomae's (1993) suggestion that we reexamine the role of basic writing in our profession, in our institutions, and in our students' lives. As this chapter attests, many thought-provoking discussions have resulted, and numerous exciting and valuable programs are being implemented on campuses across the country. It is extremely important, however, to remember that students at one institution are not the same as at another. Consequently, programs for basic writers should be designed to meet each institution's particular needs and to help each specific student population.

References

Adams, P. D. (1993). Basic writing reconsidered. *Journal of Basic Writing, 12*(1), 22-36.

Applebee, A. (1974). *Tradition and reform in the teaching of English: A history*. Urbana, IL: National Council of Teachers of English.

Arendale, D. (1997, July). *Survey of education policies concerning developmental education at the state and federal level in the U. S.* [Online]. Available: www.umkc.edu/centers/cad/nade/nadedocs/devstate.htm

Bartholomae, D. (1983). Writing assignments: Where writing begins. In P. Stock (Ed.), *Fforum: Essays on theory and practice in the teaching of writing* (pp. 300-312). Montclair, NJ: Boynton/Cook.

Bartholomae, D. (1986). Inventing the university. *Journal of Basic Writing, 5*(1), 4-23.

Bartholomae, D. (1993). The tidy house: Basic writing in the American curriculum. *Journal of Basic Writing, 12*(1), 4-21.

Bizzel, P. (1978). The ethos of academic discourse. *College Composition and Communication, 29*, 351-355.

Bizzell, P. (1982). College composition: Initiation into the academic discourse community. *Curriculum Inquiry, 12*, 191-207.

Connors, R. (1987). Basic writing textbooks: History and current avatars. In T. Enos (Ed.), *A sourcebook for basic writing teachers* (pp. 259-274). New York: Random House.

Cross, K. P. (1971). *Beyond the open door: New students to higher education*. San Francisco: Jossey-Bass.

Duffey, S. (1996). Mapping the terrain of tracks and streams. *College Composition and Communication, 47*, 103-108.

Elbow, P. (1991). Reflections on academic discourse: How it relates to freshmen and colleagues. *College English, 53*, 135-155.

Enos, T. (1987). *A sourcebook for basic writing teachers*. New York: Random House.

Glau, G. (1996). The "Stretch Program": Arizona State University's new model of university basic writing instruction. *Writing Program Administration, 20*(1/2), 79-91.

Gray-Rosendale, L. (1996). Revising the political in contemporary basic writing scholarship. *Journal of Basic Writing, 15*(2), 24-49.

Greenberg, K. (1993). The politics of basic writing. *Journal of Basic Writing, 12*(1), 64-73.

Greenberg, K., & Smoke, T. (1995). Editors' column. *Journal of Basic Writing, 14*(1), 2.

Grego, R., & Thompson, N. (1996). Repositioning remediation: Renegotiating composition's work in the academy. *College Composition and Communication, 47*, 62-84.

Gunner, J. (1997, Spring). CBW: A recent history. *Conference on Basic Writing Newsletter, 13*, 4.

Hallahan, D., & Kauffman, M. (1982). *Exceptional children: Introduction to special education*. Englewood Cliffs, NJ: Prentice-Hall.

Harris, J. (1995). Negotiating the contact zone. *Journal of Basic Writing, 14*(1), 27-42.

Kitzhaber, A. R. (1963). *Themes, theories, and therapy: The teaching of writing in American colleges*. Boston: Allyn & Bacon.

Kogen, M. (1986). The conventions of expository writing. *Journal of Basic Writing, 5*(1), 24-37.

Laurence, P. (1993). The vanishing site of Mina Shaughnessy's *Errors and expectations*. *Journal of Basic Writing, 12*(2), 18-28.

Lunsford, A. (1977). *An historical, descriptive, and evaluative study of remedial English in American colleges and universities*. Unpublished doctoral dissertation, Ohio State University, Columbus.

Lunsford, A. (1987a). Politics and practices in basic writing. In T. Enos (Ed.), *A sourcebook for basic writing teachers* (pp. 246-258). New York: Random House.

Lunsford, A. (1987b). Cognitive development and the basic writer. In T. Enos (Ed.), *A sourcebook for basic writing teachers* (pp. 449-459). New York: Random House.

Lu, M. Z. (1991). Redefining the legacy of Mina Shaughnessy: A critique of the politics of linguistic innocence. *Journal of Basic Writing, 10*(1), 26-40.

Lu, M. Z. (1992). Conflict and struggle: The enemies or preconditions of basic writing? *College English, 54,* 887-913.

McCormick, J. (1997, July). *Writing lab adaptations of supplemental instruction.* [On-line]. Available: www.umkc.edu/centers/cad/si/sidocs/jmwrit93.htm

McMillin, J. (1993). Adapting SI to English composition classes. In D. Martin and D. Arendale (Eds.), *Supplemental instruction: Improving first-year student success in high-risk courses* (pp. 34-37). Columbia, S.C.: National Resource Center for The Freshman Year Experience, University of South Carolina.

Miller, C., Brothen, T., Hatch, J., & Moen, N. (1988). Beyond functional literacy: An integrated writing across the curriculum package for basic writers. *Research and Teaching in Developmental Education, 6*(5), 5-16.

Perl, S. (1979). The composing processes of unskilled college writers. *Research and Teaching of English, 13,* 317-36.

Pratt, M.L. (1991). Arts of the contact zone. *Profession, 91,* 33-40.

Rodby, J. (1996). What's it worth and what's it for? Revisions to basic writing revisited. *College Composition and Communication, 47,* 108-111.

Rose, M. (1983). Remedial writing courses: A critique and a proposal. *College English, 45,* 109-128.

Rose, M. (1985). The language of exclusion: Writing instruction at the university. *College English, 47,* 341-359.

Roueche, J., & Snow, J. (1977). *Overcoming learning problems.* San Francisco: Jossey-Bass.

Royer, D., & Gilles, R. (1997). *Putting assessment in its place with directed self-placement.* Manuscript submitted for publication, Grand Valley State University.

Segall, M. T. (1995). Embracing a porcupine: Redesigning a writing program. *Journal of Basic Writing, 14*(2), 38-47.

Shaughnessy, M. (1977). *Errors and expectations: A guide for the teacher of basic writing.* New York: Oxford.

Sheridan-Rabideau, M. P., & Brossell, G. (1995). Finding basic writing's place. *Journal of Basic Writing, 14*(1), 21-26.

Shor, I. (1980). *Critical teaching and everyday life.* Boston: South End.

Soliday, M. (1996). From the margins to the mainstream: Reconceiving remediation. *College Composition and Communication, 47,* 85-99.

Sommers, N. (1980). Revision strategies of student writers and experienced adult writers. *College Composition and Communication, 31,* 378-388.

Stygall, G. (1994). Resisting privilege: Basic writing and Foucault's author function. *College Composition and Communication, 45,* 320-341.

Trimmer, J. (1987). Basic skills, basic writing, basic research. *Journal of Basic Writing, 6*(1), 3-9.

Troyka, L. Q. (1987a). Defining basic writing in context. In T. Enos (Ed.), *A sourcebook for basic writing teachers* (pp. 2-15). New York: Random House.

Troyka, L. Q. (1987b). Perspectives on legacies and literacy in the 1980s. In T. Enos (Ed.), *A sourcebook for basic writing teachers* (pp. 16-26.) New York: Random House.

White, E. (1995). The importance of placement and basic studies: Helping students succeed under the new elitism. *Journal of Basic Writing, 14*(2), 75-84.

Writing at Washington State University. (1997, August). *WSU writing program: Online brochure.* [On-line]. Available: www.wsu.edu:8080/~bcondon/wpbroch.html

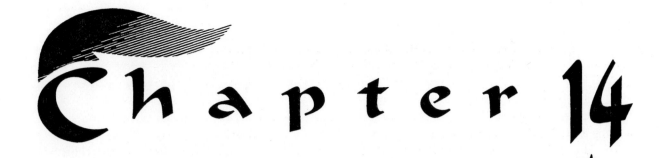

Chapter 14

A COMMENTARY ON THE CURRENT STATE OF

DEVELOPMENTAL READING PROGRAMS

Martha Maxwell

Many reputable studies report that required college developmental reading courses are ineffective. Although filled with the best of intentions, developmental reading programs are not producing the necessary results. This chapter will explore the failure of these reading courses by analyzing how the stigma of taking a remedial course, the course goals, design and strategies, the tests used for placement, the course materials, and the experience, training, and philosophy of teachers all contribute to the problem. Indeed, many college reading courses not only fail to deliver what they promise, but also have several negative effects on students, such as increasing dropout rates, lowering self-confidence, and slowing their progress toward graduation.

College administrators long have assumed that reading courses are necessary and helpful, but they rarely require these courses to be evaluated systematically in order to determine their outcomes. Reading program directors usually do not report on how developmental students fare in mainstream courses. The few follow-up studies that have been done fail to show that there is any difference between the reading skills or academic achievement of those who took developmental reading courses and high-risk students who should have taken the courses but did not.

On the one hand, nobody denies that many students need to improve their reading skills. Administrators, faculty, and students themselves all agree that good reading skills are essential for a successful completion of most college courses. In fact, the need to improve reading skills is intensifying as more than half of our high school graduates enter college, and more than one quarter of incoming freshmen are required to enroll in developmental reading courses. Why? Many of today's college entrants either did not take college preparatory programs or made poor grades in the high school courses they did take (Smittle, 1996). Others are high school dropouts or adults returning to school after a hiatus of many years.

On the other hand, there is little evidence that taking required developmental reading courses makes a significant difference in students' reading ability or college achievement (Bohr, 1994-95; Grant & Hoeber, 1978; Keimig, 1983; Losak, 1972; Maxwell, 1979; Richardson & Marten, 1982; Roueche & Roueche, 1993). A number of studies describe the negative effects of forced placement in a college reading course, including increased dropouts, decreased self-confidence, low morale, and retarding the student's progress in completing a degree (Dimon, 1993; Keimig, 1983; Maxwell, 1979; Utterback, 1989). Dimon (1993), for example, found that four years after taking a reading course, former developmental reading students were 20 credits behind high-risk students who did not take a reading course, more than the three credits they lost by taking one reading course. Some studies also show that for high-risk students, taking mainstream courses improves reading test scores, retention, and academic grades significantly while taking a developmental reading course does not (Bohr, 1996; Dimon, 1993; Losak, 1972; Tarabon, 1997).

Although the California system's developmental reading courses usually test to determine student placement, they typically do not test to decide whether students are ready for college-level reading.

A recent example, Adelman's (1996) National Center for Education Statistics report on a 10-year follow-up study of developmental students, is the latest in the long history of studies that have found college developmental reading courses ineffective. Based on his follow-up study, Adelman recommends that reading courses be restricted to community colleges where most of the developmental courses are taught; furthermore, faculty in community colleges know how to help determined students obtain degrees. He concedes that students can improve math and writing skills through developmental courses in four-year colleges because these skills are readily fixable, but he believes reading deficits signal comprehensive literacy problems that lower students' chances of completing a degree. He further argues that four-year colleges are not very efficient in handling cases of reading deficiencies and that they defraud students if they pretend otherwise.

Community colleges are better suited than four-year colleges to address a combination of multiple remedial needs and a lingering adolescent attitude toward education—but the comprehensive literacy problems that force students to take remedial reading courses require solutions more far-reaching than even community colleges can provide. (Adelman, 1996, p. 56)

Earlier researchers were somewhat kinder. Losak (1972) found there were no subsequent academic gains for high-risk students who took a developmental reading course compared to a control group who did not. Grant and Hoeber (1978) asked whether basic skills programs were working and answered that although the basic skills instructors were working very hard indeed, there was little evidence that the courses were successful. Keimig (1983) declared that skills should be integrated directly into academic courses and that stand-alone developmental courses were the least cost-effective way of providing academic support to students. These warnings have made little difference; colleges have continued to add required reading courses while avoiding their evaluation. Dimon (1993) traced the history of college developmental reading courses under California's Master Plan, learning that although administrators from community colleges, state universities, and the University of California regularly discussed the "developmental problem" and made recommendations about the need for evaluation and the need for change, studies were not completed, nor changes made. In fact, reading and study skills courses continued to proliferate universally, expanding in all levels of public postsecondary institutions over a 30-year period. Systematic evaluation was not conducted to assess the effects of participation in developmental courses on retention, dropouts, parity, or transfer to senior colleges, though these were considered high-priority concerns. During that period some people even suggested that administrators did not insist on evaluating their programs because they knew the outcomes would be negative.

Although the California system's developmental reading courses usually test to determine student placement, they typically do not test to decide whether students are ready for college-level reading. Students who complete the required sequence of courses are assumed to have gained the necessary skills. Many other systems use both pre- and post-testing.

Standardized Reading Tests: Cure or Curse?

Experts have long complained that standardized reading tests are artificial, minimally useful in placing students, and punitive. But they still continue to be the primary factor determining who must take developmental reading. It is as if administrators and policy makers, in their desire to fix the national reading problem, have found a panacea (i.e., give a standardized test and force students who have low scores to take developmental courses). Not only do individual institutions use this procedure, but a number of states, such as Florida, Texas, and Tennessee, mandate reading tests and developmental courses for low-scoring students in all public colleges.

The number of poor readers entering college has remained high, but little else has changed. They are still tested and placed in reading courses, and there is little evidence that most of today's programs are effective. There is even disagreement on whether college reading courses should be required or voluntary. Although voluntary programs have been shown to be more successful than mandatory ones, surveys show that less than one third of the students who are recommended to take developmental courses do so when they are given the option and one half believe the courses are not needed (Utterback, 1989). Because it has been difficult to show that taking courses improves reading skills, perhaps the students are right.

In the 1960s, 95% of the college reading programs evaluated students' reading skills and progress with standardized tests (Maxwell, 1979), and this is probably still true in community colleges where standardized reading tests have been adopted as a matter of convenience to place students in developmental courses (Kerstiens, 1997). The Nelson-Denny Reading Test is the most frequently used test for pre- and post-assessment, probably because it is easy and quick to administer (30 minutes), and its subscores (reading speed, vocabulary, and comprehension) reflect the skills traditionally taught in college reading courses. In addition, scores can be converted to grade equivalent norms so that one can readily decide upon and justify cutoff scores. In fact, for those who are naive about psychometrics, it seems like the ideal reading test. However, critics contend that the Nelson-Denny Reading Test is the most misused and abused test in the reading field. First of all, it is not a placement test. It is a norm-referenced test in that it shows how a student scores in comparison with a particular norm group. Placement tests should be criterion referenced and indicate how well a student reads, not how he or she compares with others (Keimig, 1983; Kerstiens, 1979, 1986, 1990, 1993, 1997; Maxwell, 1979, 1997; Sternberg, 1991; Utterback, 1989; Wood, 1997). Secondly, the Nelson-Denny Reading Test is a highly speeded test. In fact, if students are told to read faster on the post-test, they can easily increase their scores significantly because there is no penalty for guessing (Maxwell, 1997). Speeded tests bear little relation to the kinds of reading freshman students do in college, and the Nelson-Denny Reading Test measures an artificial or test-specific kind of reading, not realistic reading. Kerstiens (1997) adds that although time-critical assessment instruments unfairly appraise students' reading skills, a look at the Nelson-Denny Reading Test content should discourage anyone from administering it to students. The 100 vocabulary words, many of which are obsolete, are tested out of context within a 10-minute time limit that encourages students to guess; the 600-word reading passages followed by questions are invariably elitist, including topics like Greek poetry, Swinburne, Browning, Shelley, and Virgil, all written in conceptually dense prose. Kerstiens asks "Is this the kind of prose we want to inflict on thousands of entering and reentering developmental students?" (1997, p. 42). Despite its obvious inadequacies, the NDRT remains a favorite. "Ironically, the popularity of speeded reading comprehension tests, like the Nelson-Denny Reading Test, continues to be inversely proportional to the negative comments of critics" (Kerstiens, 1997, p. 42).

Some other standardized reading tests share the same weaknesses in that they contain short passages with multiple choice questions and are closely timed, while reading actual textbooks requires students to read longer, more difficult chapters with no time constraints. Sternberg (1991) further cautions that standardized reading tests reveal only a narrow measure of student aptitude and achievement and that reading test scores provide an incomplete and distorted picture of how students actually read. He describes other differences between reading as it is done on tests and reading in school, explaining that on tests, reading passages are short and recall is immediate; in school, reading passages are moderate to long and recall is delayed. On tests, recall is entirely intentional, while recall in school is incidental. Comprehension on tests is based on a single type of question, usually multiple choice; in school, multiple assessments are made. Reading passages on tests are often boring and tend to be emotionally neutral, which may not be true in school reading. On tests, the reading situation minimizes distraction, while in school there may be many distractions. Tests evaluate reading for a single purpose: Students try to get a high score. Depending on the type of reading test, students might read more carefully (e.g., when there are penalties for guessing) or more carelessly (e.g., when speed of response is important) than they would in normal reading. Furthermore, reading tests measure the reader's ability to evaluate, but not to construct arguments (Sternberg, 1991).

The problems are compounded when single test scores are used in forced placement of students into developmental courses. Although some students are undoubtedly helped by taking reading courses, the dropout rate for required reading courses is as high as 48% (Utterback, 1989). Many students do not want to take special classes for which they receive no credit. Utterback concludes that the misuse of tests may discourage students and drive them away from college, although administrators

may not be aware of this because there are very few evaluative studies or reviews of results.

Despite the fact that single test scores have little or no value (Morante, 1989), placement in college reading courses still relies heavily on single test scores. Multiple criteria are seldom used to decide who must take the developmental courses. Utterback (1989) suggests that one solution would be to substitute advising ranges for cutoff scores and to eliminate forced placement that takes control away from students. He argues that open access rather than forced placement is needed with more flexible advisement ranges rather than rigid cutoff scores. Also, other aspects of placing students in developmental programs should be used and made more effective, such as tutoring, career and personal counseling, and mentoring.

Another problem in using current tests for placement into reading courses is that although researchers have warned that developmental programs are inefficient and ineffective in the absence of specific diagnoses of difficulties, many of today's tests neither diagnose nor reflect the reality of college study (Utterback, 1989). There is also evidence that without diagnosis, students' weaknesses are not addressed in developmental reading courses (Kerstiens, 1978).

The misuse of standardized tests for reading placement has a long history. Some colleges continue to disregard basic psychometric principles. One example is the inappropriate use of the Scholastic Aptitude Test (SAT) or American College Testing (ACT)—norm-referenced tests of scholastic aptitude—to place students in developmental courses. Newer tests, including customized computerized placement and instruction programs, attempt to minimize test-taking skills and reflect students' reading skills more accurately. One example, the Texas Academic Skills Program (TASP) test is untimed so that students can take up to five hours to complete its three parts. Reading passages on the TASP are much longer and better reflect college reading tasks (D. Garnett, personal communication, August 13, 1997). Although the TASP offers more alternatives, including classes and individualized services, students are still required to participate and pass the post-test before they can take advanced college courses.

Teaching to the Test

Another negative effect of using standardized reading tests is that they encourage teachers to teach to the test and reinforce their adherence to traditional methods (Wood, 1997). Wood states that reading teachers who feel obligated to demonstrate gains on traditional multiple choice tests will have a difficult time abandoning these methods; this is especially true of those working with poor readers in situations where testing and remedial courses are mandated. Traditional methods are easier to teach and more predictable to follow; teachers don't have to relinquish their authority. "In traditional teaching, the teacher's knowledge is privileged; while in modern methods, the student's knowledge is privileged" (Wood, 1997, p. 91).

What Can Be Done about Reading Tests?

Although placement in reading should be voluntary, testing should be mandatory. Too many students, especially those who most need assessment, will avoid it wherever possible (Morante, 1989). However, reading tests should only be used when counseling and advisement services are available. Reading tests are best used to indicate where students should start in a reading program, not to brand them "poor learners." Test scores should be one of the factors students use in deciding which courses they need. Although multiple criteria rather than cutoff scores have long been recommended, only a few programs are using multiple criteria either for placement or for ongoing diagnosis in their reading courses. For example, Peers (1993) describes a performance based placement assessment that integrates reading and writing as a diagnostic tool. She required students to read three articles on water problems in California, learn about the problem, devise a solution, and present their solution in written form to a specified audience. She looked at three aspects of the process: the methods used, the extent to

which a controlled structured assignment help them focus and organize their information, and the appropriateness of the scoring criteria. Specifically, she looked at the information gained from reading, the accuracy and appropriate selection of information, the control of content-task accomplishment, the development of a paper, the organization of material, and the control of language (i.e., word choice, sentence variety, grammar, and mechanics).

Simpson and Nist (1992) have developed a comprehensive assessment model that reflects current reading research and theory while still being tailored to the philosophy and goals of their particular program. They use a multidimensional assessment involving a variety of formal and informal instruments that sort, diagnose, and evaluate. Changes are made as the students progress so the assessment becomes an integral part of the instruction and shapes decisions about materials, tasks, pacing, and feedback in future lessons. Also, this approach involves students in diagnosing their own problems and evaluating their own progress.

> *Too many students, especially those who need assessment, will avoid it [taking a reading test] wherever possible (Morante, 1989).*

The Stigma of Forced Placement

In education, as in legal situations, there is a fine line between remediation and punishment, and sometimes a given action can be both. Educators and policy makers underestimate how much students feel stigmatized when they are forced to take a developmental college reading course. Further, this humiliation also affects the attitudes of their reading instructors who sometimes feel like second-class citizens in their institutions.

College students perceive taking a required developmental reading course as more shameful and punitive than taking similar courses in writing and mathematics, perhaps because people associate learning to read with what one learns in first grade. Perhaps being forced to take a college reading course is more painful because, unlike math and writing, reading courses do not fit into any discipline or department. Indeed, reading skill underlies them all. At any rate, the stigma of taking a course for "dummies" serves as a major deterrent for aspiring college students with poor reading skills. Labeling the course as remedial worsens the problem.

As Uri Treisman, the mathematician, is quoted as saying about math courses, "Call them intensive, call them honors courses, call them anything, but don't call them remedial!" I would add, "and don't call them reading!" However, not only are reading courses identified as remedial, sometimes they are labeled as "reading for those who read below the eighth-grade level." What a put-down for an adult! At least Triesman takes his own advice and calls his math seminars "The Developing Scholars' Program."

The shame of being forced to take a developmental reading course lowers expectations, increases resistance, and makes students even more difficult to teach. Being labeled dumb can destroy self-confidence and have long lasting effects on students' self-image. When we assign students to a developmental course, we are, in effect, committing those who do not meet our expectations to an intellectual ghetto in hopes that they will not contaminate the rest of the students. Indeed, most developmental reading courses isolate the students from other students and from the rest of the college curriculum, producing lasting negative results. Astin (1993) found that having been tutored was negatively related to scores on a graduate record examination taken years later. Being labeled as "needing help" lingers on while the experience of having been a tutor was positively related to later graduate exam scores.

Dimon (1993) suggests that instead of asking the question of whether taking a reading skills course improves the student's chance of success, we should investigate the possible frustration and loss of self-esteem that accompanies any remedy (in this case, a reading course) that does not produce the desired results. In follow-up interviews with high-risk students who completed a reading course, Dimon found that students generally gave the course poor ratings and most said that it had not helped them. None rated the reading course as their favorite, and although they complained about not being able to understand the content of some of the mainstream courses they were taking, they did not believe that their reading skill was the problem. In fact, taking general education courses like English composition or a communications course increased high-risk students' self-esteem, while completing a reading and study skills course did not.

Knowing that administrators, politicians, and indeed the general public complain that they are paying twice to teach skills that should have been learned in high school does not add to a student's self-confidence. What the policy makers fail to realize is that improving reading skills is a continuous process that varies by discipline as one moves through school. In other words, the reading skills needed to pass freshman literature probably will not get you through law school or medical school, just as fourth-grade skills will not get you through college. Furthermore, students' motivation and feelings of self-efficacy play a large part in their willingness to study, which impacts their eventual success or failure in college.

Are College Reading Teachers Adequately Prepared?

Many of the problems with developmental reading courses seem to stem from the fact that reading teachers may be unaware and unappreciative of the reading demands of college faculty in other disciplines. Convinced that their students are unable to read textbooks, they do not try to teach them how, but concentrate on "basic skills." Furthermore, reading teachers usually lack training or experience in working with adults and may be uninformed about current theory, research, and practice in the college reading field. Because there are few graduate training programs for college reading specialists, most learn on the job.

College reading teachers rarely, if ever, come from the ranks of college professors, but are usually former local public school reading or English teachers. They may have been trained to teach elementary or high school students, but lack experience in teaching adults. They know little about what different faculty members mean by academic literacy in their fields, what faculty expect students to learn, or the criteria they use to assess student progress. Although reading teachers have been college students themselves, they may have very limited knowledge about the skills necessary to read genres outside of their own college majors (usually English or education).

More than half of today's college students are over age 22, so Friedman (1997) stresses the importance of training teachers in adult education so that they can understand the unique characteristics that adult learners bring to the developmental classroom. This training should emphasize not only the special learning needs of adults, but also the importance and implications of teacher self-awareness in the classroom. Reading teachers should also be aware that the techniques they use in teaching children may not work with adults. As Friedman points out, adults tend to be independent and self-directed learners and have had many life experiences that younger students lack. College teachers should focus on special problems of adult readers and evoke genuine examples drawn from real-life situations.

In addition, many college reading teachers are part-time or adjunct teachers, which limits their financial ability and their opportunities to get further education. The degrees and training in reading that a reading teacher may have earned in the past may well be as out of date as the philosophy of reading and teaching strategies they learned.

Teacher Attitudes

The results of a survey of college reading instructors who attended a professional meeting showed that they disagreed about the definition of reading, nor could they agree on what should be taught in a reading course (Dimon, 1993). Many teachers said they regard reading as a skill and believe in teaching it as a separate subject worthy of inclusion in college catalogs. The majority agreed that the reading classes should not focus on the content of other courses that students might be taking. All

heavily supported continuing existing reading and study skills classes and were unwilling to support any decrease in the number of reading classes should their college face budget cuts. Although most teachers said they preferred teaching "reading improvement" courses over teaching study techniques, none of them preferred to teach vocabulary development as it relates to college textbooks. Only a small percent of teachers were willing to focus on subject matter, content areas, or students' life experiences.

It is clear that different college reading courses in different institutions focus on quite different goals. Some assert that college reading assumes a higher degree of literacy than high school work and that college reading demands are much more specific, requiring that students be competent in reading the different kinds of academic textbooks and other materials assigned in college classes. In other words, teaching students to read newspaper and magazine articles is not enough (Bohr, 1996; Burrell, Tao, Simpson, & Mendez-Berrueta, 1997; Cohen & Quinn, 1995).

Many teachers seem to believe that their goal is to focus on basic skills with the aim of getting students up to the 12th-grade level in reading (or as close to it as possible). It may be that some college reading teachers, at least those in community colleges, need training in phonics and how to teach beginning literacy skills (Kerstiens, 1978), but it is crucial for all of these teachers to understand that the goal is to train students for academic literacy (Bohr, 1994-1995). The recently proposed International Reading Association/National Council for Teachers of English (IRA/NCTE) Standards on Language Arts calls for a broader definition of literacy to include listening, computer literacy, and alternatives to a curriculum currently driven by standardized test subskills. However, these new standards have had little effect on college reading teachers, many of whom still cling to traditional methods and textbooks.

Problems with Reading Courses

Today's developmental reading courses have many problems, including teachers who are unprepared to teach adults and often have a limited knowledge of current theories and practices in teaching reading. Compounding these difficulties are teachers who adhere to out-of-date reading texts, do not assign enough reading or writing, and do not teach students how to apply newly acquired reading skills to their mainstream course work.

New Reading Theory and Research

Since the 1970s, new theories and research in psycholinguistics and cognitive psychology (Smith, 1994) have changed our understanding of the reading process, but they have made little difference to college programs. Developmental reading courses remain much as they have always been. Nancy Wood (1997) contrasts the traditional way of teaching developmental reading based on behaviorist theory with today's model, which is based on psycholinguistic theory. She explains that one result of the impact of traditional behaviorist theory on reading was that experts began to divide reading into skills and subskills under the belief that if students improved in the subskills they would become stronger readers and that they could transfer reading skills learned on one set of practice material to their textbooks. Furthermore, reading was thought to be a linear process so that one progressed from easier skills (such as reading for facts) to the more complex skill of critical reading. We now know that reading is discipline-specific and skills learned in one genre may or may not transfer to other academic fields.

Today, most authorities no longer believe that meaning lies in the text and that the teacher's job is to see that students understand the author's meaning. Psycholinguistic theory argues that reading and writing are modes of learning and share common purposes and processes. That is, they are ways that students construct meaning or ways of thinking and knowing. Reading involves an interaction between a learner's prior knowledge, text, and context; reading and writing are viewed as a single act of literacy that should be taught together (Quinn, 1995).

Traditionally, college reading teachers focused on teaching reading skills through drills on

graded paragraphs and exercises on cards, but we recognize now that the academic support curriculum must be directly relevant to the courses freshmen are taking. Walter, Gomon, Guenzel, and Smith (1989) state it clearly:

> For many years it was common practice for reading and study skills courses to use standardized materials and texts such as the SRA Better Reading Books and the survey part of the Diagnostic Reading Test. It was assumed that once freshmen were trained to master reading strategies with these materials, they would apply them to their own course assignments. Unfortunately, what many freshmen learned in these study skills courses did not generalize to their day-to-day reading and studying. When they learn reading skills by directly applying them to their own texts, completing their own assignments more efficiently, they are likely to continue to use the new approach to reading. (p. 111)

The Skills Approach as an End in Itself Lingers On

Current reading course descriptions inevitably list the necessity of bolstering vocabulary, word attack, and comprehension skills. In analyzing the content of California community college reading and study skills courses, Dimon (1993) reported that they begin by giving poor readers training in materials below the sixth-grade level: "When students feel comfortable with reading sixth grade essays or stories, they are advanced to intermediate-level reading courses where the scenario repeats itself with more difficult material" (p. 71). She concludes that, in general, teachers make no effort to relate reading skills to textbook reading in the other courses the students are taking.

If developmental courses give students nothing important to read about and nothing to write about that remotely resembles college work, how can they hope to improve? After observing the materials used in community college reading classes, Dimon (1993) wrote, "Those who teach reading skills courses seem to believe that practice of any kind makes perfect, but can real practice be effective without real purpose?" (p. 73).

Bohr (1994-1995) examined general freshman courses that were associated with reading gains when initial ability was controlled in students enrolled in three different types of four-year colleges. She reported that taking a developmental reading course did not improve students' reading scores. The courses that contributed most significantly to gains in reading ability were applied science and humanities courses, especially English literature and composition courses (as expected), but also freshman classes in engineering, music, and foreign language. The limited amount of reading assigned in most reading courses may explain why students taking required courses in general education subjects like freshman composition improve their reading skills even when they do not take a reading course (Bohr, 1994-1995; Dimon, 1993; Tarabon, 1997). Students in engineering, drawing, music, or foreign languages improve their reading skills significantly; those taking developmental reading do not (Bohr 1994-1995). These mainstream courses are probably more rigorous than reading classes and require not only more effort during class but a significant amount of homework, while students in reading courses may get by with doing short exercises with few outside assignments.

Bohr's (1996) results question the effectiveness of college developmental reading courses and the validity of reading tests. Do students fail to improve in reading because they feel they are labeled unteachable by being placed in a developmental course, thus lowering their motivation and expectations? Do the reading instructors have low expectations and place minimal demands on their students? Is failure to improve reading skills due to the nature of the courses? Are they too easy, not challenging enough, do not require enough "time on task," or do they overstress methodology rather than empowering students to monitor and control their own reading efforts? These questions are also raised by Maxwell (1997).

How Does College Reading Differ from Reading Instruction in Lower Grades?

Bohr (1996) points out that reading instruction in elementary grades prepares readers for all reading; college reading instruction is limited to helping students succeed in college—that is, it involves academic literacy and not general literacy. The teacher's definition of reading also affects student motivation. If teachers believe that reading is a process, not a discipline, they realize that students do not come to college expecting to major in reading and resent having to take sequences of noncredit reading courses. Poor readers differ from their better prepared classmates in degree; their skills are weaker but they are capable of improving (Tarabon, 1996).

Different Courses Require Students To Read Different Types of Academic Genres for Different Purposes

Students who have never learned to read for their own purposes usually have great difficulty reading for other people's purposes; some educators suggest that getting into the habit of reading for one's self should precede reading for other people (Henry, 1995). Certainly, many poor readers do not read for pleasure. David Caverly suggests that we should be teaching students to read to satisfy various tasks: standardized tests (if that be one task), course requirements (a necessary task), and reading task demands of other college courses where reading is peripheral (read if you want, but I am going to tell you what is in the book anyway), supportive (read and confirm what I am saying in my lectures), or vital (read and share in class your understanding). Any developmental program must prepare students for all of these tasks. A course that prepares for only one type of reading task is not doing the students justice. (David Caverly, personal communication, July 19, 1997).

There Is Not Enough Reading in College Reading Courses

Alliterate students (those who can read but do not, and rarely, if ever, read books) need total immersion in an intensive reading experience to become the fluent, habitual readers who characterize successful college students. Unfortunately, what they receive in developmental reading courses may be too little and too late (Henry, 1995). Developmental reading teachers often complain that they cannot assign homework or give extra work to students who do not get credit for the course because their students refuse to do it. To be sure, intensive reading is emphasized by some reading teachers, such as Nist and Hynd (1985), whose students engage in sustained silent reading on their reading assignments during their lab class, or Henry (1995), whose course stresses free reading during class time. These, however, are exceptions. Henry uses a whole language approach reminiscent of the "Hooked on Books" movement popularized by David Fader and colleagues in the 1960s and 1970s. This movement intended to turn non-readers into readers at the junior high school level by focusing on their reading interests, not those of the teacher (Fader & McNeil, 1968). Apparently, Fader's junior high movement had few lasting effects; we find teachers still using the same approach with college students.

Out-of-Date Reading Textbooks Restrict What Teachers Offer

The reading textbooks and materials used in college reading courses may also limit the effectiveness of reading courses. Kerstiens (1979) warned about the problems of community college reading courses when he pointed out that the objectives as well as the methodologies applied in most developmental reading courses had not changed in 48 years. Teachers and textbooks still emphasized the same skills: comprehension, vocabulary, reading rate, and study skills. Usually new, untrained instructors choose the same text as was used last term, and if students complain, search around for an easier text. Those same instructors are the ones who, about six weeks before classes begin, will start flooding the Internet listservs with questions about what text to use in reading class. Few seem to plan reading activities or assignments around the other classes a student is taking.

Despite the fact that more than 500 reading textbooks have been published since the 1890s,

If developmental courses give students nothing important to read about and nothing to write about that remotely resembles college work, how can they hope to improve?

Stahl, Simpson, and Brozo (1988), in a review of content analyses of reading textbooks, discovered that authors who write college reading textbooks tend to ignore the research on verbal cognitive development. Their books rarely deviate from the same old patterns of earlier texts; they use the same kinds of exercises and apparently choose topics based on marketing surveys rather than on theory and research.

Wood (1997) found a little improvement in her review of 20 popular reading texts, which she classified as traditional, modern, or mixed. Her criteria to classify texts as modern included the variety of passages used, including those from text and multicultural passages, whole language approach using real reading, strategy exercises in place of skills and drills, predicting questions, collaborative exercises, writing-to-learn activities, assessing reading at different stages, and placing significant emphasis on critical reading and critical thinking. She classified books that contained mainly skills and drill activities as traditional. Of the 20 texts, she rated eight as traditional, eight as modern, and four as mixed. Thus Wood's content analysis shows that authors of reading text books are slow to update their materials and implies that 40% or more of the reading texts may still focus primarily on skills-based exercise.

Most experts agree that "The value of training materials depends on their ability to teach freshmen to perform course-related tasks successfully. Often it is better to design special exercises based on the actual course text than to use commercial materials" (Walter et al., 1989, p. 12). Yet the numbers of reading textbooks that ignore college content proliferate and continue to sell.

Successful Courses

Certainly the quality of reading courses varies immensely. On the one hand, there are highly successful reading courses such as those offered at the University of Georgia and at Middle Tennessee State University, but they seem to be the exception rather than the rule. On the other hand, there are still some that would fit Traub's (1991) account of a developmental course at the City College of New York, which he describes as having the ambience of an oncology ward. The problem is, however, that most do not demonstrate that they help students read better or make better grades in college.

Poor Readers

Poor readers tend to underestimate how important and how difficult college reading requirements are. They reason that because they have passed high school courses with Ds they will be able to do the same in college. They may hate to read and have avoided it or still carry the scars of earlier unhappy academic experiences and low self-efficacy about school work. They need much more than a reading course to orient them to the realities of college.

Some developmental students in open-admission schools may be reading a great deal below college level, even below the sixth-grade level. Some may be nonreaders, but even those who can read may have very restricted reading experiences. Further, they may have had minimal exposure to reading textbooks because there were not enough textbooks in high school to allow them to take books home. In community colleges in Texas, for instance, most students who need remediation in reading are not taking college-level courses at the same time, and are instead offered three tiers of reading classes. Teachers feel that the poorest readers find the reading workbooks that simulate textbook chapters too difficult and do not understand how demanding college texts really are. Only the top students, not those at intermediate or low levels, can handle reading workbooks with exercises that approximate college textbooks.

So, what can you do if you are teaching a course for poor readers who are not permitted to take regular college courses until they complete your reading course? There are still intellectually honest ways to teach these students using simulated precollege-level or college-related content, but it takes a great deal of effort, planning, and

skill. However, having them also enrolled in a mainstream course is certainly more motivating because it enables students to apply immediately the reading and study strategies they are learning. Thus, in teaching at-risk students who are not quite ready to read college textbooks, you have a dual task: acculturating them to the real reading demands of college as well as helping them develop the vocabulary acquisition and critical thinking skills they will need to succeed in mainstream courses. Even then some teachers have discovered that it is better to use realistic college course materials than easier exercises. Kasper (1995) had English as a Second Language (ESL) students read selections from psychology texts even though they were not taking a psychology course. She taught them the vocabulary and discussed the textbook concepts with them. Students made greater gains in reading and were better satisfied with the "real college" material than those taking traditional ESL courses.

Another strategy is to use a simulation model that replicates the tasks and texts of a typical required lower-division course (Stahl, Simpson, & Hayes, 1992), although students may complain that this approach is dull and difficult. However, it is better to use sections from a real college textbook or to pair a reading and study skills course with a regular course (even a course such as "Introduction to Computers" that requires little outside reading).

Historically, the most successful model for high-risk students who enter college with limited reading skills involves a core of intensive, interdepartmental courses that are team-taught and include reading, writing, mathematics, and a mainstream course, usually in social science. Counseling is a key component and is integrated into the content courses (Clark, 1987; Obler, 1977; Roueche & Roueche, 1993). Also, recent studies show that high-risk students who are poor readers respond well to courses in which content and skills are paired, as in Supplemental Instruction (SI) or adjunct skills classes (Dimon, 1993; Garland, 1987; Ramirez, 1993, 1996). In fact, Ramirez (1996), in a 10-year follow-up study of high-risk students who took SI, found that students with the poorest grade averages in high school made greater grade improvement than their better prepared peers in the SI classes. The new Video Supplemental Instruction (VSI) has also had dramatic effects on underprepared students with poor ACT scores, low high school percentile ranks, and even those on academic probation. These underprepared students made higher final course grades, more A, B, and C grades with fewer Ds and Fs than a group of average students who did not take VSI (University of Missouri-Kansas City, 1997).

Conclusion

As discussed in this chapter, the traditional required developmental reading course has many shortcomings. Students are stigmatized by forced placement; they resent the course. Their dropout rates are higher, and high-risk students who take the course take longer to complete degrees and shed the "high-risk" label. The skills taught tend to be speed, vocabulary, and comprehension. Furthermore, these skills are taught in traditional ways and are often unrelated to those needed to understand college textbooks. Also, college reading teachers may be untrained in modern theory and research, may lack skills in teaching adults, and may not be knowledgeable about what other faculty members consider academic literacy (Burrell, Tao, Simpson, & Mendez-Berrueta, 1997; Cohen & Quinn, 1995). Courses are rarely evaluated systematically, so there is no incentive to change topics or teaching strategies. Perhaps most damning of all: There is little evidence of the value of developmental reading courses in improving reading skills or college success.

Possible Solutions

Students need testing, counseling, advising, and mentoring so they understand the necessary ingredients for college success. Those who need to improve their reading should be given a choice of different programs rather than being sectioned into compulsory courses based on a low test score.

The best solution is to integrate reading, writing, and study skills directly into content courses. Rutgers' Gateway Program does this for under-

prepared freshmen who take an additional skills lab course along with their mainstream course such as psychology. Learning skills specialists co-teach the skills lab, but both lab and course are offered under the aegis of the academic department. An ever-increasing number of studies show that course-related skills programs like adjunct skills (Dimon, 1994), Supplemental Instruction (Blanc, DeBuhr, & Martin, 1983; Martin & Arendale, 1992, 1994), and paired courses (Bullock, Madden, & Harter,1987; Gabelnick, MacGregor, Matthews, & Smith, 1990; Luvaas-Briggs, 1984; Resnick, 1993; Tinto, Goodsell-Love, & Russo, 1990) effectively raise students' course grades, result in higher grade-point averages, and improve retention and graduation rates. Further information regarding Supplemental Instruction is available on the SI homepage at http://www.umkc.edu/centers/cad/si/sidocs/sibib97.htm.

The best solution is to integrate reading, writing, and study skills directly into content courses.

What Reading Teachers Need To Do

Drawing on research that examines the impact of different types of reading and writing activities on comprehension and learning, Quinn (1995) suggests that teachers can design innovative strategies to teach for reading and writing—strategies that base learning on the interaction between these two language activities. For example, extended analytical writing, note taking during and after reading, and summary writing influence learning in different ways. Tasks that require (separately and in different combinations) reading, note taking, annotation, summarizing, discussion, analysis, revision, and review are critical if students are to use reading and writing as models of learning. Teachers need to incorporate tasks that promote a metacognitive awareness of the different reading and writing strategies appropriate in various contexts. Students need to recognize how diverse experiences in language, literacy, and learning affect their success in learning academic discourse. Quinn (1995) summarizes,

> By committing to a content-based literacy program which actively engages students in learning how to use purposeful, self-directed reading and writing strategies

for learning across disciplines, I believe college reading and writing teachers are well placed to lead in efforts to promote reading and writing as modes of learning. (p. 26)

Because of their insularity, college reading teachers have generally been excluded from the current Writing Across the Curriculum and Content Based Reading initiatives that offer promise, as do discipline-specific literacy strategies for learning content (Quinn, 1995).

Why Not Revive Preparatory Programs?

Another solution is to revive intensive college preparatory programs that were commonly offered by state universities prior to the 1930s and are still available in private preparatory schools or the military academy prep schools. Preparatory courses should offer basic skills that are fully integrated with the content that is prerequisite for college courses.

Core Courses in Summer Bridge Programs

The core programs mentioned earlier are another alternative; these core programs offer team-taught, interdisciplinary courses including a reading course, a writing course, plus a mainstream course. Such a curriculum is particularly effective for poor readers and can be offered as a summer bridge program. In fact, as the evidence mounts, one can only conclude that successful developmental students, especially more highly motivated, older students, succeed despite having taken a required reading course, not because of it.

Dimon (1993) strongly recommends the following: Funds that presently support reading and study skills courses should be redirected toward programs that help students succeed in their core curriculum by combining skills and college content. This combination of teaching process plus content is available today in many effective course-related programs. It is high time that colleges redirect their time, effort, and money to programs that help students succeed in college courses rather than perpetuating reading courses that waste both the students' and the institution's time and money.

References

Adelman, C. (1996, October 4). The truth about remedial work: It's more complex than windy rhetoric and simple solutions suggest. *The Chronicle of Higher Education*, p. 56.

Astin, A. (1993). *What matters in college: Four critical years revisited*. San Francisco: Jossey-Bass.

Blanc, R. A., DeBuhr, L. E., & Martin, D. C. (1983). Breaking the attrition cycle: The effects of Supplemental Instruction on undergraduate performance and attrition. *Journal of Higher Education, 54*(1), 80-90.

Bohr, L. (1994-1995). College courses which attract and generate good readers. *Journal of College Reading and Learning, 26*(2), 30-44.

Bohr, L. (1996). College and precollege reading instruction: What are the real differences. *The Learning Assistance Review, 1*(1), 14-28.

Bullock, T., Madden, D., & Harter, J. (1987). Paired developmental reading and psychology courses. *Research & Teaching in Developmental Education, 3*(2), 22-29.

Burrell, K. I., Tao, L., Simpson, M. L., & Mendez-Berrueta, H. (1997). How do we know what we are preparing our students for? A reality check of one university's academic literacy demands. *Research and Teaching in Developmental Education, 13*(2), 55-70.

Clark, C. S. (1987). *An evaluation of two types of developmental education programs as they affect student's cognitive and affective domains*. Unpublished doctoral dissertation, University of Pittsburgh.

Cohen, J. S., & Quinn, K. B. (1995, April). *Faculty views of college student literacy: The missing factor in the retention equation*. Paper presented at the College Reading and Learning Association Conference, Tempe, AZ.

Dimon, M. (1981). Why adjunct courses work. *Journal of College Reading and Learning, 21*, 33-40. Reprinted in M. Maxwell (Ed.). (1994). *From access to success*. Clearwater, FL: H & H.

Dimon, M. (1993). *The effect of reading/study skills courses on high-risk students*. Unpublished doctoral dissertation, The Claremont Graduate School.

Fader, D. N., & McNeil, E. G. (1968). *Hooked on books: Programs and proof*. New York: G. P. Putnam Sons.

Friedman, A. R. (1997). Fostering

student retention in developmental reading through understanding adult learning theory. In P. L. Dwinell & J. L. Higbee (Eds.), *Developmental education: Enhancing student retention* (pp. 25-36). Carol Stream, IL: National Association for Developmental Education.

Gabelnick, F., MacGregor, J., Matthews, R. S., & Smith, B. L. (1990). Learning communities: Creating connections among students, faculty, and disciplines. *New Directions for Teaching and Learning*. San Francisco: Jossey-Bass.

Garland, M. (1987). Effectiveness of Supplemental Instruction with minority students. *Supplemental Instruction Update*. Kansas City, MO: University of Missouri-Kansas City.

Grant, M. K., & Hoeber, D. C. (1978). *Basic skills programs: Are they working?* Higher Education Research Report, No.1. (ERIC Document Reproduction Service No. ED 150 918)

Henry, J. (1995). *If not now: Developmental readers in the college classroom*. Portsmouth, NH: Boynton/Cook Heinemann.

Kasper, L. F. (1995). Using discipline-based texts to boost college ESL reading instruction. *Journal of Adolescent & Adult Literacy, 385*(4), 290-306.

Keimig, R. T. (1983). *Raising academic standards: A guide to learning improvement*. Washington, DC: Association for the Study of Higher Education. (ERIC Document Reproduction Service No. ED 233 669)

Kerstiens, G. (1978). *The effect of a typical community college developmental reading course on the phonic disablement of students*. Unpublished doctoral dissertation, Nova Southeastern University, Fort Lauderdale.

Kerstiens, G. (1979). Yet another look at developmental reading courses. In G. Enright (Ed.), *Proceedings of the 12th annual conference of the College Reading Association, 12*, 12-18.

Kerstiens. G. (1986, April). *Time-critical reading comprehension tests and developmental students*. Paper presented at the annual meeting of the American Educational Research Association, San Francisco, CA.

Kerstiens, G. (1990). A slow look at speeded reading comprehension tests. *Research in Developmental Education, 7*(3).

Kerstiens, G. (1993). Postsecondary student and placement: History, status, direction. *Proceedings of the 13th and 14th Annual Institutes of Learning Assistance Professionals*, Tucson, AZ.

Kerstiens, G. (1997). Almost too bad to be true. *Journal of Developmental Education, 21*(1), 42-43.

Losak, J. (1972). Do remedial programs really work? *Personnel and Guidance Journal, 50*(2), 383-386.

Luvaas-Briggs, L. (1984). Integrating basic skills with college content instruction. *Journal of Developmental and Remedial Education, 7*, 6-9, 31.

Martin, D. C., & Arendale, D. (1992). *Supplemental Instruction: Improving first-year student success in high-risk college courses* (Monograph No. 7). Columbia, SC: University of South Carolina, National Resource Center for The Freshman Year Experience.

Martin, D. C., & Arendale, D. (Eds.). (1994). *Supplemental Instruction: Increasing achievement and retention*. San Francisco: Jossey-Bass.

Maxwell, M. (1979). *Improving student learning skills: A comprehensive guide to successful practices and programs for increasing the performance of underprepared students*. San Francisco: Jossey-Bass.

Maxwell, M. (1997). *Improving student learning skills* (Revised ed.). Clearwater, FL: H & H.

Morante, E. A. (1989). Selecting tests and placing students. *Journal of Developmental Education, 13*(2), 1-6. Reprinted in M. Maxwell (Ed.). (1994), *From access to success*. (pp. 121-128). Clearwater, FL: H & H.

Nist, S. L., & Hynd, C. R. (1985). The college reading lab: An old story with a new twist. *Journal of Reading, 28*(4), 305-309. Reprinted in M. Maxwell (Ed.). (1994), *From access to success*. (pp. 169-171). Clearwater, FL: H & H.

Obler, M. (1977). Combining of traditional counseling, instruction, and mentoring functions with academically deficient college freshmen. *Journal of Educational Research, 5*, 192-197.

Peers, M. G. (1993). A teacher/researcher's experience with performance-based assessment as a diagnostic tool. *Journal of Reading, 36*(7), 544-548.

Quinn, K. B. (1995). Teaching reading and writing as modes of learning in college: A glance at the past, a view to the future. *Reading Research and Instruction, 34*(4), 285-314.

Ramirez, G. M. (1993). Supplemental Instruction. In S. Miodoski & G. Enright (Eds.), *Proceedings of the 13th and 14th Annual Institutes for Learning Assistance Professionals*. Tuscon, AZ.

Ramirez, G. M. (1996, October). *Where are they now? The long-term impact of SI*. Paper presented at the Second National Conference on Research in Developmental Education, Charlotte, NC.

Resnick, J. (1993). A paired reading and sociology course. In P. Malinowski (Ed.), *Perspectives of Practice in Developmental Education* (pp. 62-64). Canandaigua, NY: New York College Learning Association.

Richardson, R. C., & Marten, K. J. (1982). *A report on literacy development in community colleges*. Washington, DC: National Institute of Education.

Roueche, J. E., & Roueche, S. E. (1993). *Between a rock and a hard place: The at-risk student in the open-door college*. Washington, DC: The American Association of Community Colleges.

Simpson, M. L., & Nist, S. L. (1992). Toward defining a comprehensive assessment model for college reading. *Journal of Reading, 35*(6), 452-458.

Smith, F. (1994). *Understanding reading: A psycholinguistic analysis of reading and learning to read* (5th edition). Hillsdale, NJ: Lawrence Erlbaum.

Smittle, P. (1996, October). *Why do many high school graduates require basic skills remediation in college*. Paper presented at the Second National Conference on Research in Developmental Education, Charlotte, NC.

Stahl, N. A., Simpson, M. L., & Hayes, C. G. (1992). Ten recommendations from research for teaching high-risk college students. *Journal of Developmental Education, 16*(1), 2-8.

Stahl, N. A., Simpson, M. L., & Brozo, W. G. (1988). The materials of college reading instruction: A critical and historical perspective from 50 years of content analysis research. *Reading Research & Instruction, 273*, 16-34.

Sternberg, R. I. (1991). Are we reading too much into reading comprehension tests? *Journal of Reading, 34*(7), 539-544.

Tarabon, R. (1996). Reading comprehension development in college reading. *NADE Newsletter*, 10.

Tarabon, R. (1997). Using statewide data to assess the effectiveness of developmental reading programs. *Journal of College Reading and Learning, 27*(3), 119-128.

Tinto, V., Goodsell-Love, A., & Russo, P. (1990). *Building learning communities for new college students*. University Park, PA: National Center on Postsecondary Teaching, Learning, and Assessment.

Traub, J. (1991). *City on a hill: Testing the American dream at City College*. Reading, MA: Addison-Wesley.

University of Missouri-Kansas City. (1997). *Video-Based Supplemental Instruction Data*. Kansas City, MO: The Center for Academic Development, University of Missouri-Kansas City.

Utterback, J. (1989). Closing the door: A critical review of forced academic placement. *Journal of College Reading and Learning, 22*(2), 14-22.

Walter, T. L., Gomon, A., Guenzel, P. J., & Smith, D. E. P. (1989). Academic support programs. In M. L. Upcraft & J. N. Gardner (Eds.), *The freshman year experience: Helping students survive and succeed in college* (pp. 108-117). San Francisco: Jossey-Bass.

Wood, N. V. (1997). The status of college reading instruction as reflected in current reading textbooks. *Journal of College Reading and Learning, 27*(3), 79-95.

Chapter 15

Establishing Personal Management Training in Developmental Education and First-Year Curricula

Robert Nelson

Higbee (1996) writes of developmental educators: "We envision our mission as the development of the whole student, not just the development of intellectual competence" (p. 66). Consequently, we must assume responsibility for providing an educational curriculum that includes, to use Loehr's (1994) term, "training for life." Because the term "developmental" is relative to standards of individual institutions and because many students enter universities underprepared for their responsibilities (Farmer & Barham, 1996; Higbee, 1996; Nelson, 1996; Payne & Lyman, 1996), this "training for life" is applicable to all first-year student programs. As Upcraft and Gardner (1989) state: "Freshmen cannot be left to sink or swim. Institutions should have a clear definition of freshman success, and the freshman year must be strategically planned. It is too important to be left for chance" (p. 5).

As "trainers for life," developmental educators and first-year program coordinators have a responsibility to incorporate personal management training within developmental and first-year programs. Personal management skills can be defined as those behaviors that assist people in establishing appropriate goals, planning complicated projects, organizing daily and long-term schedules, and coping with the emotional, mental, and physical challenges that accompany such activity. Smith (1994) refers to this as "life management;" Covey (1994) refers to this as "life leadership."

Educators who teach developmental writing courses and work with students referred by professors, counselors, and administrators have become increasingly aware of the students' need for personal management skills. Indeed, much research in the 1990s has substantiated both the need for personal management training for students and the positive impact such training has on academic performance.

Britton and Tesser (1991), for instance, examined the time management skills and attitudes of 90 first-year college students at the University of Georgia and found that personal management skills and attitudes were more highly correlated with grade point averages than were SAT scores. Students who indicated on a questionnaire that they spent time organizing their daily activities and focused on making constructive use of their time were more likely to earn higher grade point averages at the completion of their undergraduate work. Macan, Shahani, Dipboye, and Phillips (1990) found similar results in a survey of 288 college students. They concluded that "students who perceived control of their time reported significantly greater evaluations of their performance, greater work and life satisfaction, less role ambiguity, less role overload, and fewer job-induced and somatic tensions" (p. 760).

Further studies advocate the implementation of personal management skills training through a supportive, organized college intervention program. Higbee and Dwinell (1992a; 1995) implemented a developmental studies counseling course at the University of Georgia "that focuses primarily on self-awareness issues such as setting goals and objectives, time management, career exploration, relationships and communication skills, academic anxiety, and health and wellness" (1992a, p. 28). At the end of the first academic year, 81 of 83 underprepared students who participated in the course were "still enrolled at the institution" (1992a, p. 31). Starks (1994) reiterates the importance of such an interactive retention model by identifying several successful first-year orientation programs that "stress the importance of academic integration of students in college" because they "integrate students' affective and academic needs" and provide "comprehensive student-help services" (pp. 22-23).

Further indicating the importance of social support for first-year students, Schwitzer, Robbins, and McGovern (1993) investigated the impact of psychosocial support for 113 first-year students and determined that students "with low goal instability and high natural social support had sig-

nificantly higher levels of post-test academic, institutional, and personal adjustment than people with low goal instability and low naturally occurring support" (p. 23). As a result, their findings advocate "a social support component in orientation seminars, residence hall programs, or other freshman adjustment interventions" (p. 24). This type of social support occurred in a newly established developmental program at Miami-Dade Community College, where the "teachers and advisors provide intensive monitoring of students' work" and students "were given more direction, fewer choices of curriculum, more information about college requirements, and closer follow up by advisors and counselors" (Roueche & Baker, 1994, p. 304). As a result, student graduation rates increased by nearly 30%. Starks (1994) confirms that "small classes for individualized learning," "frequent student/faculty contact in the classroom setting," and "cooperative or collaborative learning" are key elements to retaining developmental students "because they support academic and affective needs" (pp. 23-25).

The importance of a supportive, personal management program for first-year students is again confirmed by Starke's (1994) comparison of retention rates for students who attended an orientation course at Ramapo College in New Jersey with those students who did not participate in the program. The course contained units on study skills and interpersonal skills, as well as time and stress management. Students who attended the orientation "bonded more to the institution and experienced more benefits in both the academic and personal spheres" (p. 1) and "retention rates into the subsequent years of college favored those students who enrolled in the seminar" (p. 1). After two years of implementing this course, Ramapo required all first-year students to take the seminar.

Despite the overwhelming evidence of the positive impact of personal management training for college students, personal management skills

Despite the overwhelming evidence of the positive impact of personal management training for college students, personal management skills are not addressed in many developmental courses.

are not addressed in many developmental courses (e.g., math, reading, and writing) because instructors primarily attend to basic skills competencies so their students can eventually succeed in regular courses (see Boylan & Bonham, 1994). Consequently, as the courses become increasingly difficult, students may find themselves constantly struggling to get by and may never really gain confidence in themselves during their collegiate experience. To enable students to gain control of their academic agendas, personal management training must become integrated within the developmental and first-year curricula as our appropriate response to the "disequilibrium inherent in working with students during a period in their lives that is charged with opportunity for growth" (Higbee, 1996, p. 64). Students must have the opportunity to observe, recognize, develop, and exercise goal-setting principles, project-planning techniques, time management habits, and stress management strategies.

Some college developmental and first-year programs currently provide models for developing and exercising our students' personal management skills, and some study skills manuals provide helpful materials for the implementation of personal management training. The utilization of such personal management skills should ultimately permit these students simultaneously to control their schedules, acquire an intimate mastery of course content, and meet their individual academic objectives with confidence. Therefore, it is important to identify what constitutes an effective personal management training program and to discuss ways in which we can better prepare our students with personal management skills that will continue to empower them long after their undergraduate experience.

To begin personal management training, we must first request that our students think about their long-term goals. To do this, students must identify their personal values and principles so they have a foundation on which to base their goals. Once they have a general direction (e.g., graduating in five years, majoring in a particular academic field, or developing their awareness in a career area), they need to expand upon their repertoire of planning techniques that help them advance incrementally toward their long-term

goals. In addition to planning, they need to be made aware of fundamental time management behaviors that will allow them to utilize their time effectively and efficiently. Finally, to ensure a thorough, comprehensive personal management training program, students need direction on how to minimize the interference and discomfort caused by the stress that is inextricably intertwined with setting goals, planning projects, and managing time.

Goal Setting

Students must set general goals that provide them with a constructive direction and appropriate framework in which they can pursue their adult education. The first year of college is a particularly critical goal-setting period for college students. Moffatt (1989), after having conducted a 10-year ethnographic study of Rutgers University students, observed that "incoming freshmen usually had two goals for their first year in college: to do well in classes and to have fun (or to make friends, or to have a good social life)" (p. 33). Fiske and Chiriboga (1990) corroborate this observation, pointing out that young adults are at a period of shifting from hedonistic "fun and games" goals to goals that show they are "striving toward a semblance of adulthood" (p. 220) as they begin "changing their goals to match their circumstances" (p. 241). Unfortunately, as Starke (1994) calculates, "30% of America's freshmen are dropping out during their first year of college" (p. 2). Levitz and Noel (1989) write: "If we are to reduce the dropout rate, we must help students move toward goal-directed thinking and behaviors. At the same time, we must recognize that the uncertainties faced by freshmen are to be expected, and are usually healthy" (p. 73). As students enter their undergraduate education, they need to begin shaping their long-term objectives so they know what direction to take and ultimately what they want to accomplish. Below are three areas of appropriate goal setting principles for college students.

1. Successful students establish their own goals. Often, students who pursue degrees based upon others' expectations either lack the motivation to fulfill such expectations or do not feel a sense of achievement after the goal is accomplished.

Smith (1994) writes: "It takes great inner strength to stand up for your own values and live your life in harmony with them, rather than living according to the values of others" (p. 88). It is difficult but imperative for first-year students to determine the difference between what others want them to do and what they themselves want to do. As Covey (1994) warns, students must avoid "'the ladder against the wrong wall' syndrome, meaning, we climb the proverbial ladder of success only to find that it's leaning against the wrong wall for us" (p. 138). Consequently, students must begin planning their educational objectives according to their own values and principles. Fiske and Chiriboga (1990), after interviewing over 200 adults five different times over a 12-year period, also warn about what can occur when goals are reached that are not connected to a sense of personal purpose: "Several of our participants commented on the sense of loss they experienced after achieving some long-sought-after goal: the birth of a child, graduation, even retirement" (p. 241). Thus, we must do what we can to make our students aware that "mountains must be climbed to reach the other side" (Browne & Keeley, 1997, p. 1). In other words, students must want to graduate from college, but they must also have a sense of why they want to graduate and what they want to do afterward.

> As Covey (1994) warns, students must avoid "'the ladder against the wrong wall' syndrome, meaning, we climb the proverbial ladder of success only to find that it's leaning against the wrong wall for us" (p. 138).

College students must determine for themselves what is right and wrong, what educational goals are worth pursuing and sacrificing for, and what type of education will bring them happiness when their college experience has been completed. Maxwell (1997) refers to a study on developmental students conducted in 1949 which determined that high-risk students were more likely to be successful if "they themselves had selected a goal or major and felt their own interests had influenced the choices they made. In contrast, unsuccessful students felt that their goals had been selected for them and gave more

superficial reasons for wanting to attend college" (p. 138). Hirsch (1994) agrees: "There is a well-documented positive relationship between the degree to which students feel in control of their education (internal locus of control) and positive academic achievement" (p. 12). For our students to be committed to their education, they need to know for themselves that they are doing "the right thing, for the right reason, in the right way" (Covey, 1994, p. 146).

2. Successful students establish general academic goals first, then state specific goals. Lewallen (1993), who conducted a longitudinal study of 27,064 first-year students from 433 colleges and universities, determined that "being undecided about major choice or career choice was not significantly associated with persistence" and that "being undecided is not the exception, but the norm" (p. 110). Levitz and Noel (1989) support this, claiming, "Of the one million students who take the ACT assessment annually, two thirds indicate that they are not fully sure of their vocational choice" (p. 69). Thus, it is acceptable for students to enter college not knowing the field in which they want to major. Advisors should encourage these students to take courses in a variety of fields to get a sense of what they personally find interesting and purposeful.

Students (and their parents) must value a college education as an exploratory experience that will enable them to make choices for their future career paths. As students hone their general academic goals into more specific pursuits, such as moving from knowing that they want a college education to knowing that they want to major in business, they can set incremental markers and deadlines that will move them toward goal accomplishment. During this process, successful students will attempt to get the best grades they can, even if they believe a course to be boring or irrelevant, knowing that an overall higher grade point average will better enable them to be selected into a major, undergraduate or graduate program, or career field to which they ultimately wish to commit. Browne and Keeley (1997) observe that successful students do this by making active attempts to treat professors as expert sources of information, by associating with other students who want to take the course seriously, and by staying involved in class activities such as taking notes and asking appropriate questions.

3. Successful students set academic goals that are both challenging and attainable. Successful students become "action-oriented" (Smith, 1994, p. 84) toward fulfilling these goals. As they become more focused on what they want to do within their college experience, they dare themselves to strive toward the accomplishment of a certain number of degree credits with a desirable grade point average by establishing specific goals that are ambitious enough to create a sense of adventure, yet grounded in reality so that the goals will be achievable with the appropriate plans and hard work. They are aware that the accomplishment of goals must require sacrificial actions rather than wishes and good intentions. Consequently, they focus on the performance of activities to reach goals, and they take immediate action to progress toward the fulfillment of these goals. They approach their college studies with a daily "sense of urgency—a bias for action" (Smith, 1991, p. 21) by identifying the ultimate rewards associated with their academic goals (e.g., job opportunities in a career of interest or acceptance to a graduate program).

In short, successful students' goals are daring enough to create a personal contest of sorts, but they are not so farfetched that the slightest obstacle or lapse into procrastination will completely thwart the quest. Covey (1994) writes: "To set and work toward any goal is an act of courage" (p. 152). Successful students have both the confidence and the ability to challenge themselves with realistic, measurable goals that require great sacrifices, and they know that the rewards associated with their goals will make the sacrifices worthwhile.

Project Planning

Once they have established general goals, such as acquiring a college education, students need to implement planning strategies that will enable them to move incrementally toward their long-range goals. Proficient project planners "make time to plan" (Day-Timers, 1994) and have a repertoire of strategies to accomplish complicated assignments. Listed below are four characteristics of successful student planners of which first-year students need to be made aware when entering college.

1. Successful student planners break projects into manageable tasks with realistic deadlines. Those deadlines include: (a) establishing steps that will lead them toward the completion of important projects, (b) generating realistic deadlines for the completion of these steps, and (c) working to meet these deadlines. Once they have immediate tasks to perform, they take on a "bias for action" (Smith, 1991, p. 21) and begin working. They even give themselves "false due dates" (S. M. Swiderski, personal communication, March 5, 1997) to force themselves to work ahead of schedule in case they encounter unanticipated obstacles. They take a few minutes to plan their activities for the day, utilizing the "bundle of sticks" method (Pauk, 1997) for accomplishing complicated assignments. Simply put, the best way to break a bundle of sticks in half for kindling is to take out a few at a time rather than try to break the whole bundle at once. This echoes Browne and Keeley (1997), who advise students to "start small, and then take small steps" (p. 23).

In a sense, they have the ability to pace themselves appropriately in the present while thinking ahead to what must be accomplished in the future. They operate in "two time horizons" (Smith, 1994) by utilizing an assortment of short-term and long-term planning aids such as action lists and monthly calendars. These devices enable them to plot out activities according to due dates and establish daily objectives that will move them toward the completion of multiple tasks. As they are continually working to meet these short-term objectives, they continually review long-term goals so they don't "lose sight of the forest for the trees."

2. Successful student planners begin projects early. Getting an early start on an assignment provides them with the time and freedom to brainstorm about the best alternatives for accomplishing their objectives. The early start on an assignment gives the student the opportunity to gather information, ruminate over the matter, collaborate with others for assistance, and modify plans for convenience or effectiveness. This enables students to operate in what Covey (1994) refers to as "quadrant two" of the Covey Time Management Matrix, in which a student is involved with "activities that are important, but not urgent" (p. 37). In other words, beginning an important academic assignment early permits a student to become engaged in serious activity without the stress of an immediate deadline. Furthermore, working within this quadrant minimizes the amount of time spent in a "quadrant one" framework where students must concern themselves with "crises, pressing problems, and deadline-driven projects" (p. 37).

3. *Successful student planners willfully seek advice from others.* They eagerly accept input from anyone in a position to assist them or offer them information, and they view this action "as an enhancement-related behavior rather than a dependent behavior" (Maxwell, 1994, p. 166). They make use of what Gardner (1993) designates as interpersonal intelligence—"the ability to understand other people: what motivates them, how they work, how to work cooperatively with them" (p. 9). Bruner (1996) writes: "The cultural contexts that favor mental development are principally and inevitably interpersonal, for they involve symbolic exchanges and include a variety of joint enterprises with peers, parents, and teachers" (p. 68). Students making use of their interpersonal awareness will review other students' notes and old exams, converse and correspond with expert sources, and consider others' ideas as they chart out a course of action to complete an assignment (this, of course, does not justify plagiarism, when a student might submit someone else's work as his or her own). As students consider advice from others, they shuttle between their ability to understand others (interpersonal intelligence) and their ability to be candid with themselves (intrapersonal intelligence). They are both "people smart" and "self smart" (Armstrong, 1993, pp. 109-146), and they are capable of being honest with themselves about how their plans are going in comparison to alternative approaches

while being amenable to modifying their original plans for improved results.

4. *Successful student planners remain flexible, persistent, and optimistic.* They have a "Plan B." They anticipate obstacles. They are "proactive rather than reactive" (Covey, 1989), and thus can shift to other plans to ensure that the overall goal is accomplished. Covey (1994) refers to this as the "MacGyver Factor," after the television adventure hero, who "is the embodiment of the power of creative imagination" (p. 71). Covey accredits the fictional "master of ingenuity" with "understanding and being able to apply principles in a wide variety of situations" (p. 71). It is this flexible, persistent, and optimistic attitude with which successful planners operate to accomplish their mission. They are emotionally tough, meaning they are "able to deal with life in flexible, responsive, strong, and resilient ways" (Loehr, 1994, p. 120). They can endure adversity, thereby enabling themselves to consider instantly other avenues of approach when encountering barriers. They also have the self-discipline to be "able to stop unprofitable routines or activities" (Britton & Tesser, 1991, p. 409). It is this "emotional toughness," that "buffers people against falling into apathy, hopelessness, or depression in the face of tough going" (Goleman, 1995, p. 88). As Goleman (1995) reports of several empirical investigations, college students' levels of hope and optimism are better predictors of college grades than SAT scores (pp. 86-88). Simply put, there is a lot to be said for "having the right attitude."

Time Management

Once they develop strategies for planning their daily and long-term schedules to plot out the successful completion of multiple complicated tasks, students need to incorporate time management habits to ensure that they are performing their routines efficiently. Ironically, the term "time management" is a misnomer. Time itself is continuous, nonrecoverable and noncontrollable, finite and limited. We cannot manage it. We cannot slow it down when we are enjoying ourselves, and we cannot speed it up when we are miserable. Consequently, people must consider how they manage themselves rather than how they manage time. Perhaps Ellis (1990) has the best one-sentence definition for time management, which is simply a person's ability to "do what you say you will do, and to do it when you say you will do it."

Unfortunately, research shows that many college students are not experienced time managers. Thombs (1995) surveyed 576 first-year students in a public college in western New York state to find that "54% indicated that they did not manage their time effectively" (p. 283). A similar survey by Gallagher, Golin, and Kelleher (1992) conducted at the University of Pittsburgh with 806 students indicated that 52% of them reported a high or moderate need for assistance with overcoming procrastination. As Maxwell (1994) points out, "That management tips and schedules are the most popular handouts that students request from learning centers suggests that managing their time is a major adjustment problem of freshmen" (p. 162).

This is not surprising when we consider our high school students' previous experiences with time management responsibility. From the moment they arrive in school, they are directed where to go and when to go there. When they arrive home, especially if they arrive late because of involvement with extracurricular activities or part-time employment, they eat, and then have only a few hours before bedtime to decide how they are going to spend their time. Thus, their time management responsibility involves deciding during the last few hours of the evening how much to study and how much to entertain themselves. As Maxwell (1997) comments, "Whether they attend Harvard or an open-admission college, freshmen share a common problem—learning how to manage their own time" (p. 1). Because time management principles enable students to control their own agendas while minimizing stress levels, this dearth of time management experience can itself be distressing for college students who suddenly find themselves responsible for how they are going to spend their time. Consequently, college stu-

dents who may never have had to take any responsibility for managing their time (particularly first-year students and underprepared students) need to recognize the behaviors of good time managers, and they must exercise these behaviors until they develop into habits. Below are five general behaviors of effective time managers.

1. Effective time managers habitually reflect on how they spend their time. They make use of their intrapersonal intelligence. Intrapersonal intelligence is an area of private intellect that Gardner (1993) describes as "the capacity to form an accurate, veridical model of oneself and to be able to use that model to operate effectively in life" (p. 9). Students who exercise an intrapersonal intelligence recognize when they are being productive, and they are honest with themselves when they are wasting time. Gardner speculates that our intrapersonal abilities provide humans with "the capacity to transcend the satisfaction of instinctual drives" (p. 25).

Perhaps, then, it is this capacity that enables students to refuse to acquiesce to such temptations as procrastination and the errant rationalization of unproductive behavior. Moffatt (1989) observed that first-year students believed "that academic work and friendly fun were, or ought to be, about equally important activities during one's undergraduate years," but "they also almost all worked more and played less around exams or when big papers or other projects were due" (p. 33). We can say then, that successful students (as a result of their intrapersonal intelligence) exercise their ability to sacrifice personal entertainment (or at least delay such personal gratification) when there is work to be done.

It is also this intrapersonal intelligence that enables students to recognize their limitations, preventing them from "the hero syndrome that some of us get trapped into by thinking we can do more than we actually can" (Smith, 1994, p. 43). Successful students have the ability to identify a

Perhaps Ellis (1990) has the best one-sentence definition for time management, which is simply a person's ability to "do what you say you will do, and to do it when you say you will do it."

level of "just manageable difficulty" that is "both challenging and attainable" (Armstrong, 1993, p. 135). In other words, as a result of their intrapersonal awareness, their academic ambition is curbed within a candid sense of reality.

2. Effective time managers can prioritize responsibility. They know how to "separate the vital from the trivial" (Eagle International Institute, 1996, p. 5). A student should be able to wake up each day, review his or her action list and long-term planner, and determine what needs to get done that day, what needs to be started, and what can wait. Effective time managers are aware that there is a difference between being busy and being productive and will not allow themselves to become preoccupied with a menial task (e.g., cleaning out the closet) that will sabotage the completion of more important activities (e.g., preparing for exams and completing assignments).

3. Successful time managers establish realistic, flexible schedules. They know when they are most productive and can get major tasks out of the way. They "maximize the missing minutes" (Keim, 1995, p. 29) by studying during daylight hours when they are most alert. Pauk (1997) points out that "each hour used for study during the day is equal to one and a half hours at night" (p. 27). Unfortunately, many college students are not accustomed to studying during the day because they have graduated from an educational system that plans every daylight hour for them.

Successful time managers also make sure they plan more than enough time for the important things. If they feel they need three hours to prepare adequately for an exam, they will set aside four or five hours of study time. This extra "flat tire" time enables a student to prepare comfortably for what is most important, and allows the student time to recover in case an emergency arises or the studying takes longer than anticipated (see Day-Timers, 1994).

4. Effective time managers reward themselves for planned accomplishments. They position a "carrot in front of their noses" by promising themselves a gratuity after the accomplishment of a task. Consequently, they self-induce positive behav-

ior by rewarding themselves for accomplishing tasks, and they have the seriousness of purpose to deny themselves the reward if the tasks are not accomplished. A planned trip to a party, movie, or mall after a big exam or the completion of a writing assignment might be all that is needed to "jump start" the student into accomplishing priority tasks with a positive "let's get this done now" attitude.

5. Effective time managers write everything down. To ensure the accomplishment of simultaneous projects, they list everything they need to do so they will not forget to do it. They have simple, accessible "to do" lists in addition to long-term planners such as monthly calendars that provide a framework in which they can continually decide what present action to take, what to schedule for a specific later time, what can be delegated to others, and what can be ignored for the moment but not forgotten later (Ellis, 1990). There are a variety of publications with weekly, monthly, and daily planners. Perhaps the most comprehensive are those provided by Smith (1994), Pauk (1997), Ellis (1994), and Haynes (1994).

Writing things down on "to do" lists and monthly planners enables students to formulate their personal schedules because, as Risko, Alvarez, and Fairbanks (1991) point out, the amount of time needed for learning is "highly idiosyncratic" (p. 201). Underprepared students are at particular risk for lacking a sense of how much time they will need to learn information or complete an assignment, and they may make the mistake of establishing study schedules and routines comparable to their peers who may be more skilled in self-management techniques. Consequently, these students need to be encouraged not only to "make time to plan" (Day-Timers, 1994) but also to "over-plan" in case they need more time than originally expected.

Stress Management

As students clarify goals and develop routine plans to complete assignments and prepare for exams, they must prepare themselves for the stressful situations they are likely to encounter. Just the ecological transition (i.e., the displacement from one environment to another) creates stress for an individual (Banning, 1989). There is further potential for extreme stress because of the demands on first-year students to consider career goals as they begin to design for themselves a sense of purpose and identity in the adult world. Because they continue to value personal relationships, and because they are introduced to an elevated level of academic responsibilities (and for many, an elevated level of financial responsibilities as well), first-year students are likely to encounter an amount of stress previously unknown to them. They must suddenly concern themselves with "the often stressful task of meshing educational goals, sex roles and work roles" (Roberts, 1990, p. 201; see also Leafgren, 1989; Rayman & Garis, 1989; Roueche & Roueche, 1993; and Sher, Wood, & Gotham, 1996). Developmental first-year students may be the most at risk to encounter extreme stress. As Higbee and Dwinell (1992b) point out, "High-risk students may experience greater pressure than other freshmen to prove themselves and join the mainstream" (p. 35). This greater pressure is of particular concern because, as Macan, Shahani, Dipboye, and Phillips (1990) state: "Affective stress may cause poor time management. That is, students who are performing poorly and are dissatisfied with the present situation may, as a result of the accompanying stress, be less able to manage and control their time" (p. 767). The experience of extreme stress and accompanying loss of control can create a synergistic snowball effect that can lead these students into becoming completely overwhelmed.

In addition to interfering with students' academic pursuits, stress can lead to long-term debilitation. Barrow (1986) warns: "When unchecked, stress can lead directly to certain health problems. Degenerative illnesses, such as ulcers and heart disease, can be an outgrowth of uncontrolled stress. These conditions are likely to become problematic well after university years; however, the unhealthy patterns probably originate during university years or earlier" (p. 275; see also Roberts, 1990). Goleman (1995) echoes this warning and cites studies demonstrating that "many adults who suffer panic attacks say the attacks began during their teen years" (p. 219). He also lists the variety of diseases linked to the effects of prolonged stress.

Alarmingly, recent studies of college students indicate that today's undergraduates are experiencing more stress than students in previous decades. Murphy and Archer (1996) surveyed 639 students at a large Southeastern university to identify the major stressors during their undergraduate experience. They concluded that the students of the 1990s "continue to be highly stressed by exams, competition for grades, and too many demands on their time" (p. 26) as were the students in the 1980s. However, Murphy and Archer (1996) note that the 1990s students are further stressed "as class sizes increase and faculty is reduced" (p. 26), as there continues to be "the increased competition for professional employment" (p. 26), and as "the stress of never having enough money" (p. 27) accompanies the increased challenge of financing college (see also Keim, 1995; Maxwell, 1997; and Roueche & Roueche, 1993). Keeping Higbee's (1996) introductory comment in mind, that "we envision our mission as the development of the whole student, not just the development of intellectual competence" (p. 66), we undoubtedly have a responsibility to help our students manage stress. We can assist our students in minimizing the effects of stress by making them aware of the five points below.

1. Successful students minimize stressful encounters through time management techniques. They set goals, plan projects, and use time management strategies to assist them in their quest for identity and purposefulness while maintaining control. Macan et al. (1990) report that for college students, "feeling in control of the situation is related to lower levels of stress" (p. 767). Students who develop and exercise personal management skills have an internal control of their own schedules. Hammond (1990) cites several studies of undergraduates and determines that students "believing in the power of forces other than self are high-risk students" (p. 297). Having a repertoire of personal management skills enables students to have a personal sense of control over what happens to them and, when becoming temporarily alarmed, to regain that sense of control.

Acquired personal management skills enable students to operate in "quadrant two" of the Covey Matrix (Covey, 1989, 1994), a paradigm in which students are working on important projects (those projects that are attached to their long-term goals) well in advance so that they can function, as often as possible, without having to resort to crisis management. As a result of advanced attention to "things that matter most" (Covey, 1989), when urgent problems do arise, they are more easily managed. Students can operate on a daily basis in Covey's "quadrant two" paradigm by proactively previewing the scheduled activities for the day, prioritizing, and utilizing a "time-sensitive" planning technique that "empowers you to look at the best use of your time through the paradigm of importance rather than urgency" (Covey, 1994, p. 100).

2. Successful students use stress reduction techniques. They minimize their stress levels by identifying the sources of stress, by recognizing when they are reacting to stress, and by establishing a repertoire of strategies to reduce the negative effects of stress. King (1995) offers "The College Readjustment Rating Scale," which assigns values to "the amount of readjustment a person has to make in life as a result of change" (p. 348). This scale shows students the various life events that are likely to create additional stress in their lives and provides a sense of the relative levels of stress that might result by including a weight for each event (e.g., death of a parent versus a change in dating behavior). Students also need to know the symptoms of stress as well. To summarize King, breathing becomes more rapid, the heart rate increases, shoulder, neck, and chest muscles tighten, hands sweat, the stomach is disturbed, and the voice, hands, and knees may shake. To encourage students to identify both their personal sources of stress and their individual reactions to such stressors, Higbee and Dwinell (1992b) have developed "The Developmental Inventory of Sources of Stress (DISS)." This survey, which is both comprehensive and easy to administer, requires students to reflect on lifestyle, academic behavior, time management practice, and interactions with other people.

Students can minimize the effects of stress by being aware of the physical and mental exercises that can enable them to regain their immediate sense of control. For reducing the physical reactions to stress, Pauk (1997) advocates the "count-of-three" breathing method. This four-step method is easy to remember and easy to perform when anxiety levels begin to rise. It involves inhaling through the nose, holding the breath, exhaling through the nose, and pausing, all to the count of three (p. 48). This cycle, repeated several times, will almost always induce a more relaxed state. Ellis (1994) offers the following mental exercises for dealing with mental stress: yell "stop!" (to yourself if you are with others) to "break the cycle of worry," then try one of the following techniques—fill your mind with a daydream, visualize success, focus attention on a specific object, or use a positive monologue to induce a state of comfort and confidence (pp. 172-173).

3. Successful students minimize performance anxiety by over-preparing for tests and presentations. In a study by Murphy and Archer (1996) involving 639 students, undergraduates indicated that tests and finals were the most prevalent causes of stress among the undergraduate population. Maxwell (1997) verifies the degree to which test anxiety can be detrimental to academic performance: Test-anxious students "spend so much time worrying about how well they are doing that they have trouble concentrating" (p. 259) and they develop a "tunnel vision, a narrower attention to test cues, which leads them to overlook the important clues and misread key words" (p. 259). Maxwell (1997) discusses the many reasons why students may have test anxiety to the extent that it is academically debilitating. For example, they may have a genuine fear of failing, a simple overreaction to the importance of an exam, or even a severe anxiety attack that can render them both mentally and physically incapable.

Underprepared students who may not have studied in high school are particularly prone to test anxiety. They may not have been challenged before, and they may not have developed the coping skills necessary to compensate for such anxiety. As Hirsch (1994) writes, developmental students have "long-established negative perceptual/cognitive sets about the educational process" (p. 14); they also are more likely to lack a sense of internal control over what happens to them in college (Hashway, Hammond, & Rogers, 1990).

These underprepared students may lack the confidence it takes to relax and focus when taking exams. Affirming this, Higbee and Dwinell (1996) examined inventory responses from 71 first-term freshmen in a developmental program and "a significant negative correlation ($r = -.63$, $p < .01$) was found between self-esteem and test anxiety" (p. 44).

Thus, it is a challenge for developmental educators to assist students in overcoming both the negative perceptions of institutionalized education and the inferior sense of themselves. Sapp (1996) found in a study of 45 undergraduates that supportive counseling "allowing students to find solutions to their issues related to test anxiety" (p. 82) was more effective than hypnosis and relaxation therapy. At the College of Lake County in Illinois, Ross (1994) conducted "School Anxiety Reduction" courses that involved weekly meetings in small groups, a workbook, and audio tapes that covered study strategies and coping strategies for stress and which resulted in an "improvement in grades and course completion" (p. 12). Practicing relaxation exercises, predicting exam questions, testing oneself in a simulated testing environment, and over-preparing for exams (studying harder than the student thinks he or she needs to) are the best methods for developmental students to reduce exam anxiety. Browne and Keeley (1997) advise students to "focus on the process of learning, not just the results" (p. 14), and they encourage students to think of themselves as active learners who will challenge themselves, make some mistakes, then "accept the need to practice, practice, and practice again those things you find most difficult" (p. 15).

4. Successful students minimize the effects of stress by taking care of themselves. Murphy and Archer (1996), in their survey of 639 undergraduates to identify the major stressors for college students, found that the students in the 1990s indicated that there were "emerging categories related to

> *Thus, it is a challenge for developmental educators to assist students in overcoming both the negative perceptions of institutionalized education and the inferior sense of themselves.*

sleep and health problems" (p. 26). Pauk (1997) discusses in detail the importance of sleeping, eating, and exercising (pp. 54-66). Loehr (1994) states that "sleep clearly is the most important recovery activity in our lives" (p. 75) and advises people to keep a routine sleep-wake schedule by going to bed the same time each evening, getting up the same time each morning, avoiding caffeine in the evenings, and exercising regularly (pp. 74-79). Carter and Kravits (1996) advise students to think "balance" and "moderation" when it comes to healthy eating. They suggest "eating small meals at regular intervals" (p. 154) that represent the major food groups and are low in fat, sugar, and salt.

In partnership with sleep and proper diet, exercise will round out the health cycle. Many first-year students have had no physical training during high school unless they participated in an athletic activity after school. Others may be accustomed to a regular athletic regime until they begin college, when they no longer believe they have time for exercise. Students need to be aware of the benefits exercise will have on their future health, and they need to be encouraged to incorporate such activity into their daily routines. Loehr (1994) offers such guidelines as starting slowly into an exercise regime, seeking professional supervision, participating in an enjoyable activity, and increasing the activity over time (pp. 178-179).

5. Students can further minimize the effects of stress by asking for help when needed. Students exhibiting symptoms of depression are likely to experience a reduction in their ability to perform to their academic potential (see Haines, Norris, & Kashy, 1996). Sher, Wood, and Gotham (1996) examined 457 undergraduates over a four-year period and found that "the freshman year is most strongly associated with psychological distress" (p. 50), and although "much 'freshman distress' is relatively transient" (p. 49) their research also revealed that there were students "who experience significant distress during the freshman year and continue to experience some distress over the next several years" (p. 49). On the most serious note, Ellis (1994) reminds us that "suicide is the second leading cause of death among young adults between the ages of 15 and 25" (p. 174). Of the 10,000 suicide attempts among college students, 1,000 take their lives every year (Mitchell, Elmore, & Fygetakis, 1996, p. 698).

First-year and developmental students must be made aware that "people who talk to counselors are healthy people who will often gain new insights into the issues facing them" (Keim, 1995, p. 36). Educators must be accessible to and honest with troubled students, referring them to appropriate counselors and clinicians who can diagnose individual situations and provide professional direction.

Discussion

Citing the studies indicating the increasing number of "underprepared" and "misprepared" students entering college, Maxwell (1997) believes that today's students "seem to need even more help in adjusting to college than did their predecessors" (p. 2). Maxwell proposes that "one reason is that both high school teachers and college professors are subject matter specialists and have not been as concerned with teaching students how to learn their subjects" (p. 2). College instructors of first-year and developmental courses may be so concerned with improving the basic math, writing, and reading competencies of their students "for success in later college courses" (Boylan & Bonham, 1994, p. 309) that they cannot help students develop the "strategic control and regulation" of management techniques necessary for them to become "effective independent learners" (Stahl, Simpson, & Hayes, 1994, p. 154). Since it is unfair to burden these basic skills instructors with the task of both increasing their students' subject matter competencies and developing their students' personal management skills, colleges need to provide personal management training programs for as many of their incoming students as possible.

First-semester seminar courses for which first-year students receive academic credit provide the ideal opportunity to encourage students to exercise goal-setting principles, project-planning techniques, time management behaviors, and stress management strategies. The length and intensity of such a course and the amount of academic credit given to the students is subject to the needs of the student population, the standards of the university, and the resources available to provide such training.

Fortunately, the framework required to implement such training is extremely flexible. A college can offer a three-hour, self-management workshop to all incoming students or a three-credit, full-semester, self-management course. Higbee and Dwinell (1992a) argue that "for any program for underprepared students to reach its target audience it must be mandatory" (p. 32) because students who need such training may not even be aware that they lack personal management skills.

To accommodate any framework, there are a variety of training materials available, whether they be personal management handouts created by the individual instructors themselves or comprehensive personal management and study skills manuals. We must remember, however, that the most effective training programs are those that provide students with the opportunities to witness, recognize, develop, and exercise personal management skills while simultaneously enabling them to develop relationships with counselors, instructors, mentors, and peers.

For those educators who wish to go beyond instilling basic skills competencies by taking on a responsibility to educate students for life, we must concern ourselves with providing direction for, instilling confidence in, and modeling appropriate behavior for our students. We can do this by implementing a personal management training agenda that identifies the goal-setting principles, project-planning techniques, time management habits, and stress management strategies that our students must develop and exercise in order to graduate as confident, self-fulfilled adults.

References

Armstrong, T. (1993). *Seven kinds of smart: Identifying and developing your many intelligences*. New York: Plume.

Banning, J. H. (1989). Impact of college environments on freshman students. In M. L. Upcraft & J. N. Gardner (Eds.), *The freshman year experience* (pp. 53-64). San Francisco: Jossey-Bass.

Barrow, J. C. (1986). *Fostering cognitive development of students.* San Francisco: Jossey-Bass.

Boylan, H. R., & Bonham, B. S. (1994). The impact of developmental education programs. In M. Maxwell (Ed.), *From access to success: Readings in learning assistance and developmental education* (pp. 305-310). Clearwater, FL: H & H.

Britton, B. K., & Tesser, A. (1991). Effects of time-management practices on college grades. *Journal of Educational Psychology, 83*(3), 405-410.

Browne, M. N., & Keeley, S. (1997). *Striving for excellence in college.* Upper Saddle River, NJ: Prentice Hall.

Bruner, J. S. (1996). *The culture of education.* Cambridge, MA: Harvard University Press.

Carter, C., & Kravits, S. L. (1996). *Keys to success: How to achieve your goals.* Upper Saddle River, NJ: Prentice Hall.

Covey, S. R. (1989). *The seven habits of highly effective people* (Cassette Recording No. 68796-4). New York: Simon and Schuster Sound Ideas.

Covey, S. R. (1994). *First things first.* New York: Simon and Schuster.

Day-Timers, Inc. (1994). *Day-timer solutions for success: Time power for today* [Film]. (Available from Day-Timers, Inc., One Day-Timer Plaza, Allentown, Pennsylvania, 18195-1551)

Eagle International Institute, Inc. (1996). *How to increase your personal and professional productivity.* Rochester, NY: Author.

Ellis, D. B. (1990). *Becoming a master student: Time management* [Film]. (Available from College Survival, Inc., 2650 Jackson Boulevard, Rapid City, SD 57702-3474)

Ellis, D. B. (1994). *Becoming a master student* (7th edition). Rapid City, SD: College Survival.

Farmer, V. L., & Barham, W. A. (1996). Selected models of developmental education programs in postsecondary institutions. *Selected conference papers, 2* (pp. 10-11). Carol Stream, IL: National Association for Developmental Education.

Fiske, M., & Chiriboga, D. A. (1990). *Change and continuity in adult life.* San Francisco: Jossey-Bass.

Gallagher, R. P., Golin, A., & Kelleher, K. (1992). The personal, career, and learning skills needs of college students. *Journal of College Student Development, 33*(4), 301-309.

Gardner, H. (1993). *Multiple intelligence: The theory in practice.* New York: Basic Books.

Goleman, D. (1995). *Emotional intelligence.* New York: Bantam Books.

Haines, M. E., Norris, M. P., & Kashy, D. A. (1996). The effects of depressed mood on academic performance in college students. *Journal of College Student Development, 37*(5), 519-526.

Hammond, C. J. (1990). Effective counseling. In R. M. Hashway (Ed.), *Handbook of developmental education* (pp. 279-304). New York: Praeger.

Hashway, R. M., Hammond, C. J., & Rogers, P. H. (1990). Academic locus of control and the collegiate experience. *Research and Teaching in Developmental Education, 7*(1), 45-54.

Haynes, M. E. (1994). *Personal time management.* Menlo Park, CA: Crisp Publications.

Higbee, J. L. (1996). Defining developmental education: A commentary. In J. L. Higbee & P. L. Dwinell (Eds.), *Defining developmental education: Theory, research, and pedagogy* (pp. 63-66). Carol Stream, IL: National Association for Developmental Education.

Higbee, J. L., & Dwinell, P. L. (1992a). The development of underprepared freshmen enrolled in a self-awareness course. *Journal of College Student Development, 33*, 26-33.

Higbee, J. L., & Dwinell, P. L. (1992b). The developmental inventory of sources of stress (DISS). *Research and Teaching in Developmental Education, 8*(2), 27-40.

Higbee, J. L., & Dwinell, P. L. (1995). Affect: How important is it? *Research and Teaching in Developmental Education, 12*(1), 71-74.

Higbee, J. L., & Dwinell, P. L. (1996). Correlates of self-esteem among high risk students. *Research and Teaching in Developmental Education, 12*(2), 41-50.

Hirsch, G. (1994). Helping students overcome the effects of difficult learning histories. *Journal of Developmental Education, 18*(2), 10-16.

Keim, W. (1995). *The education of character: Lessons for beginners.* Fort Worth, TX: Harcourt Brace College Publishers.

King, K. W. (1995). Managing Stress. In John N. Gardner & A. J. Jewler (Eds.), *Your college experience: Strategies for success* (pp. 345-357). Belmont, CA: Wadsworth Publishing Company.

Leafgren, F. A. (1989). Health and

wellness programs. In M. L. Upcraft & J. N. Gardner (Eds.), *The freshman year experience* (pp. 156-167). San Francisco: Jossey-Bass.

Levitz, R., & Noel, L. (1989). Connecting students to institutions: Keys to retention and success. In M. L. Upcraft & J. N. Gardner (Eds.), *The freshman year experience* (pp. 65-81). San Francisco: Jossey-Bass.

Lewallen, W. (1993). The impact of being "undecided" on college-student persistence. *Journal of College Student Development, 34,* 103-112.

Loehr, J. E. (1994). *Toughness training for life.* New York: Penguin Books USA.

Macan, T. F., Shahani, C., Dipboye, R. L., & Phillips, A. P. (1990). College students' time management: Correlations with academic performance and stress. *Journal of Educational Psychology, 82*(4), 760-768.

Maxwell, M. (1994). Are the skills we're teaching obsolete? A review of recent research in reading and study skills. In M. Maxwell (Ed.), *From access to success: Readings in learning assistance and developmental education* (pp. 161-167). Clearwater, FL: H & H.

Maxwell, M. (1997). *Improving student learning skills.* Clearwater, FL: H & H.

Mitchell, S. L., Elmore, K., & Fygetakis, L. M. (1996). A coordinated campus response to student suicide. *Journal of College Student Development, 37*(6), 698-699.

Moffatt, M. (1989). *Coming of age in New Jersey.* New Brunswick, NJ: Rutgers University Press.

Murphy, M. C., & Archer, J. (1996). Stressors on the college campus: A comparison of 1985 and 1993. *Journal of College Student Development, 37*(1), 20-28.

Nelson, R. R. (1996). Peer tutors at the collegiate level: Maneuvering within the zone of proximal development. *Journal of College Reading and Learning, 27*(1), 43-51.

Pauk, W. (1997). *How to study in college* (6th edition). New York: Houghton Mifflin.

Payne, E. M., & Lyman, B. G. (1996). Issues affecting the definition of developmental education. In J. L. Higbee & P. L. Dwinell (Eds.), *Defining developmental education: Theory, research, & pedagogy* (pp. 11-20). Carol Stream, IL: National Association for Developmental Education.

Rayman, J. R., & Garis, J. W. (1989). Counseling. In M. L. Upcraft & J. N. Gardner (Eds.), *The freshman year experience* (pp. 129-141).

San Francisco: Jossey-Bass.

Risko, V. J., Alvarez, M. C., & Fairbanks, M. M. (1991). External factors that influence study. In R. F. Flippo & D. C. Caverly (Eds.), *Teaching reading and study strategies at the college level* (pp. 195-236). Newark, DE: International Reading Association.

Roberts, G. H. (1990). Stress and the developmental student. In R. M. Hashway (Ed.). *Handbook of developmental education* (pp. 197-216). New York: Praeger.

Ross, D. B. (1994). *Group reduction of test anxiety: Does it really work?* (ERIC Document Reproduction Service No. ED 379 312).

Roueche, J. E., & Baker, G. E. (1994). A case study on an exemplary developmental studies program. In M. Maxwell (Ed.), *From access to success: Readings in learning assistance and developmental education* (pp. 303-304). Clearwater, FL: H & H.

Roueche, J. E., & Roueche, S. D. (1993). *Between a rock and a hard place: The at-risk student in the open-door college.* Washington, DC: Community College Press.

Sapp, M. (1996). Three treatments for reducing the worry and emotionality components of test anxiety with undergraduate and graduate college students: Cognitive-behavioral hypnosis, relaxation therapy, and supportive counseling. *Journal of College Student Development, 37*(1), 79-87.

Sher, K. J., Wood, P. K., & Gotham, H. J. (1996). The course of psychological distress in college: A prospective high-risk study. *Journal of College Student Development, 37*(1), 43-51.

Smith, H. (1991). *Franklin International Institute: Seven ingredients for success.* Princeton, NJ: Princeton University Press.

Smith, H. (1994). *The 10 natural laws of successful time and life management.* New York: Warner Books.

Schwitzer, A. M., Robbins, S. B., & McGovern, T. V. (1993). Influences of goal instability and social support on college adjustment. *Journal of College Student Development, 34,* 21-25.

Stahl, N. A., Simpson, M. L., & Hayes, C. G. (1994). Ten recommendations from research for teaching high risk college students. In M. Maxwell (Ed.), *From access to success: Readings in learning assistance and developmental education* (pp. 147-167). Clearwater, FL: H & H.

Starke, M. C. (1994). *Retention, bonding, and academic achievement: Effectiveness of the college seminar in promoting college success.* (ERIC Document Reproduction Service No. ED 374 741)

Starks, G. (1994). Retention and developmental education: What the research has to say. In M. Maxwell (Ed.), *From access to success: Readings in learning assistance and developmental education* (pp. 19-27). Clearwater, FL: H & H.

Thombs, D. L. (1995). Problem behavior and academic achievement among first-semester college freshman. *Journal of College Student Development, 36*(3), 280-288.

Upcraft, M. L., & Gardner, J. N. (1989). A comprehensive approach to enhancing freshman success. In M. L. Upcraft & J. N. Gardner (Eds.), *The freshman year experience* (pp. 1-12). San Francisco: Jossey-Bass.

Chapter 16

Increasing Efficiency and Effectiveness of Learning for Freshman Students through Supplemental Instruction

David Arendale

Some educational leaders proclaim a new emphasis is taking root in higher education. They expose the time honored myth that teaching and learning are two sides of the same coin, posing the question: "How can we be teaching if students are not learning?" The answer is simple: Some students are ready for the curriculum, while others are not. Professors cannot be expected to design a perfect lesson or devise a magical test that will effectively bridge all the gaps between the different learning abilities of the students in their class. The reality of higher education is that no traditionally taught, teacher-centered course's curriculum (no matter how gifted the professor) can be universally mastered by every student without some additional form of assistance.

This new change in emphasis of the educational model is reflected in several areas. The first area concerns the central focus of education. Rather than the traditional teacher-centered model, the focus shifts to being learning-centered. Instead of focusing on the broadcaster of information, emphasis is now on the effectiveness of the transmission process. The traditional instructional model encourages an increase not only in the quantity of information that is presented to students, but also in the use of new instructional technologies for transmission. After a long period of focusing energies on and committing scarce resources to improving teaching, many bruised and battered educators are turning their attention to improving the efficiency and effectiveness of the learning environment. Rather than examining how much information is delivered, the new focus is upon how much the student understands. This new emphasis embraces the appropriate use of state-of-the-art technology to enhance instructional delivery without sacrificing the importance of a stable learning environment.

A second dimension of the new educational model measures the effectiveness of education. Have students deeply understood and mastered the material? Can students discuss the material in their own words and transform it into novel applications and expressions? The traditional periodic examinations, although perhaps effective in assessing the degree to which students have copied a field of data, are insufficient measures of higher levels of learning. The new model uses continuous formal and informal classroom assessment to provide feedback to both students and instructors concerning the effectiveness of learning. The old model made the assumption that if teachers broadcast information, it would be received by students. Students, however, are more complicated than television sets that receive programs from the broadcasters.

The new educational model recognizes that professors cannot deliver the perfect lecture and that there is no perfect test; therefore, we must change what we do. We must recognize who our students are; we must change the way we think about ourselves and our students. Professors must acknowledge that the gender balance is shifting in higher education and that the mean age is rising, but also that many of the changes go beyond demographics. Many students expect relevance of the course material and bring a wealth of personal experiences to the classroom to integrate with the course material. Traditional-age students come from secondary education where collaborative learning activities have accustomed students to working in small groups and engaging in peer discussions. Although previous generations of students took seriously the admonition that required two hours of preparation for each hour in class, a growing number of the present generation expect satisfactory grades regardless of understanding and preparation because higher education is just one part of their busy lives. Many students have a low tolerance for frustration, and delayed gratification is a foreign concept. Some students view themselves as "consumers" who have "purchased" a product (traded tuition dollars for a college degree),

and they expect it to be delivered in an acceptable fashion. They have high expectations regarding support services to make the process convenient and trouble-free. We do not have to approve or support these expectations or behaviors, but it is critical that we understand them.

Role of Developmental Education with the Changing Educational Model

As the focus of education shifts from the professor to the learner, developmental educators have a historic opportunity to reinvent themselves as resources for the entire campus (students and faculty alike) as partners in the new enriched learning environment. The learning process must be expanded beyond the traditional classroom walls. The new process must be released from the shackles of the fixed number of traditional class time periods. New partners must be added to the learning environment in addition to the classroom professor. Developmental educators are vital change agents in renewing the learning environment.

The following vision statement was developed by the National Association for Developmental Education (NADE) (1997), "By 2003, NADE will be a nationally recognized association of professionals with expertise to help students academically succeed throughout the entire educational experience from high school through college and graduate/professional school." Building upon service to developmental education students, many NADE leaders at the local, state, and national level encourage developmental educators to expand their mission to support learning achievement by all students, not just those at the margins of academic success.

The first year of college has always presented challenges to both students and institutions. For students it is one of life's most critical transitions. The first- to second-year attrition rate of nearly 50% is a national trend among two-year

Many NADE leaders at the local, state, and national level encourage developmental educators to expand their mission to support learning achievement by all students, not just those at the margins of academic success.

institutions. Attrition rates have also increased at many four-year institutions over the past decade, except those with highly selective admission policies (American College Testing Program, 1997). Moreover, most institutions are faced with severe budget constraints and limited flexibility in assigning personnel to student retention activities.

Effective models of retention stress the need for students to be integrated into the academic and social dimensions of the college community (Tinto, 1993). These connections need to be established during the initial weeks of students' first year of college. This interpersonal support system is important for all first-year students despite their background and experience.

In addition to concerns about student dropout rates, there is a particular concern with student persistence in mathematics, science, and engineering for all student subpopulations, but particularly for females and students of color. Some researchers (Shlipak, 1988) have found a positive correlation between persistence in science courses and involvement in study groups outside of class for female students. Researchers (Hilton & Lee, 1988) also suggest that increased student involvement is an important strategy to help stem the dropout rate for all science and math students.

Developmental educators have many of the skills needed to promote student learning and to increase graduation rates. Some of those skills include the following: academic assessment, counseling, academic advisement, high-school-to-college bridge programs, classroom assessment techniques, instructional technology, collaborative peer-assisted learning, curriculum development, program evaluation, and many others, including the adaptation of instruction to meet affective needs of diverse students. These skills uniquely position developmental educators to expand the services of their centers or departments to a wider population. Georgia State University, for example, has moved away from offering traditional developmental classes and a tutoring center and has expanded to include course related services such as Supplemental Instruction and linked courses (Commander,

Stratton, Callahan, & Smith, 1996; Stratton, Commander, Callahan, & Smith, 1997).

Numerous developmental education centers have been transformed into full-service learning and teaching centers. Rather than focusing exclusively on developmental students, these departments have changed their mission. This "value-added" mission expands service for all students, not just those at the institution's two extremes (i.e., the developmental and gifted students) who have traditionally received additional help. In addition, some of these expanded centers also provide faculty development services. An overview of some of these centers is provided through the NADE home page (http://www.umkc.edu/centers/cad/nade/nadedocs/lrnteacn.htm). Some of the common practices of these expanded centers include using academic support programs to provide requested feedback to professors, publishing teaching effectiveness newsletters, conducting learning effectiveness workshops, providing teaching mentors, and consulting on instructional delivery innovation.

Some programs report innovative means to facilitate faculty development activities concurrently as the faculty members participate in learning assistance activities. The Educational Development Center at Central Missouri State University coordinates the new student orientation course for hundreds of students each year. While the course obviously has benefit for the students, one of the original purposes of the course was faculty development. Instructors for the course are drawn from volunteers throughout the campus. Many of them are faculty members who receive additional funds for various professional development activities (e.g., journal subscriptions and conference registrations) in lieu of extra pay. In addition, orientation teachers gather on a weekly basis to discuss common course issues and share effective teaching strategies.

Overview of Supplemental Instruction (SI)

Many developmental educators can help faculty improve the effectiveness and efficiency of the learning environment. One of the learning assistance programs that offers diverse opportunities to enrich the learning environment is Supplemental Instruction (Martin & Arendale, 1994). Supplemental Instruction (SI) is used by more than 800 campuses in the United States and 12 other countries to increase understanding of content in historically difficult courses. There are more than 350 citations in the professional literature concerning the use of SI in the United States and abroad (Arendale, 1997). The SI program was created at the University of Missouri-Kansas City (UMKC) in 1973 by Deanna C. Martin. Extensive literature regarding SI can be found at its web site: www.umkc.edu/cad/si.htm.

SI is a student academic assistance program that increases academic performance and retention through its use of selected collaborative learning and study strategies. The SI program targets traditionally difficult academic courses, those that typically have 30% or higher rate of D or F final course grades or withdrawals (e.g., algebra, chemistry, anatomy). SI provides regularly scheduled, out-of-class, peer-facilitated sessions that offer students an opportunity to discuss and process course information (Martin, Lorton, Blanc, & Evans, 1977).

SI Addresses Needs of New Education Emphasis Areas

SI sessions are extensions of the classroom in which students continue the learning process initiated by the professor (Wilcox, 1995). Rather than being limited by the prescribed classroom time, students are able to attend SI sessions as often as they desire throughout the academic term to receive the assistance they need and to engage in intellectual inquiry. Students receive continuous feedback regarding their comprehension of the classroom material, thereby giving them the opportunity to modify their study behaviors before taking examinations. Immediate feedback received during SI sessions enables students to modify study behaviors quickly to adapt to the academic rigor and requirements of the course. Many students are responsive to SI because they perceive that the sessions meet their need for academic assistance. Professors participate in the SI program at the level they choose. Some faculty members report significant professional development opportunities for

themselves that are described later in this chapter. SI sessions provide a way to integrate "what to learn" with "how to learn." SI allows students to develop the needed learning strategies while they are currently enrolled in college-degree credit courses.

SI Program Activities

Assistance begins in the first week of the term. The SI leader, a former successful student of the same class, introduces the program during the first class session and surveys the students to establish a schedule for the SI sessions. Attendance is voluntary. Students of varying abilities participate, and no effort is made to segregate students based on academic ability. Many underprepared students who might otherwise avoid seeking assistance will participate in SI because it is not perceived to be remediation, and there is no potential stigma attached that can cause motivation problems for developmental students (Somers, 1988). SI increases student persistence and graduation rates and is more cost-effective than one-on-one tutoring programs (Martin & Arendale, 1993).

Glendale Community College in Glendale, California has reported success with SI in calculus courses. The following student comments are illustrative of the benefits of the SI sessions:

> What I really liked about the SI was that if I had any questions, Dr. Kolpas or the other helpers didn't tell us the answer. Instead, they let us think about the problem, set it up, and solve it ourselves. I also liked the one-on-one help and the friends I made. . . . Having more opinions and minds to work a problem helped a lot. The groups discussed problems from many different points of view. (Allen, Kolpas, & Stathis, 1992, p. 9)

Some UMKC students noted that the learning environment in SI provided them a comfortable place to work; one SI leader said, "Students realize at the SI sessions what they do not understand; after determining this, students are less likely to be intimidated and more eager to tackle the more difficult concepts." A UMKC sophomore stated, "I felt comfortable about being wrong in front of other students in SI sessions, no insecurities." A first-year student at Colorado State University said that "SI gives us a chance to talk about the problem and to work through it ourselves instead of the professor telling us what it ought to be. You work it yourself. This way it sticks in your mind."

Concurrent Development of "What to Learn" and "How to Learn"

SI sessions provide a way to integrate "what to learn" with "how to learn." Students develop the needed learning strategies while they are currently enrolled in college-degree credit courses. SI avoids the remedial stigma often attached to traditional academic assistance programs because it does not identify "high-risk students" but identifies "historically difficult classes." Because SI is open to all students in the targeted course, prescreening of students is unnecessary. The SI program begins the first week of the academic term, so the program provides academic assistance during the critical first six-week period of class before many students face their first major examination. Attrition is thought to be highest during this period (Noel, Levitz, & Saluri, 1985).

> *SI avoids the remedial stigma often attached to traditional academic assistance programs because it does not identify "high-risk students" but identifies "historically difficult classes."*

Focus on Historically Difficult Courses

Historically difficult courses often share the following characteristics: large amounts of weekly readings from both difficult textbooks and secondary library reference works, infrequent examinations that focus on higher cognitive levels, voluntary and unrecorded class attendance, and large classes in which each student has little opportunity for interaction with the professor or the other students. Christie and Dinham (1991) concluded that it is difficult to rely solely upon the analysis of high school grades and standardized college entrance examination scores to identify all students who will withdraw from college. Less than 25% of all students who drop out of college do so because the institution has academically dismissed them (Tinto, 1993). Many leave the institution due to extreme difficulty and frustration in high-risk courses.

A designation of "historically difficult" for a course makes no prejudicial comment about the professor or the students. It is a numerical calculation that suggests many students have difficulty in meeting academic requirements for the class. Rather than blaming the students or the professor, the designation suggests that additional academic support is needed for students to raise their level of academic performance to meet the level deemed appropriate by the classroom professor. In recent years, the popular and professional literature has been replete with extensive discussions about who is at fault for the perceived lower quality of student academic achievement. Supplemental Instruction bypasses this issue and provides a practical solution that helps students meet the professor's level of expectation.

Key SI Program Personnel

There are three key persons involved with SI on each campus: 1. the SI student leaders, 2. the SI supervisor, and 3. the course instructors. Each plays an important role in creating the environment that allows the SI program to flourish.

1. The first key person, the SI leader, is a student who has successfully completed the targeted class or a comparable course. It is ideal if the student has taken the course from the same instructor for whom he or she is now providing SI assistance. The SI leader is trained in proactive learning and study strategies and operates as a "model student," attending all course lectures, taking notes, and reading all assigned materials. The SI leader conducts three or more out-of-class SI sessions per week during which he or she integrates "how to learn" with "what to learn."

189

The SI leader is a facilitator, not a mini-professor. The role of the leader is to provide structure to the study session, not re-lecture or introduce new material. The SI leader should be a model student who shows how successful students think about and process course content. He or she facilitates collaborative learning, an important strategy that empowers students to become more self-sufficient and less dependent as learners. In contrast, traditional tutoring often increases dependency. Furthermore, research suggests that tutoring relationships do not always promote transfer of academic skills (Keimig, 1983).

A central responsibility of the SI leader is to integrate study skills with the course content. As someone who has performed well in the course, the SI leader has displayed mastery of the course material. However, it is important for the SI leader to share learning strategies with the other students in the SI sessions. If the students learn only content material and not the underlying study strategies, they will have a high probability of experiencing academic difficulty in succeeding courses. The integration of study skills with course content is a key difference between SI and other forms of collaborative learning. The SI model is more than students simply working together; it is the planned integration of study strategies with course content that sets SI apart. By combining "what to learn" with "how to learn it," students can develop both content competency and transferable academic skills. Supplemental Instruction sessions capitalize on the use of the "teachable moment" to integrate learning strategies with the course material.

SI provides many opportunities to address study skills within the content of the course. Research has shown that teaching study skills in isolation from content has little impact on the students' academic performance (Dimon, 1988; Keimig, 1983; Stahl, Simpson, & Hayes, 1992). Although students can be taught elaborate note-taking and text-reading strategies, these skills usually are not applied in subsequent courses. Different classes and texts often require different note-taking and text-reading styles; for example, a science text is read differently from a social science text. As SI leaders model appropriate

questioning and reasoning, students begin to internalize aspects of thinking strategies that will carry over into their individual and group study.

A qualitative study from the United Kingdom (Ashwin, 1993) suggested the following benefits to SI student leaders from their participation in the program: increased confidence, greater understanding of course material, and increased interest by potential employers due to cocurricular nature of SI-leader experience. Maloney (1992) reported the use of the SI-leader experience as an alternative field experience for secondary education majors prior to student teaching.

2. The second key person in the SI program is the SI supervisor, a faculty or staff member who has received formal training to supervise the program and whose responsibilities include: selecting courses for support, hiring and supervising SI student leaders, and completing evaluation reports every academic term that SI is offered. Supervision of SI leaders during their SI sessions is critical. It is not enough to conduct an initial workshop at the beginning of the term and then have a party at the end. SI student leaders need helpful feedback from the SI supervisor on the following behaviors that occur during the SI sessions: modeling appropriate study strategies, allowing students to set the agenda for the SI session, insuring that the SI leader does not talk too much, and using effective collaborative learning strategies to encourage active learning.

3. The third key person in the SI program is the faculty member. SI is only offered in connection with classes that have the full support of the classroom instructor. Instructors choose their level of involvement with the SI program. At a minimum, the instructor makes an announcement at the beginning of the academic term endorsing the SI program and encouraging the participation of all students. Some instructors spend a few minutes each week with the SI leader reviewing SI session plans. Increasing levels of involvement could lead to the instructor helping the SI leader prepare mock practice exams or practice problems.

Jean Jubelirer (personal communication, August 15, 1995), campus SI Coordinator for Milwaukee Area Technical College (MATC), finds the collaborative nature of SI very powerful. The SI program at MATC started with two classes in 1989 and now operates in 13 classes each term, serving over 1,000 students each year. Jubelirer says that SI helps to form learning communities composed of the SI leader, participating students, and the classroom instructor. Strong bonds are formed among all three. Beyond quantifiable results of increased persistence and better grades, students frequently describe the personal impact of the SI program on their ability to learn. Faculty members appreciate SI leaders because they help students learn material presented in class lectures.

SI Adds Value to the Professor's Lecture and Assigned Readings

SI adds value to the professor's lectures and assigned readings through the out-of-class, peer-facilitated review sessions. As one United Kingdom student said, "the fact that SI sessions followed lectures added value" (Wallace, 1996). Professors have an ever-expanding knowledge base to consider as they deliver their lectures and make reading assignments. Since the number of class periods will not increase, strategies must be developed to help students manage study time outside of class in order to master the instructional content.

The SI leader can teach the students to use appropriate strategies. This is why it is critical that the SI leader attend class with the students. The students need specific assistance with the day's reading material and lecture notes as well as appropriate use of study skill strategies. Supplemental Instruction activities can enhance both study skills and comprehension of the course content. It is generally not advisable to label these activities as study skill instruction, but rather to weave skills into the context of the course material. Supplemental Instruction leaders need to recognize "teachable moments" and introduce appropriate skills, tying them directly to the content review. Often these discussions last at most only a few minutes.

Processing lecture notes requires students to consider the adequacy of their own note-taking techniques. It quickly becomes evident to many of them that there may be a better note-taking method than the one they presently use. SI student leaders suggest the following: using summary margin notebook paper (which has a wide left margin), recopying notes that are particularly difficult to decipher, writing potential test questions that can be used to review the material in their notes, correlating notes with outside reading assignments, and highlighting notes when appropriate. In addition to modeling the strategies of the SI leader, other students in the study group are encouraged to share their own methods as well.

Students find that organizing and processing information during the SI session are very beneficial. They see that course content is manageable and that with some work and mutual support, they can make sense out of even the most difficult material. One SI participant said that SI sessions, "clarified things in your own mind if you had to explain it." A student at UMKC reported about actively listening during the SI sessions, "From the other people talking, I get a better understanding than what I get in the lecture. The other students put it into better words."

After each exam, the SI leader can guide the group in reviewing the questions that were particularly troublesome. This process gives the students a chance to reexamine the way they initially interpreted the questions and the manner in which they derived their answers. If they originally made an error, this will give them a chance to see the reasons why and help avoid repeating the mistake in the future. Reviewing the test will also help students to understand more thoroughly the kinds of questions the professor asks and to predict future test questions more accurately. This activity helps students select the most important concepts in the lecture. Sometimes students who attempt to record every statement made in the course can have the same level of academic difficulty as those who take very few notes. The ability to value and prioritize information is as important a skill as the ability to quickly record notes from live lectures or textbooks.

If the textbook includes graphs, charts, or diagrams, students must learn to include these aids in their study of the materials. Occasionally, when graphs are used extensively, it is appropriate to review how to read and interpret graphs, as well as to review the material they contain.

Text reading efficiency can be enhanced through a procedure called "reciprocal questioning" (Martin & Blanc, 1984). In brief, a small section of the text is selected for silent reading, and both the SI leader and the students take turns asking and answering questions. When students become active readers, as this procedure requires, they find that the time they must spend in rereading material is greatly reduced because they comprehend more information during their initial reading.

At times during the term it will be helpful to direct the students' attention back to the course syllabus. From the syllabus students can anticipate the dates of future tests and the amount of material to be covered between tests. Some discussion can result that will include tips on time management.

SI as a Follow-Up to The First-Year Experience

The SI program is uniquely suited to serve as a companion of a campus first-year experience program. Supplemental Instruction provides immediate application of learning strategies to content courses, formation of learning communities composed of students who seek higher academic achievement, a solution to common factors in student attrition, and an expectation of higher levels of academic performance for historically difficult first-year courses (Martin & Arendale, 1993). Supplemental Instruction is an excellent follow-up activity for students who have participated in first-year experience programs since it provides a supportive environment for the immediate application and use

of study strategies that were discussed or demonstrated during those programs.

First-year student programs conducted before the beginning of the academic term often teach study strategies by lecture only with no opportunities for students to practice. Such sessions are isolated from the actual content material in college courses. Students often feel frustrated when faced with abstract lectures on study skills that are dissociated from college content material. Rather than seeing the need for such instruction, many students associate reviewing study skill strategies as appropriate for "other students" (i.e., those who need remedial assistance). Students understand the need for more efficient study skill strategies when the skills are directly applied to content courses that the students are currently taking. Faced with an impending exam, students are receptive when they might otherwise be uninterested.

In addition to increasing students' understanding and retention of course material, the SI program has been effectively used for faculty development and renewal.

Use of SI for Faculty Development and Renewal

In addition to increasing students' understanding and retention of course material, the SI program has been effectively used for faculty development and renewal. Faculty can choose to do one or more of the following: adopt strategies used in the SI sessions during regular class time, receive informal feedback from the SI sessions concerning what the students understand and where they may need additional assistance, and learn new strategies from the SI student leaders. Additional benefits mentioned by Australian faculty members include increased rapport with students, membership in the national and the international SI network, increased recognition from their colleagues, additional opportunities to obtain grant funds, and increased satisfaction with their teaching role (Gardiner, 1996).

Angelo (1994) identified several barriers to the employment of effective faculty development programs most efforts focus primarily on improving teaching, and only secondarily, if at all, on improving learning; many programs do not recognize the importance of discipline-specific "ways of knowing," teaching, and learning; many teachers fail to recognize the need to improve their own teaching; and many faculty development programs are not planned and organized for student success.

One of the strengths of the SI program is that faculty members select their level of involvement. Professors can select from three broad areas of participation. The first is to receive anonymous feedback from SI leaders regarding student comprehension. This gives them an opportunity to revisit previous lectures for review and clarification and to modify future lectures. It is difficult for students to reveal their ignorance or lack of understanding to a person who has placed great effort on delivering carefully crafted lectures. Students do not want to admit that they do not understand the lecture to the person who also determines their final grades and whether or not they move on to the next class. In Australia and the United Kingdom, the SI program is frequently used as a feedback loop.

The second level of involvement is to incorporate SI strategies into class period activities (Martin, Blanc, & Arendale, 1994). The faculty member may attend a portion of the SI leader training workshop to learn how to adopt these activities for in-class use. Supplemental Instruction activities often used by SI leaders also could be used by faculty members during class to do the following: give the "big picture" of the course throughout the academic term; illustrate the "messy" process of solving problems and thinking about issues; refer to the syllabus throughout the academic term; provide an early "low impact" exam to provide feedback regarding comprehension before the first major exam; organize course content through visual tools (e.g., matrix boxes); and be explicit about expectations for excellence.

The third and highest level of involvement is for the faculty member to co-plan activities that occur inside the classroom and within the out-of-class SI sessions. Faculty members might also serve as SI supervisors and provide helpful feedback to SI leaders and to other faculty.

SI Fosters Self-Development of Faculty Members

Wolfe (1990) describes the use of SI at Anne Arundel Community College in Arnold, Maryland to provide services for both students and faculty members. Some faculty members serve as SI supervisors. Faculty have several options to earn promotion credit for increased salary, one of which is to earn "professional development credit." Faculty who choose this option and are approved by the SI program help supervise the SI leaders (Wolfe, 1990). A faculty member who agrees to serve in this role is called a "Faculty Mentor." Initially, Wolfe received a grant from the Fund for the Improvement of Post-Secondary Education to implement this activity. Since the conclusion of the grant, the institution has continued the mentor faculty program.

Faculty supervise SI leaders in areas outside the faculty member's content specialty; thus, the faculty "mentors" focus on general learning skills, not on critiquing the content of the course for which SI is being offered. These faculty attend classes and SI sessions with student SI leaders for the first four weeks of the term. During this time these faculty assume the role of a student in the course by attending class and taking notes with the SI student leader. Before the SI review sessions, these faculty mentors work with the SI leaders in preparing materials and activities. Following SI sessions, mentors offer constructive comments.

Faculty, who become students in a class outside their discipline, have the opportunity to observe and learn different approaches and teaching techniques. They may also become a nonthreatening resource for ways to integrate study skills into course lectures, readings, and assignments. Reported changes in behavior of the classroom teacher and the faculty mentor occur in three areas: procedural strategies (e.g., include board work and handouts, refer to course syllabus throughout the term); study strategies (e.g., classroom assessment techniques, review to reinforce major points); and group interaction (e.g., redirect questions back to other students or to the textbook, coach problem solving among small groups).

Marshall (1994) reported on the use of SI for faculty enrichment at Salem State College and found frequent interaction between faculty members and SI leaders through joint participation in SI leader training workshops, monthly meetings to discuss pedagogical issues, and weekly meetings to discuss SI participant comprehension of in-class material by SI student leaders and by all students enrolled in SI courses. Faculty members reported numerous positive changes in their behaviors and attitudes.

Research Findings Concerning Supplemental Instruction

The U. S. Department of Education has designated SI as an Exemplary Educational Practice and has validated the following three research findings:

1. In the targeted historically difficult courses, students participating in SI earn higher mean final course grades than students who do not participate in SI. This difference holds despite ethnicity and prior academic achievement.

2. Again, despite ethnicity and prior academic achievement, students participating in SI within targeted historically difficult courses succeed at a higher rate (i.e., withdraw at a lower rate and receive a lower percentage of D or F final course grades) than those who do not participate in SI.

3. Students participating in SI persist at the institution, reenrolling and graduating at higher rates than students who do not participate in SI.

The basic design of the various quasi-experimental research studies compares performance of the voluntary treatment group (SI participants) with the control group (non-SI participants). All final course grades were based on a 4.0 grade scale (4 = A; 3 = B; 2 = C; 1 = D; 0 = F). The research does not meet the standards for true experimental design, but results have been replicated across many institutions. For the foregoing analyses, all students within the targeted SI courses are included across institutions

where SI has been adopted and evaluative data have been collected. Dozens of research studies from UMKC, the national database from 270 institutions, and other studies from individuals campuses are available through the SI home page: www.umkc.edu/cad/si.htm.

The following are three studies that illustrate the variety of research studies: frequency of SI attendance and final course grades, graduation rates of UMKC students, and final course grades of students from a national study ($N \sim 5,000$). The national study examined classes with total enrollments over one-half million students.

The data provided in Table 1 suggest that increased frequency of SI attendance has a relationship with higher final course grades. The data in Table 1 show that students who attended SI sessions 12 or more times (12+) earned a slightly lower mean final course grade (2.64) than did other SI attendance groups. However, the 12+ attendees received a higher mean final course grade (2.64) than the non-SI attendees (2.37). Interviews with these 12+ attendees suggest that a large group were students who nearly withdrew from the course but persisted through frequent attendance at SI sessions.

The data in Table 2 suggest that SI makes a positive difference in terms of increased college graduation rates. The studies only considered students from University of Missouri-Kansas City because other institutions had not yet reported on their own persistence studies. The reenrollment rates were significant at the $p < .05$ level, and the graduation rate was significant at $p < .01$.

Nearly 100 colleges and universities submit data reports annually to the Center for Supplemental Instruction at University of Missouri-Kansas City. Table 3 was compiled from 270 institutions of varying types. These institutions submitted nearly 5,000 individual studies concerning the use of SI in classes with a combined enrollment of over one-half million students. A cross section of institutions was selected with (a) a sufficient number of SI sections in place, (b) sufficiently rigorous data collection procedures, and (c) transmission of data in a timely fashion. These findings are similar to those drawn

Table 1

Frequency of Supplemental Instruction (SI) Attendance upon Mean Final Course Grades: Winter 1996 (N = 1,590)

	Final Course Grades		
Number of SI Sessions Attended	Percent Receiving A or B	Percent Receiving D, F, or W	Mean Final Course Grade
None	42.2	39.3	2.37
1 or more	59.1**	18.2**	2.79*
1 - 3	56.3**	21.4**	2.77*
4 - 7	63.0**	17.4**	2.82*
8 - 11	63.7**	12.8**	2.88*
12 or more	56.7**	10.5**	2.64*

*Each SI-participant group was significantly better than non-participants ($p < .05$). These course grades are based on a 4.0 scale.

**More SI participants earned better grades than non-participants ($p < .01$).

from the University of Missouri-Kansas City campus which show that in comparison with their non-SI counterparts, SI-participants received a higher final mean course grade ($p < .01$) and a lower percentage of D and F final course grades and withdrawals ($p < .05$).

A variety of research studies have been conducted concerning the SI model by educators outside of UMKC. One of the most rigorous was a regression analysis conducted by Kenney (1989). Three variables were found significant at the .05 level: SAT math score, number of times students attended SI sessions, and whether or not they participated in SI. Studies of SI have also been conducted in other countries: United Kingdom by Bidgood (1994); Sweden by Bryngfors and Bruzell-Nilsson (1997); and

Australia by Hamilton, Blakeley, Critchley, Playford, Kelly, McNamara, and Robertson (1994).

Conclusion

It has been nearly two decades since Supplemental Instruction first appeared in higher education. After starting at the University of Missouri-Kansas City in 1973, SI has been implemented at a variety of institutions across the United States and around the world. Borrowing ideas from the field of cognitive development in psychology, SI encourages students to become actively involved in their own learning. By integrating appropriate study skills with the review of the course content, students begin to understand how to use the learning strategies they

Table 2

Graduation Rates of Fall 1989 University of Missouri-Kansas City First-Time, First-Year Students. Cumulative Graduation Rate at End of Four Time Periods

Supplemental Instruction	Fall 1993	Fall 1994	Fall 1995	Fall 1996
Participant	15.9%*	31.3%*	38.1%*	46.0%*
Non-Participant	12.3%	21.1%	27.4%	30.3%

Note. Includes all University of Missouri-Kansas City first-time, first-year freshmen who were not enrolled in professional degree programs. Supplemental Instruction was offered in 19 courses during Fall 1989.

*$p < .01$ using chi-square test.

Table 3

National Supplemental Instruction (SI) Field Data: 1982-1983 to 1995-1996 from 4,945 Courses in 270 Institutions for 505,738 Students

Student Grades[a]	SI	Two-Year Public (931)	Two-Year Private (20)	Four-Year Public (3,001)	Four-Year Private (993)	All Institutions (N = 4,945)
Final Course Grade	SI	2.56*	2.55*	2.36*	2.55*	2.42*
	Non-SI	2.09	2.26	2.07	2.31	2.09
Percent A & B Final Grades	SI	50.2**	53.1**	53.1**	52.1**	46.8**
	Non-SI	32.4	38.9	38.9	43.2	35.9
Percent D, F, & W Final Grades	SI	24.3**	24.6**	24.6**	19.1**	23.1**
	Non-SI	32.4	31.5	31.5	28.4	37.1

Note. Parentheses indicate number of courses.

[a]Based on 4.0 scale

*$p < .01$ using independent t-test

**$p < .01$ using chi-square test

have heard about from teachers and advisors. As new educational theories and practices have surfaced, the SI model has been adapted to incorporate the best in educational research.

The SI program serves as a catalyst for an improved and effective learning environment. Supplemental Instruction is flexible enough to meet the learning needs of students and complement an enriched learning environment managed by the classroom professor. It extends the classroom learning environment and helps organize student study time to master difficult course material. Supplemental Instruction serves as a valuable tool to increase the efficiency and effectiveness of learning.

References

Allen, M., Kolpas, S., & Stathis, P. (1992). Supplemental Instruction in calculus at a community college. *Collaborative Learning Exchange*, 8-9.

American College Testing Program. (1997). *ACT institutional data, 1997.* Iowa City, IA: Author.

Angelo, T. A. (1994). From faculty development to academic development. *American Association of Higher Education Bulletin, 46*(10), 3-7.

Arendale, D. (Ed.). (1997). *Annotated bibliography of Supplemental Instruction and Video-Based Supplemental Instruction.* Unpublished manuscript, Center for Supplemental Instruction, University of Missouri-Kansas City.

Ashwin, P. W. H. (1993). *Supplemental Instruction: Does it enhance the student experience of higher education?* Unpublished doctoral dissertation, Kingston University, London, England.

Bidgood, P. (1994). The success of Supplemental Instruction: Statistical evidence. In C. Rust & J. Wallace (Eds.), *Helping students to learn from each other: Supplemental Instruction* (pp. 71-79). Birmingham, England: Staff and Educational Development Association.

Bryngfors, L., & Bruzell-Nilsson, M. (1997). *Supplemental Instruction: An experimental project with the method of SI.* Lund, Sweden: The Lund Institute of Technology and The Faculty of Science.

Christie, N. G., & Dinham, S. M. (1991). Institutional and external influences on social integration in the freshman year. *Journal of Higher Education, 62*(4), 412-436.

Commander, N. E., Stratton, C. B., Callahan, C. A., & Smith, B. D. (1996). A learning assistance model for expanding academic support. *Journal of Developmental Education, 20*(2), 810, 12, 14, 16.

Dimon, M. (1988). Why adjunct courses

work. *Journal of College Reading and Learning, 21,* 33-40.

Gardiner, R. (1996, December). *Supplemental Instruction: A cost-effective, student-centered collaborative learning program.* Paper presented at The Second International Open Learning Conference held in Brisbane, Australia.

Hamilton, S., Blakeley, R., Critchley, C., Playford, J., Kelly, B., McNamara, E., & Robertson, R. (1994). *Supplemental Instruction at the University of Queensland: A pilot program.* Brisbane, Australia: University of Queensland.

Hilton, T. L., & Lee, V. E. (1988). Student interest and persistence in science: Changes in the educational pipeline in the last decade. *Journal of Higher Education, 59*(5), 510-526.

Keimig, R. T. (1983). *Raising academic standards: A guide to learning improvement.* Washington, DC: Association for the Study of Higher Education. (Eric Document Reproduction Service No. ED 233 669).

Kenney, P. A. (1989). Effects of Supplemental Instruction on student performance in a college-level mathematics course. *Dissertation Abstracts International, 50*(2), 378A. (University Microfilms No. 8909688)

Maloney, R. S. (1992). *The Supplemental Instruction program as an alternative field experience for secondary education majors.* Unpublished undergraduate honors thesis, University of New Orleans, LA.

Marshall, S. (1994). Faculty development through Supplemental Instruction. In D. C. Martin & D. Arendale (Eds.), *Supplemental Instruction: Increasing achievement and retention* (pp. 31-40). San Francisco: Jossey-Bass.

Martin, D. C., & Arendale, D. (Eds.). (1993). *Supplemental Instruction: Improving first-year student success in high-risk courses* (Monograph No. 7). Columbia, SC: National Resource Center for The Freshman Year Experience.

Martin, D. C., & Arendale, D. (Eds.). (1994). *Supplemental Instruction: Increasing achievement and retention.* San Francisco: Jossey-Bass.

Martin, D. C., & Blanc, R. A. (1984). Improving comprehension through reciprocal questioning. *Life Long Learning, 7*(4), 29-31.

Martin, D. C., Blanc, R., & Arendale, D. (1994). Mentorship in the classroom: Making the implicit explicit. *Teaching Excellence, 6*(1), 1-2.

Martin, D. C., Lorton, M., Blanc, R., & Evans, C. (1977). *The learning center: A comprehen-sive model for college and universities.* Kansas City, MO: University of Missouri (ERIC Document Reproduction Service No. ED 162 294).

National Association for Developmental Education Strategic Plan. (1997). [On-line]. Available: http://www.umkc.edu/cad/nade/nadedocs/straplan.htm

Noel, L., Levitz, R., & Saluri, D. (Eds.). (1985). *Increasing student retention: Effective programs and practices for reducing the dropout rate.* San Francisco: Jossey-Bass.

Shlipak, A. M. (1988). *Engineering and physics as cultural systems: Impressions of science students at Harvard/Radcliffe.* Thesis submitted to the Harvard University Department of Anthropology for the degree of Bachelor of Arts with Honors, March 26, 1988.

Somers, R. L. (1988). *Causes of marginal performance by developmental students.* Boone, NC: National Center for Developmental Education, Appalachian State University.

Stahl, N. A., Simpson, M. L., & Hayes, C. G. (1992). Ten recommendations from research for teaching high-risk college students. *Journal of Developmental Education, 16*(1), 2-4, 6, 8, 10.

Stratton, C. B., Commander, N. E., Callahan, C. C., & Smith, B. D. (1997). From DS to LS: The expansion of an academic preparation program from developmental studies to learning support. *Selected Conference Papers. (pp. 42-44).* Carol Stream, IL: National Association for Developmental Education.

Tinto, V. (1993). *Leaving college: Rethinking the causes and cures of student attrition.* (2nd ed.). Chicago: The University of Chicago Press.

Wallace, J. (1996). *Supplemental Instruction: The challenging way forward.* [Videotape] G. Mair (Producer). Glasgow, Scotland: Glasgow Caledonia University .

Wilcox, F. K. (1995). Supplemental Instruction and efficiency in learning. In M. T. Keeton, B. Mayo-Wells, J. Porosky, & B. Sheckley (Eds.). *Efficiency in adult higher education: A practitioner handbook* (pp. 102-107). College Park, MD: University of Maryland University College, Institute for Research on Adults in Higher Education.

Wolfe, R. (1990). Professional development through peer interaction. *The Journal of Professional Studies, 14*(1), 50-57.

Conclusion

Jeanne L. Higbee and Patricia L. Dwinell

These chapters portray the many faces of developmental education: past, present, and future. Even in states where legislators are calling for an end to outdated remedial courses, developmental educators often find themselves in the both enviable and lamentable position of designing new services and programs that expand rather than reduce their workload. Political pressure can have a positive impact on developmental education by forcing educators to evaluate and refine current practices and seek new solutions to address such problems as underpreparedness and inadequate retention rates. The chapters in this monograph reflect just a few of the areas in which developmental educators have taken the lead in educational reform.

In Chapter One of this monograph Boylan and Saxon estimate that developmental education courses serve approximately three million college students per year in the United States. Similar programs, such as access education in Europe, provide learning support for countless millions around the world. Furthermore, developmental education is no longer limited to the provision of basic courses in reading, writing, and mathematics for high-risk freshmen. Although Boylan and Saxon's estimate would include students who enroll in core curriculum courses offered through General College at the University of Minnesota as described by Wambach and delMas (Chapter Seven), it would not include students who elect to participate in the following: adjunct courses, summer bridge programs like those discussed by Garnett and Hood in Chapter Five, Supplemental Instruction, nor courses created to enhance skill development that are available to all students at an institution, such as the University (UNV) courses offered at the University of Georgia. Nor would this figure include the millions of students who seek academic assistance each year through workshops, learning centers, and tutorial services that are now often housed within developmental education facilities or staffed or administered by developmental educators.

Numbers are important. In this age of accountability, developmental education programs should be required to justify their existence not just through the quality of services provided but also in terms of the numbers of students who benefit. However, for most professionals committed to the goals of developmental education, even more important is the impact of developmental education on the individual student, as emphasized by Hardin in Chapter 2. The students, each with their own success stories, are what attract someone to a career in developmental education. The profession is rich in personal satisfaction, despite the long hours, relatively low pay, and common sources of misunderstanding and frustration. Most developmental educators have experienced a student who is a "user," certainly the least attractive of the types described by Hardin. Yet sometimes it is the "users" who become a teacher's most rewarding students over a period of time. Their success stories become even more meaningful when considered within the context of their attitudes toward learning at the time of matriculation. As explained by Klein, Vukovich, and Alderman in Chapter Eight, developmental educators must remain optimistic. It is their job to "ignite the spark," instilling in students the desire to learn. Viewed through the framework of Astin's (1985) talent development model, it is not surprising that developmental educators take pride in devoting their lives to a profession that may not be valued highly by other constituencies, but is often treasured by the students they serve. Spann and McCrimmon (Chapter Four) ask whether developmental educators can take the lead in the reprioritization of American higher education by once again putting the student first.

Although they represent different disciplines, these chapter authors—Weinstein, Best, Craig, Duranczyk and Caniglia, Deming, Maxwell, Nelson, and Arendale—all communicate the same message: Developmental educators must continue to explore new ways to solve old problems. Through a greater emphasis on research in the profession, we know more about our students than ever before. Through investigation and evaluation we have a more accurate picture of how, why, and to what extent myriad strategies work for students with varying academic needs. Transitions in the profession, such as

those delineated in Stratton's interviews with Boylan and Arendale in Chapter Three, mirror advances in knowledge as well as demographic changes.

Through developmental education programs, students who otherwise might have been denied access to higher education have the opportunity to participate fully in the college experience. But the impact of developmental education extends well beyond the college years. Students develop a lifelong love of learning. They become critical thinkers. They practice metacognitive and personal management skills. They communicate effectively. Developmental education programs play a significant role in preparing students for success in college and in life.

Reference

Astin, A. S. (1985). *Achieving educational excellence*. San Francisco: Jossey-Bass.

About the Editors

Jeanne L. Higbee has a B.S. in Sociology from Iowa State University and an M.S. in Counseling and Guidance and a Ph.D. in Educational Administration from the University of Wisconsin-Madison. Prior to pursuing her graduate degrees, she served two years in VISTA, the domestic Peace Corps. Dr. Higbee held a variety of positions in student affairs at the University of Wisconsin-Madison, Western Maryland College, and Johns Hopkins University before accepting a faculty position in developmental education at the University of Georgia.

Dr. Higbee has served on numerous editorial boards, and currently sits on the American College Personnel Association Media Board and the advisory boards of the *Journal of College Reading and Learning* and *Academic Exchange Quarterly,* as well as serving as coeditor of the National Association for Developmental Education's monograph series.

Patricia L. Dwinell has a B.A. in English from Colorado State University and a M.Ed. and Ph.D. in Educational Psychology from the University of Georgia. Dr. Dwinell has been associated with developmental education/learning support for 18 years. She has served as cochair of the Publications and Monograph committees for the National Association for Developmental Education (NADE), and as coeditor of the NADE monograph series. She has also served as president of NADE/Georgia. Dr. Dwinell is presently Associate Director of the Division of Academic Assistance at the University of Georgia.